POLITICAL

ANALYSIS

Series Editors:
B. Guy Peters, Jon Pierre
and Gerry Stoker

Political science today is a dynamic discipline. Its substance, theory and methods have all changed radically in recent decades. It is much expanded in range and scope and in the variety of new perspectives – and new variants of old ones – that it encompasses. The sheer volume of work being published, and the increasing degree of its specialization, however, make it difficult for political scientists to maintain a clear grasp of the state of debate beyond their own particular subdisciplines.

The *Political Analysis* series is intended to provide a channel for different parts of the discipline to talk to one another and to new generations of students. Our aim is to publish books that provide introductions to, and exemplars of, the best work in various areas of the discipline. Written in an accessible style, they provide a 'launching-pad' for students and others seeking a clear grasp of the key methodological, theoretical and empirical issues, and the main areas of debate, in the complex and fragmented world of political science.

A particular priority is to facilitate intellectual exchange between academic communities in different parts of the world. Although frequently addressing the same intellectual issues, research agendas and literatures in North America, Europe and elsewhere have often tended to develop in relative isolation from one another. This series is designed to provide a framework for dialogue and debate which, rather than advocacy of one regional approach or another, is the key to progress.

The series reflects our view that the core values of political science should be coherent and logically constructed theory, matched by carefully constructed and exhaustive empirical investigation. The key challenge is to ensure quality and integrity in what is produced rather than to constrain diversity in methods and approaches. The series is intended as a showcase for the best of political science in all its variety, and demonstrate how nurturing that variety can further improve the discipline.

POLITICAL
ANALYSIS

Series Editors: B. Guy Peters, Jon Pierre *and* Gerry Stoker

Published

Peter Burnham, Karin Gilland, Wyn Grant and Zig Layton-Henry
Research Methods in Politics

Colin Hay
Political Analysis

David Marsh and Gerry Stoker (eds)
Theory and Methods in Political Science (2nd edition)

Jon Pierre and B. Guy Peters
Governance, Politics and the State

Forthcoming

Keith Dowding
The Philosophy and Methods of Political Science

Colin Hay
Globalization and the State

Colin Hay, Michael Lister and David Marsh (eds)
The State: Theories and Issues

Andrew Hindmoor
Rational Choice

Vivien Lowndes
Why Institutions Matter

David Marsh
Political Behaviour

Martin Smith
Power, Politics and the State

Dietlind Stolle and Marc Hooghe
Social Capital

Political Analysis Series
Series Standing Order
ISBN 0–333–78694–7 hardback
ISBN 0–333–94506–9 paperback
(outside North America only)

You can receive future titles in this series as they are published by placing a standing order. Please contact your bookseller or, in the case of difficulty, write to us at the address below with your name and address, the title of the series and an ISBN quoted above.

Customer Services Department, Macmillan Distribution Ltd
Houndmills, Basingstoke, Hampshire RG21 6XS, England

Research Methods in Politics

Peter Burnham
Karin Gilland
Wyn Grant
and
Zig Layton-Henry

First published 2004 by
PALGRAVE MACMILLAN
Houndmills, Basingstoke, Hampshire RG21 6XS and
175 Fifth Avenue, New York, N.Y. 10010
Companies and representatives throughout the world

PALGRAVE MACMILLAN is the global academic imprint of
the Palgrave Macmillan division of St. Martin's Press, LLC and of
Palgrave Macmillan Ltd. Macmillan® is a registered trademark in
the United States, United Kingdom and other countries. Palgrave is a
registered trademark in the European Union and other countries.

ISBN–13: 978–0–333–96253–4   hardback
ISBN–10: 0–333–96253–2   hardback
ISBN–13: 978–0–333–96254–1   paperback
ISBN–10: 0–333–96254–0   paperback

This book is printed on paper suitable for recycling and made from fully
managed and sustained forest sources.

A catalogue record for this book is available from the British Library.

Library of Congress Cataloging-in-Publication Data
Research methods in politics/Peter Burnham . . . [et al.].
        p. cm.—(Political analysis)
    Includes bibliographical references and index.
    ISBN 0–333–96253–2 (cloth)—ISBN 0–333–96254–0 (paper)
        1. Political science—Research—Methodology—Textbooks. I. Burnham,
    Peter, 1959– II. Politicial analysis (Palgrave Macmillan (Firm))
    JA86.R423 2004
    320'.072—dc 22

                                                            2003067571

10   9   8   7   6   5   4
13   12   11   10   09   08   07   06   05

Printed in China

Contents

List of Figures, Tables and Boxes

Figures

Tables

Boxes

Preface

This book arose out of the experience of the authors of teaching research methods at both undergraduate and postgraduate levels. In doing so, we used a number of the different textbooks available on the market. However, most of them were written by sociologists and did not take account of the particular needs or disciplinary perspectives of political science and international relations. Judging that we were not the only people teaching in this field whose needs were not currently served, we decided to write our own book, introducing a broad range of methods at an introductory level for those engaged in the study of politics and international relations throughout the English-speaking world.

We have tried to be as international as possible in the range of research covered, drawing on examples particularly from continental Europe, the USA and Australia as well as from the UK. However, our own greater knowledge of UK research has meant that in some cases we have not been able to go as far as we would have ideally liked in this regard and we hope our readers may be able to help us further broaden the range of examples in future editions. Please e-mail any suggestions or other feedback on the book to w.p.grant@warwick.ac.uk.

Karin Gilland would like to thank George Lutz of the Institute of Political Science, University of Berne, for his assistance with the graphics in the chapters she was responsible for drafting. Wyn Grant would like to thank Susan and David and everyone at the *Rose of Denmark*, SE7, for their friendship and much needed moral support in good times and bad.

P.B.
K.G.
W.G.
Z.L.-H.

The author and publishers are grateful to the following for permission to reproduce copyright material: Joseph Rowntree Charitable Trust for Table 4.1; Manchester University Press for Table 4.2; UNESCO for Box 7.2; NARA for Box 7.3; National Archives of Australia for Box 7.4. Every effort has been made to contact all the copyright-holders, but if any have been inadvertently omitted the publisher will be pleased to make the necessary arrangements at the earliest opportunity.

List of Abbreviations

APSA	American Political Science Association
ARCHON	Archives on-line
BSA	British Sociological Association
CESSDA	Council for European Social Science Data
ESRC	Economic and Social Research Council
EU	European Union
FRUS	*Foreign Relations of the United States*
GNP	Gross National Product
HDI	Human Development Index
IRA	Irish Republican Army
MEP	Member of the European Parliament
MORI	Market and Opinion Research International
NAIL	National Archives Information Locator
NARA	National Archives and Record Administration
NRA	National Register of Archives
NSF	National Science Foundation
OECD	Organisation for Economic Co-operation and Development
ORC	Opinion Research Centre
PAF	Postcode Address File
PR	proportional representation
PREM	Prime Minister's Office
PRO	Public Record Office
PROCAT	Public Record Office Catalogue (on-line)
PRONI	Public Record Office of Northern Ireland
PSA	Political Studies Association
SRA	Social Research Association
UN	United Nations

Introduction: Methods, Methodology and Making Sense of the Study of Politics

Politics is about power. Studying the distribution and exercise of power is, however, far from straightforward. By its very nature, as Steven Lukes (1974) famously observed, the exercise of power involves a conflict of interests characterized by observable or latent conflict or can take place in a context dominated by persuasion, inducement, manipulation or other form of influence broadly conceived.

The subject matter of political science therefore presents particular problems for the researcher. Whose views are we to believe? Can we accept the public statements of our elected (or non-elected) leaders? How can we choose between two seemingly plausible accounts of the same phenomenon?

The ability to research, and therefore provide evidence to corroborate a particular view of the world, is clearly vital to the discipline of political science. In fact, we would claim that critical reflection on method is one of the hallmarks of the discipline, separating the academic study of politics from political journalism. Methods, after all, are intrinsically linked to research findings. Without the interview, how could we question leaders on events of the day? Without analysis of documents and archives, how could we piece together the complex chain of past events? Without surveys and statistical analysis, how could popular opinion be judged and the claims of the government be assessed? In short, without carefully designed research methods serious political science would be impossible.

In this light it is somewhat ironic that whilst there are many accounts of the research process in cognate disciplines such as sociology and psychology, there are relatively few texts which provide an introduction to the range of research methods available to the student of political science. Our, relatively modest, aim is make good this deficiency and in so doing provide the necessary foundation for students of politics to progress to more advanced texts in the areas

1

of qualitative and quantitative research methods (King, Keohane and Verba, 1994; Bryman, 2001; de Vaus, 2001).

Guiding themes

Despite some inevitable (and welcome) differences in emphasis, the authors of this book are committed to three guiding principles which deserve some elucidation:

- recognition of the importance of plausible, valid and reliable evidence in political science
- recognition of the importance of theory, of the view that all knowledge is conceptually formed
- recognition of the importance of internal consistency, simplicity and fit between research model and 'reality' (however this may be conceived).

What counts as evidence?

In a democracy everyone, it is said, is entitled to hold and express an opinion. That does not, of course, mean that every opinion is equally valid or influential. In everyday conversations about politics, the use of the anecdote is regarded as an acceptable form of evidence. In academic discussion, purely anecdotal evidence is frowned upon more often than not because it results in the individualistic fallacy (i.e., generalizing from the particular to the general). Thus a college student may say to another, 'My friend isn't registering to vote because he thinks it's pointless.' One could not use this view as a basis for generalizations about voter registration rates among all American college students.

The systematic study of politics involves the assembly of evidence and subjecting it to various forms of tests of its reliability and validity (broadly speaking whether the research is replicable and whether it offers a means of studying the theories and concepts being analysed). Unlike the situation in natural science where, it is often argued, there are standardized and accepted measures, social scientists are more aware that there is a range of techniques that they can choose from and a particular problem does not necessarily suggest a particular method. In this sense we would agree with the position taken by Marsh and Stoker (2002, p.4) that 'political science is enriched by the variety of approaches that are adopted within our discipline'. Like another companion book in this series, *Political*

Analysis by Colin Hay, this book is concerned with 'the *diversity* of analytical strategies available to those engaged in the analysis of "the political" ' (Hay, 2002, p.2). There is no one correct method, even for a particular type of research. However, there are correct ways of using methods so that the results they produce can be relied upon, at least within the terms of their own limitations. This book seeks to suggest when particular methods might be appropriate, how they can be used in the study of politics and what their strengths and limitations are.

The inevitability of conceptualization

Any serious consideration of method in social science quickly runs into the thorny question of the relationship between empirical observation and theory or conceptualization (Sayer, 1992, p.45). Once it is accepted that facts do not 'speak for themselves' (Carr, 1964) but that all understanding takes place within a conceptual framework, we have begun to cross the divide between common sense understandings of the world and social science. But what is meant by theory? Sayer (1992, p.50) indicates that the term is used in at least three important senses: as an ordering-framework or set of background assumptions; as conceptualization, in which 'to theorize' means to prescribe a particular way of thinking about the world; and as a hypothesis, explanation or testable proposition. However the term is defined (and it is vital that students pay attention to these different usages) it is now widely accepted that there can be no 'theory-neutral' interpretation of events. In the 1930s Karl Mannheim coined the term 'relationism' to denote that knowledge must always be knowledge from a certain position (Berger and Luckmann, 1967, p.22) and more recently the international relations theorist Robert Cox (1996, p.87) restated this as the view that 'theory is always for someone, always for some purpose'.

The authors of this book have, in one case, diametrically opposed theoretical approaches (Marxist and pluralist/Weberian), but we share an insistence on the importance of theory and conceptualization. This is perhaps an aspect of the study of politics to which new students are particularly resistant. They will be familiar with the colloquial statement 'That's all right in theory but . . .' and with the use of 'academic' as a synonym for 'irrelevant', and to some extent it is true that a theory that does not say anything about practice is simply a collection of abstractions. It is, however, important in the study of politics at the very least to have a theory of power (how it is acquired, exercised and distributed), a theory of the state (what we mean by it and how it is situated in a broader social context) and a coherent methodological position which underpins substantive research. In this sense it is the deployment of a theoretical framework that differentiates political science from other forms of the study of politics. Serious journalism is often of a very high standard; indeed, journalists have written some excellent books about politics (e.g., Brittan, 1964; Friedman, 1989 and 2002). But, however well written and well informed it may be, an article in *The Economist* or *The New York Times*, even though it may draw on academic research, is not the same as a piece of academic research. It will have a more immediate timeframe and any theoretical framework may be implicit. Academics, by contrast, may undertake research on matters that seem to be of little immediate relevance, but will strive to contribute to both theoretical and empirical debates.

In short, political science is not simply 'story-telling'. Rather, systematic analysis, as Hay (2002, p.64) points out, is based on an assessment of what's out there to know about, what can we (hope to) know about it, and how can we go about acquiring that knowledge. This means that *methodology* (a study of the principles and theories which guide the choice of method) can be distinguished from particular *research methods* (elite interviewing or archival analysis) although, as Sayer (1992, p.3) cautions, 'methodologists need to remember that although method implies guidance, research methods are the medium and outcome of research practice; the educators themselves have to be educated – with frequent refresher courses'.

Keep it simple

Finally, alongside our emphasis on research that is theoretically informed, and that is open to the use of a variety of methods, we would stress the need to take account of the principle of parsimony. William of Occam was a minimalist Franciscan monk who, although he lived in mediaeval times (approximately from 1284 to 1349) is seen as a key figure in the development of modern social science. He built on Aristotle's principle that entities must not be multiplied beyond what is necessary. In other words, social scientists should seek to build elegant models that minimize the number of explanatory variables used. The simplest theory that fits the facts of a problem is the one that should be selected. From a set of otherwise equivalent models of a given phenomenon, the simplest one should be chosen.

Social and political reality is highly complex and probably becoming more so. For example, consider the emergence of the European Union as a 'post-modern' form of multi-level governance. Our conventional models of the state (or of international organizations) may not readily be able to cope with it. However, just to say that it is a very complex form of government is insufficient. The task of social scientists is to offer robust, clear and comprehensible explanations so that we can better understand the changing world around us. If we understand it better, there is at least the possibility that we can make it a better place to live. Unfortunately, we cannot send new Politics students down to the shops to buy an Occam's Razor to shave off unnecessary concepts or variables from their models. We can, however, give students a clear guide to the methods and techniques available to them to explore the world of politics which is what this book seeks to achieve.

Structure of the book

The ways in which an academic discipline makes use of research methods is influenced both by its objectives and by its boundaries. In the case of politics and international relations, the range of concerns is wide and the boundaries of the subject are often ill-defined, while the discipline itself is, to a considerable degree, internally fragmented. Its eclecticism is both a strength and a weakness. It has allowed the discipline to remain open to theories, perspectives and methodologies from a range of other social science disciplines. It can also mean that politics and international relations is seen as lacking a distinct perspective of its own. In Chapter 1 we develop the view that politics can be usefully seen as the 'junction subject' of the social sciences, arising out of history and philosophy and drawing in particular on the insights of economics, sociology, psychology and geography. The dominant methods used in political science reflect, to a large extent, the historical development of the discipline. We therefore provide a broad overview of the development of the discipline and discuss some of the dominant paradigms in this chapter before returning to some of the methodological concerns already raised in this introduction regarding the nature of social scientific knowledge and the link between ontology, epistemology and research methods.

In deciding how to research a phenomenon, the political scientist, like any other social scientist, is confronted with a large number of possible research strategies and methods. A key question is which research method (or methods) will provide the best test of the research hypothesis or at the very least be most appropriate to the research question? This issue is at the heart of research design. Chapter 2 analyses research design, exploring the linear and research wheel models of the research process. It also introduces the main types of research design in preparation for Chapter 3, which looks at one of the most widely used methods in contemporary political science: comparative methodology. There is, of course, a world of difference between simply 'making a comparison' (to illustrate an argument or persuade a third party) and employing the 'comparative method' to systematically test propositions. Chapter 3 provides a detailed study of the 'most similar' and 'most different' comparative research designs and probes the strengths and weaknesses of the comparative method.

Surveys and opinion polls play an increasingly important role in contemporary political life and to many political science is closely associated with the study of elections and voting behaviour. Chapter 4 introduces the principles of sampling and their application to survey design. This provides the basis for a discussion of the role of quantitative data in political science in Chapters 5 and 6 which focus on the use of descriptive statistics and the procedures adopted to gauge the statistical significance of a set of results. This involves a non-technical introduction to a range of issues including measures of central tendency and spread with numerous examples drawn from British and European Election Surveys and Organisation for Economic Cooperation and Development (OECD) and United Nations (UN) data sets.

The sheer range and diversity of documentary sources can appear bewildering to the inexperienced researcher. From newspapers to research reports, government records to personal diaries, documentary and archival material constitutes such a vast resource that the political researcher can be left feeling very much the second-rate historian. Chapter 7 provides an overview of documentary material and concentrates specifically on how political researchers can best make use of central government archives. Increasingly much documentary material is available 'on-line'. Chapter 8 assesses some of the ways in which the internet is transforming political research. Following a discussion of the most popular search engines, the chapter reviews the use of electronic resources and recent moves to conduct on-line polling and elite interviewing. There is no doubt that the Internet is becoming an increasingly important research tool. However, it is unlikely to displace more traditional approaches to research, and Chapter 9 looks at what is probably the most popular research technique in political science today, elite interviewing. Despite its centrality in the study of politics there is not a very large literature on elite interviewing. This chapter therefore carefully discusses the key stages in conducting a semi-structured interview: from tracking down interviewees to gaining access, carrying out the interview and analysing the results.

Chapter 10 focuses on two qualitative approaches that have considerable potential for use by political scientists but which are, as yet, under-utilized and, to some extent, under-appreciated: participant observation and discourse analysis. Perhaps the most anti-positivist of all research methods, participant observation requires a great deal of personal commitment but can yield rich and detailed information. The interest shown by participant observers in 'forms of life' and language has been taken further by discourse analysts who aim to reveal how shared understandings of the world legitimate and motivate collective action. Both approaches, in various ways, raise serious ethical concerns. Chapter 11 discusses the nature of ethical problems in political research and assesses the codes of conduct adopted by professional associations in social science. Finally, in Chapter 12 we analyse the arguments of those who are critical of the dominant approaches to qualitative and quantitative research in political science. In particular we focus on the feminist critique and assess the view that 'new methods' are necessary to reveal the diversity of women's experience. This chapter concludes by returning to the methodological debates introduced above and discusses the ways in which quantitative and qualitative approaches have been combined to useful effect. We end not with a list of methodological injunctions but by pointing students of politics and international relations in the direction of the best examples of research in each of the areas we have covered in the book.

Chapter 1

The Discipline of Politics

It is important to be aware that the historical development of the discipline, and in particular its openness to other perspectives, has greatly influenced the emergence and use made of research methods in politics and international relations. The first part of this chapter shows how the development of the discipline, particularly in Britain, continental Europe and the USA, reflected differing concerns of academics and policy-makers and resulted in the institutionalization of particular styles of research methodology.

However, largely under the influence of scholars in the United States, three paradigms have shaped post-war political science around the globe. The second part of the chapter charts how behaviouralism, new institutionalism and rational choice have increasingly dominated approaches to research. Although there has been constructive dialogue between these paradigms, at base rational choice and institutionalist paradigms are constructed on mutually incompatible premises. This has particular implications for choice of research method and for understandings of political 'science'. The final section of this chapter looks at what is at stake in the 'unity of method' debate and considers the relationship between ontology, epistemology and methodology.

The diverse traditions of political science

In many respects, politics is the junction subject of the social sciences, born out of history and philosophy, but drawing on the insights of economics and sociology and, to a lesser extent, the study of law, psychology and geography. This openness to other perspectives can enrich the discipline, but also leaves it open to the accusation that it lacks a distinctive theoretical and methodological core. 'We cannot talk about political science as a discipline if those who call themselves political scientists and pretend to teach it are unable to agree on its basic substance and methodology' (European

Thematic Network for Political Science, or EPSNet, 2003, p.2). This lack of a distinct core leaves the study of politics prey to the views of those who argue that politics is a field of enquiry rather than a distinctive discipline. It has been claimed, for example, that what politics attempts to do as a discipline can be better achieved by political sociology or by the deployment of the methodologies of economics to explain political phenomena.

The sense of the need to mark out clear boundaries for the discipline, to provide it with a dominant and widely accepted paradigm, and to adopt appropriate research methodologies and techniques, has been strongest in the USA. In terms of resources and intellectual power, American political science tends to dominate world political science. In 1980, about 80 per cent of the world's political scientists were American (Dreijmanis, 1983, p.214) and there is no reason to believe that the figure differs greatly at the beginning of the twenty-first century. The annual convention of the American Political Science Association (APSA) attracts upwards of 6,000 delegates. They are predominantly Americans: the rest are scholars who feel that they need to keep up to date with the latest developments in American political science.

Even in areas such as European integration, where one might think European scholars would have something of a comparative advantage, the American contribution to the body of theoretical and empirical work has been considerable. The earlier contributions to theorizing European integration 'emanated from the US, with Europeans hanging on to the coat-tails of the argument' (Wallace, 2000, p.100). Similarly, Smith argues (2000, p.399) that in the case of international relations, 'IR remains an American social science both in terms of the policy agenda that US IR exports to the world in the name of relevant theory and in terms of the dominant (and often implicit) epistemological and methodological assumptions contained in that theory.'

American political science has been characterized by repeated attempts to establish a rigorously based academic discipline that could at least bear comparison with, say, psychology, first through the behavioural movement and more recently through rational choice. British political science has been characterized by a greater intellectual scepticism in what Jack Hayward has called a 'self-deprecating discipline' (Hayward, 2000, p.1).

However, political science in continental Europe has its own distinctive traditions that are largely independent of Anglo-American influences. Public law approaches have been an important influence, reflecting the fact that there is usually a link in France between the study of politics and the possibility of a career in the elite ranks of the civil service. In France, the role of political science in the education of elites, notably at the École Nationale d'Administration gave it a special status in national life. Sciences Po (as the *École libre des sciences politiques* is usually known) in Paris was established in 1871–2 as part of a modernization effort after France's defeat in the Franco-Prussian war. 'Initially, "political science" as such played a very modest part in its teaching, the use of the plural (political *sciences*) being indicative of the fact that law and history, as well as other social sciences such as economics dominated the syllabus' (Hayward, 2000, p.25). Much political science in France is taught in law faculties. The key political science institutions are the nine Institut d'Études Politiques set up after the Second World War. Sciences Po is technically one of them, but they are essentially a network of provincial institutions. They have a broader mission than conventional political science departments, teaching their students law and some economics to prepare them for careers in business and the civil service. Effectively, the country has only two conventional political science departments. Similarly, in Italy, the weakness of departments when compared with the faculties that organize teaching undermines the institutional base for political science.

German political science was shaped in its early post-war years by a task of democratic re-education that had American influences, but since then has been able to draw on a more traditional German social-philosophical approach. Rejuvenated by the student protest movement of the late 1960s, 'This tradition may explain the perceived dominance of abstract and theoretical traditions over the empirical study of politics' (Saalfeld, 2002, p.139). The variability of national experiences within Europe is illustrated by the fact that Dutch political science went through a particularly fierce debate about behaviouralism, and 'Soon the discipline was in total disarray' (Lieshout and Reinalda, 2001, p.60). One consequence was that academics studying public administration and public policy split away from political science to form their own departments and association. Belgian political science is split on linguistic lines, while Denmark did not establish its first political science department (at Aarhus) until 1959. The early development of Danish political science was strongly influenced by American behavioural traditions (Rasmussen, 1985, p.320).

Swedish political science was influenced first by a German tradition in the first four decades of the twentieth century, then by the

United States and more recently by an Anglo-American tradition. Rather than an American hegemony, it is an Anglo-American axis that seems to be dominant. In 1971 only 8.4 per cent of the references in the leading Swedish political science journal were from the UK, but by 2000 some 25.7 per cent of the references were from that country. In the meantime, the number of references to American publications had declined from 40 per cent to 23.8 per cent (Angstrom, Hedenstrom and Strom, 2003, p.10). The Swedish case raises the question of how far political science can retain a distinctive national identity in a relatively small country with a langauge that is not widely used. According to Swedish political scientists themselves, Swedish political science 'stands less tall than it did one scholarly generation ago' (Angstrom, Hedenstrom and Strom, 2003, p.6). 'Swedish political science . . . imports more than it exports', but such small scholarly communities may nevertheless 'survive and even thrive' (Angstrom, Hedenstrom and Strom, 2003, p.15).

As in other areas of cultural and intellectual life, Canada has made a particular effort to ensure that its approach to the study of politics can be differentiated from that pursued by its powerful neighbour across the border. Of course, some Canadian political scientists are American by origin and there is necessarily much interchange of ideas. However, Canadian political science has developed a strong international reputation in areas such as federalism, the study of public policy and environmental politics. The respect with which Canadian political science is held internationally is indicated by the fact that the International Political Science Association currently has its headquarters in the country. The distinctive traditions of Quebec, expressed through the existence of a separate association for political scientists working in the province, also gives Canadian political science a special flavour.

Canadian political scientists have often worked with their counterparts in Australia on topics such as federalism where they share a common interest. Historically, the Australian National University (ANU) in Canberra, which has a strong research school, had links with universities such as Oxford. ANU and other Australian universities still recruit leading political scientists from Britain. However, the geographical isolation of Australia encourages Australian political scientists to travel extensively. They are prominent at conferences in Europe and the United States and draw from both approaches to the study of politics. Not surprisingly, Australian political science is also strong in the study of the Asia-Pacific region and such topics as the politics of international trade.

American political science emerged at an earlier date than its British counterpart, as is evidenced by the fact that APSA was preparing to celebrate its centenary at the millennium, while its British counterpart (deliberately named the Political *Studies* Association) was celebrating its golden anniversary. How can we account for the earlier development of the discipline in the USA, but in particular its more rapid professionalization (e.g., emphasis on the possession of a PhD as a necessity rather than an embarrassment) and its proneness to seek out 'scientific' paradigms?

As American universities evolved from their original function of training Christian ministers, political scientists shared in the widespread belief 'that universities must rely on science rather than revelation to inform their teachings on natural or social phenomena' (Ricci, 1984, p.66). It is therefore not surprising that early political scientists turned to the natural sciences for paradigms:

> Of the handful of political scientists who wrote on the nature of the discipline between 1880 and 1903, most held a scientistic point of view. That is to say, they believed that the methodology they associated with the natural sciences was appropriate for investigating problems of fundamental concern to political science, and that proper application of this methodology would lead to the development of 'laws' with explanatory and predictive power. (Somit and Tanenhaus, 1967, p.76)

Universities in the United States underwent a massive expansion between 1870 and 1920, a period in which the undergraduate population increased from 54,300 in 1870 to 597,900 in 1920. This created a demand for new subjects. This of itself does not explain why political science should start to develop as a distinct discipline, an event usually traced to the formation of a School of Political Science at Columbia College (as it then was) in New York in 1880. There were, however, developments in the wider society that favoured the systematic study of politics. The influx of immigrants into the United States, preponderantly from countries with monarchical or authoritarian systems of government, led to fears that the republican and democratic traditions of the country could be undermined. The new immigrants needed to undergo formal political socialisation and this led to the widespread development of 'civics' teaching in American high schools, an issue only tackled in Britain at the end of the twentieth century with a debate about political literacy. The Progressive movement of the late nineteenth century and early twentieth century was based on the concerns of a growing urban middle class about what they saw as corrupt systems of city government. Systematic ideas for reform were needed and political scientists were called upon to provide them. It should also be remembered that law is not generally available as a first degree in the USA. Majoring in political science is seen as an acceptable prerequisite to attending law school and has helped to maintain buoyant demand for undergraduate courses.

The development of the study of politics was a much more hesitant process in Britain. The London School of Economics and Political Science was founded in 1895 with an agenda of training an administrative elite and, more specifically, colonial civil servants. It was part of the 'Webbs' Fabian Socialist grand design for a meritocratic-technocratic break with the gentleman-amateur Oxford tradition' (Hayward, 2000, p.12). Oxford had established its Gladstone chair in politics before the First World War. The degree in Philosophy, Politics and Economics (PPE), which so many future political leaders were to take, was initially established in 1921. 'In 1932 changes took place which opened the way to a great increase in the amount of teaching required in Politics. The modern form of P.P.E. was introduced.' (Chester, 1975, p.155). Barry saw the combination of teachers of politics usually holding their first degrees in history, and having to teach a very wide range of courses in their colleges, as contributing to an amateurish approach to the subject. (Barry, 2000, p.433). This comment perhaps overlooks the contribution of Nuffield College in the 1930s onwards as a centre for social science research.

British political studies in the 1950s was male-dominated and characterized by a prevalent belief in the merits of British institutions. Indeed, some influential political scientists in the USA argued that it would benefit from moving closer to the model of a disciplined party system. As the 1950s came to an end, the complacency of political scientists was beginning to be punctured by the failure of Westminster-style constitutions in newly independent Third World countries. In wider political life there was an increasing realization that Britain was lagging behind the growth rates being achieved by its continental competitors. There was a general questioning of British institutions and a demand for their modernization. Political scientists such as Bernard Crick organized the Study of Parliament Group (which rather unusually brought together practitioners in the shape of Commons officials and academics) and played a leading role in calls for the reform of Parliament. Other political scientists assisted the royal commissions and committees set up in an attempt to reform the civil service, local government (and so on), with devolution being added as an agenda item in the 1970s. During this period a considerable expansion of university education took place, with politics departments being substantially increased in size in existing institutions and being an important part of the new 'plateglass' universities such as Essex and Warwick. The period from 1961 to 1974 is characterized by Hayward (1991, p.313) as 'technocratic reformism'. It was perhaps the high point of 'relevance' for British political science, although institutions remained largely unreformed.

The period since 1975 is characterized by Hayward (1991, p.315) as one of 'sceptical professionalism'. For critics from the left, the subject remained 'suffused, not to say suffocated, by a bland orthodoxy, reform-inclined at the edges but essentially emollient, apologetic and structurally unproblematic' (Miliband, 1976). After a period of expansion, there was even some contraction in the discipline in Britain in the 1980s. However, more modest expansion was renewed in the 1990s, while intellectually the discipline developed in new areas such as international political economy. The study of north–south relations attracted many able younger researchers. In both Britain and the USA, there was a marked tendency towards greater specialization in subfields of the discipline. Barry draws an important distinction between specialization and fragmentation. He sees specialization as 'the elaboration and extension of a common body of ideas to different aspects of the subject . . . In contrast, fragmentation might be defined as what happens when the centrifugal tendencies inherent in specialization are not reined in by the gravitational pull of the central core' (Barry, 2000, p.447).

Important developments have taken place in the direction of creating a European political science, although perhaps it would be more appropriate to talk of Europe-wide co-operation drawing on the distinctive traditions of the different countries. The annual workshops and other events organized by the European Consortium for Political Research since its formation in 1970 were followed by the formation in 1998 of the more teaching-oriented European Thematic Network for Political Science, later reconstituted as EPSNet. However, these events have tended to have a strong Northern European influence, with many of the participants drawn from Britain, Germany, the Netherlands and the Scandinavian countries. Norwegian political science has been particularly influential, exemplified by the work of the leading analyst of comparative politics from an historical perspective, Stein Rokkan.

The collapse of the Communist regimes in Eastern Europe, where the teaching of politics had largely been confined to the heavily ideological study of Marxism–Leninism, presented a unique opportunity and challenge: 'Immediately after the collapse of communism, political science had no institutional existence as a discipline or field of training and education. Departments had to be established, reformed or entirely redesigned. Unlike in Western Europe, political science was introduced with a single "big bang" ' (Ilonszki, 2002, pp.23–4). It is perhaps too early to assess the results of this experiment, although it does seem that the familiar problem of the lack of common themes to integrate diversity has occurred.

Dominant paradigms

Three paradigms have shaped post-war political science, especially in the USA but also with an impact elsewhere: behaviouralism, new institutionalism and rational choice.

Behaviouralism was the dominant paradigm in American political science in the 1950s and 1960s and it fell away thereafter. It emerged out of a discontent with the 'old institutionalism' which was preoccupied with the formal structures of government. This approach 'had quite spectacularly failed to anticipate the collapse of interwar German democracy and the emergence of fascism' (Blyth and Varghese, 1999, p.346). Discontent with what had gone before was not of itself enough to launch a new paradigm. However, the development of probability sampling techniques and a systematic understanding of mass surveys had opened up new areas of research for political science, particularly in the study of what shaped electoral choice (Lazarsfeld, Berelson and Gaudet, 1944). What quickly became apparent was that voters were less well informed and rational than classical democratic theory assumed. Funding foundations were eager to encourage this new 'scientific' approach to political research.

The advocates of the 'behavioural persuasion' saw 'themselves as spokesmen for a very broad and deep conviction that the political science discipline should (1) abandon certain traditional kinds of research, (2) execute a more modern sort of inquiry instead, and (3) teach new truths based on the findings of these new inquiries' (Ricci, 1984, p.140). What was the essence of this new paradigm? By combining two classic accounts (Easton, 1965; Somit and Tanenhaus, 1967) it is possible to identify eight main claims made for behaviouralism.

1. There are discoverable regularities in politics which can lead to theories with predictive value.
2. Such theories must be testable in principle. This 'proposition was repeatedly restated by behaviouralists . . . it was fundamental to the point where Easton argued that the vital difference between most pre-World War II political scientists and behaviouralists lay precisely in the latter's insistence on testability' (Ricci, 1984, p.137).
3. Political science should be concerned with observable behaviour which could be rigorously recorded.
4. Findings should be based on quantifiable data.
5. Research should be made systematic by being theory oriented and directed.
6. Political science should become more self-conscious and critical about its methodology.
7. Political science should aim at applied research that could provide solutions to immediate social problems. The truth or falsity of values could not be established scientifically and therefore political science should abandon the 'great issues' except where they were amenable to empirical investigation. 'Needless to say, the contention that political science has no proper concern with moral or ethical questions as such has been one of the most bitterly argued aspects of behaviouralism' (Somit and Tanenhaus, 1967, p.179).
8. Political science should become more interdisciplinary and draw more on the other social sciences.

The reaction against behaviouralism came from three broad directions. First, there were those who pointed out that behaviouralism had failed to fulfil its own goals. Even in an area such as voting behaviour which 'is the closest thing to a scientific theory that we have . . . even a casual review of the findings of voting research . . . shows how unstable these regularities are, and how far short of hard science our efforts to stabilize them must fall' (Almond and Genco, 1990, p.37). Much of the time political scientists were not observing actual behaviour, but trying to make sense of reports of behaviour. Political scientists were not in the voting booth with the citizen, but undertaking *post hoc* analyses of the accounts voters gave of what they claimed to have done and their reasons for it.

Second, behaviouralists were criticized for placing an 'undue emphasis on process' at the expense of the 'content and substance of political events and systems'. Moreover, 'As the behavioral methodologies became increasingly elaborate and complex, the problems seemed to get ever more narrow and insignificant. The very demand for precision of method imposed limits on the kinds of subjects that could be dealt with' (Prinati, 1983, p.192). This kind of criticism acquired additional force as the discipline developed a new interest in the analysis of public policy, stimulated by work such as that of Lowi (1964), Ranney (1968) and Pressman and Wildavsky (1973).

Third, the ferment in American politics associated with the upheavals caused by the civil rights movement and the Vietnam War, and later by the growth of feminist consciousness, penetrated the political science profession. 'In retrospect, the behavioral era in political science appears to be a time of optimism' (Ricci, 1984, p.171) both politically and within the profession. The Caucus for a New Political Science set up within the APSA in 1967 attacked the complacency, conservatism and lack of relevance of American political science, rejecting the behaviouralist paradigm. In his 1969 address to the American Political Science Association, David Easton tried to reconcile the various groups within the APSA by referring to the 'post-behavioral revolution' and calling for more applied research. Post-behaviouralism 'appeared on the political scene as a phenomenon whose name . . . indicated a shared determination to leave something definite behind rather than a common notion of the direction in which the discipline should move forward' (Ricci, 1984, p.189). Never again would a paradigm enjoy such an unchallenged position of intellectual leadership in political science.

In what ways did behaviouralism leave a mark on political science? The impulse for a more scientific and rigorous approach remained a force in American political science, as we shall see later. It was generally accepted that the behaviouralist attempt to separate value judgements and empirical research was doomed to failure. Similarly, their view that 'regularities and generalizations are the *only* proper objects of scientific political inquiry' came to be seen as 'an unnecessary delimitation of the discipline's subject matter' (Almond and Genco, 1990, p.41). Behaviouralism could lead to the neglect of 'the fact that much social and political change has to be explained neither by strong regularities nor by weak regularities, but by accidental conjunctions – by events that had a low probability of occurring' (Almond and Genco, 1990, p.39). Indeed, new developments in chaos theory would suggest that very rare events will occur more often than the Gaussian or standard bell-shaped curve model would predict.

Three of the propositions made by the proponents of behaviouralism would probably win acceptance by most political scientists today: that the study of politics should be theory-oriented and directed; that it should be self-conscious about its methodology; and that it should be interdisciplinary. At its worst, pre-war political science offered low level descriptions of political structures which treated constitutions as an accurate reflection of political reality. Methodology was often unsystematic and rarely discussed. In those respects, behaviouralism did contribute to the development of political science as a discipline, although it was not necessary to have been a behaviouralist to recognize the importance of theory and method.

One response to the demise of behaviouralism was the rebirth of institutionalism in a seminal article by March and Olsen (1984). They sought to argue that institutions do matter, that political phenomena could not be simply reduced to the aggregate consequences of individual behaviour, 'that the organization of political life makes a difference' (March and Olsen, 1984, p.747). The choices that people make are to a significant extent shaped by the institutions within which they operate. They sought to revive the tradition within political science that saw political behaviour 'embedded in an institutional structure of rules, norms, expectations and traditions that severely limited the free play of individual will and calculation' (March and Olsen, 1984, p.736). It was a way of bringing the state back into political analysis, although in Europe it had probably never left. New institutionalism 'insists on a more autonomous role for political institutions. The state is not only affected by society but also affects it' (March and Olsen, 1984, p.738).

How does the new institutionalism differ from the old institutionalism? March and Olsen are perhaps most vague and opaque on this point, stating that the new and the old are not identical and that one could describe 'recent thinking as blending elements of an old institutionalism into the non-institutionalist styles of recent theories of politics' (March and Olsen, 1984, p.738). One difference is that old institutionalism generally held a more narrow definition of what constitutes an institution, seeing it principally in terms of formal structures. 'For example, the old institutionalism argued that presidential systems are significantly different from parliamentary systems based upon the formal structures and rules' (Peters, 1999, p.1). Such an explanation has some value, but by itself it is not sufficient. Current work tends to define institutions more broadly 'as a set of rules, formal or informal, that actors generally follow, whether for normative, cognitive or material reasons' (Hall and Soskice, 2001, p.9).

The experience of behaviouralism has probably also made the new institutionalism more methodologically systematic. Old-style structuralism tended to slip into the assumption that political structures determined behaviour. The behaviouralists particularly objected to this assumption and new institutionalists would see structure (more broadly defined than by the old institutionalists) as a shaping and constraining force rather than a dominant one. Where there is a line of continuity with contemporary historical institutionalism is the notion that institutions are historically embedded, influenced by their formation and critical junctures in their development. Old institutionalism was highly normative and displayed a bias in favour of the established democracies as offering models of good government (Peters, 1999, p.13). New institutionalists do not display a preference for one set of institutions over another; instead, they are more interested in exploring how and in what ways institutions affect the behaviour of their members.

New institutionalism has developed as a broad, almost protean approach rather than as a school that sets guidelines for what constitutes acceptable research. Peters (1999, pp.19–20) identifies seven distinct variants of new institutionalism. One of the most influential variants has been historical institutionalism. This has two central hallmarks: an interest in 'the distribution of power in the polity' (Hall and Taylor, 1998, p.960), reflecting what we have emphasized as one of the central concerns of the study of politics, and an emphasis on path dependency resulting from key historical choices made by states. Critical moments create branching points from which historical development moves on to a new path and once that new path has been taken it is difficult to change track. Thus for historical institutionalists, 'the basic point of analytic departure is the choices that are made early in the history of any policy, or indeed of any governmental system. These initial policy choices, and the institutionalized commitments that grew out of them, are argued to determine subsequent decisions' (Peters, 1999, p.19). See also Box 1.1.

Developments in economics offered the possibility of a new approach through what came to be known as rational or public choice, drawing on the methodology of economics rather than the sociological and psychological approaches favoured by behaviouralists (Ward, 2002, p.65). William Riker and his collaborators at Rochester played a key role in introducing this approach to American political science, and now 'It has arguably become the

Box 1.1   The key features of historical institutionalism

1. A broad understanding of the relationship between institutions and individual behaviour.
2. An emphasis on the asymmetries of power that arise from the way in which instututions work.
3. A view of institutional development that emphasizes path dependence and unintended consequences.
4. An emphasis on the integration of institutional analysis with that of ideas.

Source: based on Hall and Taylor (1996, p.938).

dominant approach to political science at least in the United States' (Ward, 2002, p.65). However, its apparent emerging hegemony in American political science provoked a counter-movement in the USA known as the *perestroika* movement, although it also had other concerns.

The rational choice approach was based on methodological individualism and it was this core assumption that made it unpalatable to many historical institutionalists. Like behaviouralism, it viewed individuals as the key political actors and tended to reduce 'collective behaviour to individual behaviour' (Peters, 1999, p.16). A second core assumption, borrowed from economics, is that individuals are utility maximizers pursuing their own personal goals. Thus, political actors, whether they are voters, politicians or bureaucrats, 'are assumed to be material interest maximisers, seeking benefits in the form of votes, offices, power, and so on, at least cost' (Almond, 1990, p.123). Critics argued that like behaviouralism, there was an emphasis on method rather than substance. Nevertheless, one of its important insights was to draw attention to the 'free-rider' problem. The rational pursuit of individual interests can make the collective, co-operative action that politics requires difficult to achieve (Hay, 2002, pp.9–10).

One of the advantages the advocates of rational choice enjoyed was that they were a more coherent group defined by a very clear methodology compared with the more fragmented historical institutionalists who were less convinced of the innate superiority of any one approach. To some commentators it seemed as if rational choice was in the ascendant. Some of the criticisms made of the activities of supporters of rational choice were rather exaggerated or alarmist. Rational choice has much to offer political science: for example, one of the earliest models within this tradition, Downs's median voter theorem, has turned out to be one of the most robust. First published in 1957 (Downs, 1957), it can readily be applied to contemporary elections. Rather than allowing the discipline to be divided into two opposed camps, was some reconciliation between the new institutionalism and rational choice possible? Some scholars thought so.

Utility-maximizing individuals might find 'that their goals can be achieved more effectively through institutions, and find their behavior is shaped by the institutions' (Peters, 1999, p.44). Hall and Taylor (1996, p.956) pointed to the way in which 'rational choice analysts have begun to incorporate "culture" or "beliefs" into their work to explain why actors move toward one outcome when a conventional analysis specifies many possible equilibrium outcomes'. Historical institutionalists could also benefit from an opening to rational choice. 'Many of the arguments recently produced by this school could readily be translated into rational choice terms' (Hall and Taylor, 1996, p.957). Coleman and Tangermann (1999) offer an example of a political scientist who had deployed historical institutionalist approaches working with an economist to present an analysis of agricultural trade negotiations in terms of a game theory analysis of two autonomous, linked games. A narrative account of the negotiations is linked with the theoretical perspective offered by game theory.

Nevertheless, fundamental difficulties may frustrate any attempt to generate a constructive dialogue between the paradigms of historical institutionalism and rational choice. Hay and Wincott (1998, p.951) 'argue that the prospects for such a dialogue are more limited than Hall and Taylor suggest [since] rational choice and sociological institutionalism are based on mutually incompatible premises or "social ontologies" '. A central concern of the new institutionalist project is to restore collective action to the heart of political analysis and this is at odds with the individualistic premises of rational choice. 'For historical institutionalists, institutions are ontologically prior to the individuals who constitute them' (Blyth and Varghese, 1999, p.355).

A further difficulty is that for rational choice theorists, the preferences of actors are exogenous and the ways in which they are derived is of relatively little interest. For historical institutionalists, the way in which the rational actor is viewed is difficult to accept. For them 'Actors cannot simply be assumed to have a fixed (and immutable) preference set, to be blessed with extensive (often perfect) information and foresight and to be self-interested and self-serving utility maximisers.' (Hay and Wincott, 1998, p.954). Any institutionalist version of rational choice would have to be concerned with 'how individuals and institutions interact to create preferences' (Peters, 1999, p.44).

At this point, values, culture and history would return in a way which most rational choice theorists would find unnecessary or superfluous. They would accept that they make simplifying assumptions that are sometimes distorting, but would argue that these are necessary to construct elegant models, particularly at an early stage of theoretical development. Even if they distort reality, their models and methodology are more robust than the alternatives. Indeed, it may be questioned whether the historical institutionalists have a distinctive methodology.

One fundamental problem remains the question of how far rational choice theorists are open to alternative approaches. Almond suggests that they neglect other social science literatures 'that display the variety of values, preferences and goals in time and space' (Almond, 1990, p.135). In particular he argues:

> The failure to relate the economic model of rationality in any way to the sociological, psychological and anthropological literatures and particularly to the work of Max Weber, whose great theoretical accomplishment was an analysis of modern civilization and culture in terms of rationality and rationalization, is the most striking consequence of the almost complete 'economism' of the rational choice literature. (Almond, 1990, p.134)

What is evident from our discussion so far is that political science has been 'more eclectic than most disciplines in borrowing the approaches of others' (Peters, 1999, p.20). Political science has to be understood within the broader context of social science and it is to some of the more significant methodological disputes within social science that we now turn.

Political studies or political science: some methodological considerations

Our review of the dominant paradigms of behaviourism, institutionalism and rational choice has necessarily omitted close analysis of other, less popular, heterodox contenders such as Marxism, feminism, post-modernism and environmentalism. This list is by no means exhaustive and points not only to the eclectic character of modern political science but also to the divergent methodological assumptions which exist within the discipline. These assumptions concerning the character of knowledge (epistemology) and the nature of social reality (social ontology) may seem far removed from a discussion of research methods yet, as Archer (1995, p.5) rightly emphasizes, 'the practical analyst of society needs to know not only *what social reality is*, but also *how to begin to explain it*, before addressing the particular problem under investigation'. In other words, before we can locate a researchable topic, and choose the methods most appropriate to our study, it is important to be aware of basic debates within the philosophy of social science which will allow us to form a coherent link between epistemology/social ontology and research methods (Stoker, 1995, pp.13–16; Grix, 2002). This is essential if we are to be consistent and resist the temptation of 'perspectivism', which 'denies that there are serious underlying reasons for theoretical variety and slides via instrumentalism into a marriage of inconsistent premises' (Archer, 1995, p.5). A useful way into these complex debates is to consider what is commonly seen as the primal problem of the philosophy of the social sciences: *to what extent can society be studied in the same way as nature* (Bhaskar, 1979, p.107)?

The starting point of modern versions of this debate is the recognition that the common sense 'man-in-the-street' worldview of empiricism or positivism is wholly inadequate as a philosophical theory. Positivism, as Benton (1977, p.11) points out, is a variant of the philosophical theory of knowledge – empiricism – which is usually attributed to John Locke. At its heart is the claim that all knowledge is obtained from human sense experience. For classical positivists, knowledge is gained from sensory observation (and is therefore rooted in inductive reasoning); 'facts' exist independently of the observer and his or her values; and the goal of science is thus to build an objective empirical foundation for knowledge which will produce testable and verifiable statements to explain, predict and attribute causality to events and processes in the world. Finally, it is claimed that all science, natural and social, is united in accordance with these positivist principles and that if a proposition is neither true nor false in relation to ascertainable fact nor by virtue of reason or logic, it is, by definition, non-science (and by implication, nonsense).

In terms of social ontology, positivism would seem to be perfectly consistent with Individualism (the social whole can be ultimately reduced to individual beliefs and dispositions) and, in principle but to a lesser extent, with certain versions of Collectivism (the whole is not reducible to the sum of its parts and emergent properties may arise from the collective). The emphasis placed by this approach on observation as the sole means of verification, combined in particular with a crude individualistic social ontology, gave it great appeal to behaviourists in political science, and it continues to be popular (though often unacknowledged) within the rational choice camp (Sanders, 1995; Ward, 1995). A clear line can therefore be drawn between this theory of knowledge and the practical application of specific research methods (usually statistical, all conforming to the strictures of verification, causality and prediction). However, positivism encounters problems when linked to a realist social ontology inasmuch as it cannot entertain a commitment to 'ontological depth' (hidden generative mechanisms at work in nature and society) which, as we will see below, is the hallmark of many 'critical realist' writers in the Marxist, feminist and environmentalist traditions.

This is not the place to rehearse the well known critique of positivism which emerged in philosophical circles in the post-war period (Keat, 1981; Chalmers, 1982 and 1990; Hay, 2002, pp.80–1). It will suffice simply to indicate that three broad traditions developed out of this criticism, each having important implications for political science and the researchers' choice of methods. The responses may be categorized in terms of neo-positivism, conventionalism, and critical realism.

Neo-positivism continues to endorse the naturalistic claim that there is a broad unity of method between the natural and social sciences. However, through the work of Karl Popper, and later in the hands of followers such as Imre Lakatos, neo-positivist writers came to reject induction in favour of deductive modes of reasoning and replaced verification with the notion of falsification (for an overview, see Hay, 2002, pp.81–8). Through his focus on the inevitability of conceptualization (and thereby the impossibility of empiricism) Popper developed the 'hypothetico-deductive model' of scientific reasoning. In this model, from a new idea, tentative conclusions are drawn by means of logical deduction. With the help of other statements previously accepted, certain singular statements (predictions) are derived from the theory. These are then compared with the results of practical applications and experiments. If positive, the results are acceptable for the time being; if negative, then they are falsified and rejected:

So long as a theory withstands detailed and severe tests, and is not superseded by another theory in the course of scientific progress, we may say it has 'proved its mettle' or that it is 'corroborated' ... [but] I never assume that by force of 'verified' conclusions, theories can be established as 'true' or even as merely 'probable'. (Popper, 1959, p.33)

Falsification, Popper's solution to the Kantian problem of demarcation (distinguishing between scientific and non-scientific knowledge), is not – as he admits – an absolutely sharp criterion since there are degrees of testability. But, whilst science may admit 'well testable' and 'hardly testable' theories, non-testable theories are 'of no interest to empirical scientists. They may be described as metaphysical' (Popper, 1963, p.257). In short, Popper proposes a clear unity of method, 'all theoretical and generalizing sciences make use of the same method whether they are natural or social sciences. The methods always consist in offering 'deductive causal explanations' and in testing them by way of predictions' (Popper, 1957, p.131).

The Popperian model of science has been hugely influential in the development of political science in both Europe and the USA. It can, by and large, be seen as the received model of science prevailing within the discipline (Hay, 2002, p.81). However it is not without its critics who claim that Popper merely displaces the problem of induction (since falsification rests on inductive reasoning); that he misunderstands the real development of natural science; and that crucially he fails to acknowledge that knowing subjects play an active role in constituting the world they know (Habermas, 1972; Horkheimer, 1976; Chalmers, 1980; Held, 1980). Lakatos's (1970) attempt to develop 'sophisticated methodological falsificationism' (the 'hard-core' of a research programme is not falsifiable whereas statements deriving from the 'positive heurstic' are testable) may be able to more accurately account for the development of 'real science' and yet the exercise remains bound by Popper's neo-positivist straitjacket and the postulate of methodological individualism.

The second response to the crisis of positivism is that which can be labelled the conventionalist, humanist or hermeneutic. In essence, it argues that the objects of study of the natural and social worlds are so utterly different that they require totally different methods and forms of explanation (Benton, 1977, p.12). The philosophical lineage of this tradition is traceable through Weber and Dilthey to the transcendental idealism of Kant (Bhaskar, 1979, p.107). The most usually cited representative of this tradition, whose work we will briefly review, is the philosopher Peter Winch. Winch's argument focuses on the claim 'that all behaviour which is meaningful (therefore all specifically human behaviour) is *ipso facto* rule-governed' (Winch, 1958, p.52). The social 'sciences', which thus claim to analyse aspects of human behaviour, are in essence studies of rule-following. It may be appropriate for the natural scientist to follow the rules of scientific method but, Winch claims, for the social scientist the object of study, as well as the study of it, is a human activity and is therefore carried out according to rules. It is these rules, rather than the abstract rules of science, which must be understood to gain knowledge of social activity. In short, the 'nature of this knowledge must be very different from the nature of knowledge of physical regularities' (Winch, 1958, p.88). Concepts in social science are thus, in Alfred Schutz's terms, 'second order constructs': that is, they are built on 'the actual common sense first order constructs of actors in their daily lives' (Phillipson, 1972, p.144). It follows that actions are only intelligible 'in the context of, ways of living or modes of social life . . . one cannot apply criteria of logic to modes of social life as such' (Winch, 1958, p.100). Two important consequences flow from Winch's analysis. First, since voluntary behaviour is behaviour to which there is an alternative (and since following a rule involves interpretation and allows for the possibility of making a mistake), prediction, in the sense implied by Popper, is ruled out in social science. Second, Winch rejects Popper's claim that it is possible to develop a causal analysis of action. The relationship between an act of command and an act of obedience is not the same as the relation between thunder and electrical storms, since human actions belong to the realm of concepts and 'the relation of belief to action is not external and contingent, but internal and conceptual' (Winch, 1958, pp.124–5; MacIntyre in Laslett and Runciman, 1962, p.52). Theory construction in social science is different in kind from that found in natural science and ultimately events can only be understood by rejecting Popperian forms of methodological individualism in favour of a focus on 'modes of social life' or context-specific Wittgensteinian 'language games' (Winch, 1958, p.128).

This broad approach in which human beings are seen as distinctively 'free subjects', as the agents of 'meaningful acts', and as the 'creators' of their social world (Benton, 1977, p.12) has spawned a whole new tradition of social and political analysis based on the ideas of indexical (context-specific) reasoning and situational logic.

For example, the phenomenological and ethnomethodological traditions which focus on the taken for granted, the mundane level of the intersubjective world of everyday life, (Garfinkel, 1967; Filmer *et al.*, 1972), have pioneered the development of discourse analysis and the study of natural language in political settings (Heritage, 1984; Howarth, 1995). The inherent 'relativism' of Winch's position has actually been embraced as an antidote to positivism by a number of radical sociologists committed to techniques of participant observation and new feminist methods designed to 'hear women's voices' (Reinharz, 1992). Finally, it has helped bolster wider conventionalist critiques of science such as that articulated by Michel Foucault (1980), Paul Feyerabend (1975) and, in particular, Thomas Kuhn (1962); Kuhn's view that science is not a set of universal standards guided by logic and reason but rather is part of a specific form of culture and its conventions has itself gained widespread acceptance, particularly in feminist circles (Harding, 1986).

Critical realism, the third major response to the crisis of classical positivism, breaks with both Popper and Winch and argues for a position best characterized as 'qualified anti-positivist naturalism' (Bhaskar, 1979, p.108; 1989; Hay, 2002, pp.122–6). In other words, it is possible to give a common account of the development of science but it does not deny that there are important differences in methods grounded in the real differences that exist in their subject matters. While critical realists may disagree on the precise character of the social ontology they wish to endorse, they are united in their rejection of pure forms of Individualism and Collectivism, pointing instead to notions of ontological depth, stratification and emergent group properties (Benton, 1977; Archer, 1995, p.159). There is a unity of method inasmuch as scientific explanations must make reference to 'underlying structures and mechanisms' involved in the causal process, but this idea of 'generative mechanisms underlying observed phenomena' (Keat and Urry, 1975, pp.42–3) provides, it is claimed, a basis for causal analysis without the problems which beset the positivist regularity thesis. Since the objects of social science manifest themselves in 'open systems' (Bhaskar's term for systems where 'invariant empirical regularities do not obtain': p.127) social sciences are denied 'decisive test situations' for their theories. Thus the criteria for the confirmation or rejection of theories cannot be predictive and so must be exclusively explanatory. However, the 'openness' of social systems also indicates that our knowledge is 'necessarily incomplete' (Bhaskar, 1979, p.130). In short, society is not, as the positivists would claim, a mass of separable events and sequences; and neither is it constituted by the momentary context-specific meanings we attach to events. Rather, 'it is a complex and causally efficacious whole – a totality, whose concept must be transformed in theory, and which is being continually transformed in practice' (Bhaskar, 1979, p.134). As an object of study, it cannot be read straight off the empirical world, yet its conclusions are subject to empirical check and its effectiveness in explaining events is not merely accidental (Sayer, 1992, p.4).

This approach, although not without its critics (Hay, 2002, pp.122–6), has proved remarkably popular among critical social scientists. It seems to sidestep the problems associated with positivism, whilst at the same time providing a coherent basis for understanding the development of science throughout the ages without resorting to the sociological simplicities of Kuhnian conventionalism. Moreover, its rejection of positivism's *a priori* restriction of knowledge to that which can be observed allows for the reintroduction of concepts such as 'ideology', 'hegemony' and the 'power of capital' into social science (Benton, 1977). In fact, both Marxism and psychoanalysis can, on this reading, be readmitted into the scientific community. In terms of methods, it should be clear that critical realists will not rest content with simply recounting 'actor's views' or with bald statistical presentation; instead, the aim must be to reject surface explanation and, wherever possible through the use of primary sources (particularly documentary material and elite interviews), reconstruct and reinterpret the events under investigation.

Earlier in this chapter it was proposed that the discipline of politics may be usefully seen as a 'junction subject' born out of history and philosophy but drawing on the insights of cognate disciplines such as economics and sociology. This openness has indeed been a strength, fostering not only interdisciplinary work but also reflection on the methodological problems which the discipline shares with the other social sciences. This chapter has sought to show that whilst these 'meta-theoretical' problems cannot easily be resolved, researchers in the field of politics will benefit from engagement with such issues (Grix, 2002). Methodological pluralism, in the sense of enabling all approaches to flourish, is certainly to be encouraged (Bell and Newby, 1977); yet it must also be distinguished from the slide into the theoretical morass of eclectic pragmatism where 'anything goes' and perspectives are sampled regardless of methodological consistency. Appreciating both the historical development of a discipline and the links between epistemology/social ontology and research methods is the necessary first step towards becoming a competent researcher. Once these tasks are accomplished the next stage is to focus on the complex issue of research design.

Chapter 2

Research Design

Introduction

The purpose of this chapter is to introduce researchers to the idea and importance of research design. Every research project has an implicit or explicit logic that provides the framework for the research and guides the research strategy. The research design will set out the priorities of the research: for example, describing the hypotheses to be tested, listing the research questions, and specifying the evidence needed to provide a convincing test for the research hypotheses and the data needed to answer the research questions. These priorities will determine whether the evidence should be predominantly qualitative or quantitative and how it should be collected and analysed. This chapter will thus discuss the meaning of research design, its functions, and the nature of the research process. In particular, a contrast will be drawn between linear and circular models of the research process. Finally, five different types of research design will be considered, namely experimental design, cross-sectional design, longitudinal design, case study design and finally comparative design.

The meaning of research design

Research design is the logical structure of the research enquiry that the political scientist is engaged upon. It is the plan, the structure and the strategy of the investigation, so conceived as to obtain answers to research questions or problems (Kerlinger, 1986). Research design thus provides the framework for the collection and analysis of data according to the priorities set by the researcher (Bryman, 2001). Hakim argues that 'research design is the point where questions raised in theoretical or policy debates are converted into feasible research projects and research programmes that provide answers to these questions' (Hakim, 2000). The researcher observes a phenomenon that he or she feels is interesting, puzzling, neglected or difficult to understand, and then speculates about its possible causes. Naturally the researcher's training and culture helps that person to develop a number of possible explanations, but it is the role of all scientists to question most of the explanations of phenomena in their field. It is part of their training to subject these explanations to rigorous testing and research. The aim of the research is to generate new knowledge about the phenomenon and to apply, test and refine theories to explain its occurrence and operation.

In deciding how to research a phenomenon, the political scientist, like any social scientist, is confronted with a large number of possible research strategies and methods. The key question is, which research method will provide the best test of the research hypothesis or the best answers to the research questions? In practice, a combination of methods may be used, such as observation, interviews and a survey. The use of such a combination of methods may provide complementary data which can strengthen the findings. This strategy of cross-checking data by using a variety of research methods is known as 'triangulation'.

A distinction is often made between qualitative and quantitative research. Qualitative research is very attractive in that it involves collecting information in depth but from a relatively small number of cases. Examples might be a detailed case study of a revolution, or in-depth interviews with political leaders or members of international organizations, or participant observation of a new social movement. Qualitative research's emphasis on knowledge in depth is at the expense of being able to make generalizations about the phenomenon as a whole. Thus a revolution studied in depth cannot be taken as typical of all revolutions: it may be completely unrepresentative. This is also true for a participant observation study or focus group research. Statistical analysis, based perhaps on a survey of all revolutions, or more likely on a random sample of revolutions, would be needed to provide data from which generalizations could be made about all such events. However, surveys are expensive and often provide relatively limited information. The analysis of survey information also requires specific statistical skills. The best strategy is therefore one that provides the best evidence to test the research hypotheses and one which the researcher is competent to undertake. The research questions and hypotheses will provide an excellent guide to the methods needed to collect the appropriate data. Ackoff argues that the ideal research design is 'the optimum procedure that could be followed where there is no practical restriction' (Ackoff, 1953).

The problem is, of course, that there are always practical considerations. If, for example, a researcher wished to discover why people join political parties, as Seyd, Whiteley, and Richardson have done in their studies of the British Labour and Conservative Parties (Seyd and Whiteley 1992; Whiteley, Seyd and Richardson, 1994; Seyd, Whiteley and Parry 1996), then a possible obvious research design would be to interview the whole membership or, alternatively (and more cheaply), a random sample of the membership. Generalizations could then be made about their reasons for joining (providing that they gave honest and frank answers to the interview questions). However, the practical problems involved in setting up the research project would be substantial. The parties might not have a clearly defined membership, or they might define membership in different ways by, for example, including or excluding members of affiliated organizations. They might well be reluctant to co-operate with a social scientist, regarding him or her as likely to be critical of the party and its procedures, though they might also feel that the research might benefit the party, providing useful information that they did not already have. Even if the leaders agreed to co-operate with the research, ordinary members might refuse to do so. If permission is refused, what should the researcher do? Change the research project? Or adopt a different strategy, perhaps by joining the organization and collecting the data through covert participant observation even though this would violate the ethical principle that it is essential to gain the informed consent of those being researched? (See Chapter 11.)

Whatever the research strategy adopted, whether it is a sample survey, comparative analysis, a case study or participant observation, the political scientist has to consider what is the most appropriate and logical structure for the research project about to be started. Whatever the practical considerations, it would be disastrous to be forced to adopt an inappropriate research design. A content analysis, for example, of party documents would be unlikely to shed much light on why people joined the party. Interviews with party members, particularly those who had recently joined, would provide the most valuable evidence. Many researchers feel that it is essential to use several methods to collect data so that material collected by a survey may be supplemented by observations and in-depth interviews to check the accuracy of the data and to verify that people behave in the ways that they say they do.

There are thus two functions of research design: first, to

develop or conceptualize an operational plan; and second, to ensure that the procedures adopted within the plan are adequate to provide valid, objective and accurate solutions to the research problems. It is this second function that is stressed most frequently. As David de Vaus argues, 'the function of research design is to ensure that the evidence collected enables the researcher to answer the initial research question and test the hypotheses that have been formulated, as unambiguously as possible' (de Vaus 2001). The choice of research design is thus the result of the researcher's decisions about convincing his or her audience that the hypothesis has been reliably tested, and that accurate explanations have been proposed.

The first function, however, is equally important. The researcher must develop the research questions, transform them into hypotheses, and organize these in a logical and consistent way so that they form a theoretical framework for the research. Key concepts will have to be defined. The objective is to develop a clear and logical framework for the research project. In addition, there are a number of practical considerations which play a major role in the decision about which research strategy to adopt. It is very rare for a researcher to have the luxury of being able to choose the ideal research design. Usually the researcher has limited funds and limited time to do the research. For example, a political scientist might be commissioned by a government to assess the political impact of reducing the voting age from 18 to 16 years, and in particular to assess whether these young people wished to have the vote and would use it if it were granted to them. The brief might be to present the results to the relevant government minister in three months' time. It would be impossible and far too expensive to interview all 16 to 18-year-olds, and so a sample would have to be selected. As the timescale is very short, focus group interviews with small numbers of young people in different parts of the country might be the most appropriate methodology. The focus group findings might not be representative of the age group as a whole, but they would be qualitative and indicative of the feelings of young people. In the final analysis the researcher has to balance the wish to provide the most convincing evidence possible with the time and resources available to carry out the project.

When timescales are very short, sponsors often ask researchers to collect and analyse data that is already available. The collection and analysis of secondary data, as this is known, is a very cost-effective way of discovering what research has already been done on the topic and what evidence is available. The analysis of secondary data can reveal what the likely answers to the research questions will be and highlight areas where new research needs to be done. An example of secondary analysis is provided in Box 2.1.

Box 2.1   Example of secondary analysis

The aim of Norris's book, *Democratic Phoenix: Reinventing Political Activism* (2002), was to challenge the widespread view that there has been a long-term decline in political activism in many countries since the Second World War. Norris discusses the problems of defining political participation and measuring long-term trends in a consistent and reliable way. To test her hypotheses about political activism she focuses on electoral turnout, activism in political parties, and participation in a wide range of civic associations. Norris deploys data on 193 different countries from a wide variety of sources, such as survey data from the World Values Study, Eurobarometer, International Social Survey Program, the International Labour Organization and the International Institute for Democratic and Electoral Assistance.

Norris was able to show that there was no consistent fall in electoral turnouts. Countries emerging from poverty and lack of education experienced substantial growth in electoral turnouts. In affluent countries, the costs of registration, the choice of parties and the political impact of the vote affected turnout. Young people were least likely to vote, but the political culture, especially membership of voluntary associations such as unions and churches, were important. In analysing post-modern trends, Norris suggests that new social movements, Internet activism and transnational policy networks may be harbingers of new forms of civic activism.

Source: Norris (2002).

A major practical consideration in choosing a research design is provided by the research training and skills of the researcher. It is natural for a behavioural political scientist trained in statistical analysis to formulate research problems and research designs amenable to survey research, because this methodology is closely associated with voting behaviour and opinion polling, which are central areas of the behavioural approach. Similarly, an economist may design mathematical models to test and illuminate the research problems, while an anthropologist may prefer participant observation and a historian may be most attracted to a project based on documentary analysis. Political science as a 'junction' discipline is not associated with a particular research method, and so its practitioners use a wide variety of methods and research strategies. This makes research design even more important as a guide for selecting appropriate methods for research.

The overall research plan or research design thus provides the framework for the research project. It involves spelling out the research questions, defining key terms and developing hypotheses. In the example of a project to explain why people are attracted to political parties, key terms to be defined would include the party itself and the concept of membership. Pilot interviews could be carried out to develop hypotheses about why people were attracted into membership: whether, for example, they were attracted by its policies, its literature, friendships with party members, its social events, frustration at government failures, or particular incidents which galvanized them into political activity.

Research design thus specifies the kind of evidence needed to answer the research question, test the hypotheses and evaluate the issues that may arise in the course of the research. It determines the research methods and techniques used. It describes how the research will be conducted and carried out. It should do this in a way that will convince a sceptical audience that the researcher has adopted an appropriate methodology and one that will provide convincing data. The choice of research design is thus closely linked to decisions about the appropriate ways to collect the evidence needed to test the hypotheses and to provide answers to the research questions.

The research process

There are two main ways of viewing the process of research. The first is the linear model, which assumes that the process is relatively clear and straightforward and can be broken down into various stages or steps that all research projects go through. The second model is the research wheel, which describes a more complicated process that includes false starts, re-evaluations, and replications of the research as new findings, contradictions and fresh insights reinvigorate the research process. In practice these two models overlap to a considerable degree and are as much complementary as conflictual. The linear model has the virtue of clarity while the research wheel is closer to the research process in operation.

Figure 2.1   *A linear model of the research process*

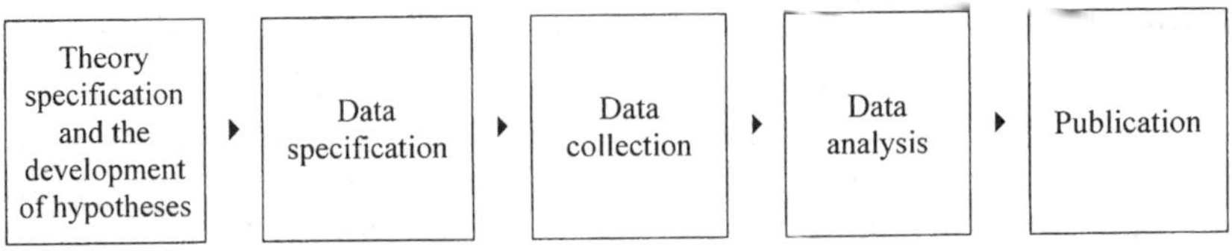

The linear model

An ideal typical description of the research process as a linear series of steps would be as shown in Figure 2.1.

The first stage consists of deciding on the topic of the research project, specifying its scope, developing hypotheses to explain its working, and developing a conceptual framework or model showing the relationships between the different hypotheses and variables the researcher wishes to investigate. This stage has been described as 'theory specification', but it includes all the thinking and theorizing that has to be done before the empirical work can begin. In the example of research on the lowering of the voting age to 16 years, a key hypothesis might be that young people in the relevant age groups are uninterested in politics and therefore would not bother to use the right to vote if it were given to them. This could be formulated as 'Lowering the voting age to 16 years will lead to lower turnouts in elections.' Questions could be designed to discover the political interest and knowledge of young people and their opinions about having and exercising the vote. The researchers might wish to investigate the impact of citizenship studies in schools, the importance of gender, the importance of politics in the family and the attitudes of parents and teachers to the proposed lowering of the voting age.

Data specification

The second stage consists of deciding what kinds of data are appropriate for answering the research questions, testing the hypotheses or investigating the accuracy of the model. This will partly depend on the nature of the research problem but also on the kinds of data that are available and that can be generated and collected. Researchers need to consider if it is possible to gain access to the relevant documents, to interview key officials, or to obtain permission to draw a sample of the relevant group. As usual, the expertise of the researchers and the resources they have at their disposal will influence decisions about the kind of data they consider to be appropriate and collectable (see Box 2.2).

Box 2.2   Designing a historical project

If the research problem is historical, such as the origins of post-war immigration policy in the UK, then documentary sources will be very important: for example, the minutes of the Foreign Labour Committee set up by the government in February 1946, the debates around the Polish Resettlement Act 1947 and the Report of the Royal Commission on Population (1949). These provide a starting point and background to debates over the recruitment of European Volunteer Workers, Irish immigration and immigration from the Caribbean and the Indian subcontinent. The papers of the Ministry of Labour lodged in the Public Record Office in Kew are particularly valuable sources of data on the development of immigration policy in this period. It may sometimes be possible to supplement documentary evidence with interviews with some of the participants, but interviews about events that occurred many years ago will have to be carefully verified. People often remember what they want to remember or firmly believe. For example, in the *Windrush* series on BBC2 television in 1998, oral testimony was presented by a witness who claimed that she had seen Enoch Powell when he was the Minister of Health visiting Barbados to recruit nurses for the British National Health Service. Powell in fact had never visited the Caribbean and the producers of the programme had to make an abject apology.

In the example of why people join political parties, we would probably decide, as did the actual researchers, that interviewing a random sample of members would be the most appropriate method. The members themselves would know best what had stimulated them to join the parties. If permission were obtained for the research, it would be a straightforward process to draw a random sample of members from a central membership list, providing the parties kept such a list. The lack of a central membership list would greatly complicate the selection of a representative sample (Whiteley, Seyd and Richardson, 1994). A questionnaire schedule could then be drawn up and tested on a small pilot sample of members and new hypotheses developed if unexpected reasons for joining were suggested. The final sample would then be interviewed and explanations developed to explain why people joined and what the profile of membership was. The study of British Labour Party and Conservative Party members found that the social characteristics of members of the two parties differed significantly and that their political views differed in significant respects from those of the party leaders. Members claimed to join the parties for altruistic and inspirational reasons, but social reasons and political ambition also played a significant role in the decisions of a minority of party members (Seyd and Whiteley, 1992; Whiteley, Seyd and Richardson, 1994).

Design of the data collection instrument

The third stage of the research process is to organize the ways in which data is to be collected. This may involve the design of a data collection instrument. In a social survey, for example, this will involve designing a questionnaire, a process which includes the framing of questions and the development of attitude scales. If people are to be interviewed in a more informal way, then interview schedules must be drawn up. These may take the form of a fairly detailed list of questions or just topic headings to guide the interviewer in a more relaxed discussion. This may be particularly appropriate when the interviewee is the person with the detailed knowledge of the policy area or the organization that the researcher is investigating.

If it has been decided to carry out a sample survey, then this stage will include the planning and design of the survey. A number of decisions have to be made, such as defining the population to be surveyed and determining the sampling design. Depending on the nature of the research project, the population might be, for example, the electorate, taxpayers, policy-makers, civil servants, party members or MPs.

If the researcher is carrying out a random sampling procedure, then a complete list (or sampling frame) of the relevant population will be required. This could be the electoral register for voters, a housing register for households or another population list. The list may have to be checked for accuracy. In the USA, electoral registers are rarely used for surveys as many people are either not registered or leave their registration to the last minute before the election. A better procedure is thus to conduct a telephone survey or to take a sample of houses and then randomly choose a member of each household.

There are several types of sample design that can be used (see Chapter 4). The most representative are based on simple random sampling procedures, but these are often not used because they are relatively expensive. Other types of sample design include quota sampling and snowball sampling, but these procedures are less rigorous and therefore less representative. Quota samples are often used by market research firms because they are quick and relatively inexpensive. Academic researchers prefer samples based on simple random sampling, as this enables the data to be subjected to tests of statistical significance. However, quota samples are a very popular means of generating information on public opinion, and market research companies claim that if quota selection procedures are carefully followed they can provide accurate and reliable results.

Pilot study

An important step in any research project is the pilot study (see Box 2.3). This is often omitted in 'ideal' type models of the research process, as in the one above, because in practice this step is often left out due to time constraints. This illustrates the difficult choices that often confront the researcher, since in any research project a trial run has considerable advantages. In particular, the data collection instruments such as the questionnaire and the sample design need to be tested.

Box 2.3   The value of pilot studies

Pilot studies enable the researcher to do the following:

1   *Test the questionnaire*
    (a)   Reveal ambiguous, meaningless or embarrassing questions.
    (b)   Convert open-ended questions into closed questions if only a limited range of answers is given.
    (c)   Discover whether new issues are raised during the pilot test and new questions need to be developed.

2   *Rehearse the actual survey*
    (a)   Provide training for interviewers.
    (b)   Alert them to difficulties that were unforeseen.
    (c)   Give them an opportunity to discover how the respondents will react to the survey and thus estimate the level of non-response.
    (d)   Test the accuracy of the sampling frame.

It is essential that the pilot study is carried out on a sample of the actual population that the researcher will investigate in the main survey. Pilot tests on other groups may not uncover the problems that the actual population will have with the survey.

Once the pilot studies have been carried out, the design of the final versions of the data collection instruments can proceed. It is impossible to eliminate every flaw in the questionnaire, so the decision must be made when to go ahead with the survey: that is, when the questionnaire is as good as the researcher can reasonably make it. The time quickly comes when further refinements bring diminish ing returns and additional complications. The researcher will also have to adhere to the timetable for the research agreed with the funding organization.

While the questionnaire is being finalized, the researcher will be deciding on the final sample design, such as whether to use a simple random sample, a multi-stage sample or a non-random design such as quota sample. The pilot study will have provided a check on the accuracy of the sampling frame and the success of the sampling procedures.

Data collection

This stage is the actual process of collecting the data. In a documentary study, this might involve long periods in libraries obtaining copies of significant documents such as minutes of meetings and files from a particular organization. Many organizsations such as the British government, political parties and politically prominent families place restrictions on access – for example, a 30-year rule – so that researchers are refused access to more recent documents (see Chapter 7).

In the case of opinion polls and sample surveys, the collection of data is crucial to the success of the project. It will involve the greatest investment of resources, especially if a commercial market research firm such as Market and Opinion Research International (MORI) has been used to interview the final sample and administer the questionnaire. If a postal sample is being used, then a telephone help line may help to resolve some of the concerns of members of the sample and thereby increase the response rate. This was a successful strategy used by the researchers undertaking the postal survey of Conservative Party members (Seyd, Whiteley and Richardson, 1994). One issue that often arises is how often should an interviewer call back if people are out. The general rule is three times if the overall response rate is to be 50 per cent or higher. Market research firms will carry out random checks to ensure that the interviews have actually been carried out. Butler and Stokes in their classic study of electoral change in Britain (Butler and Stokes, 1969), had a small part of their sample re-interviewed by experienced interviewers to check that the data collected was reliable and consistent.

Coding

Once the data has been collected, it needs to be coded so that analysis of the results can take place more efficiently. Many questions in a survey can be closed if the distribution of the responses is known. They can thus be coded while the interview is taking place by the interviewer ticking the appropriate box.

The real challenge at the coding stage is how to code open-ended questions. This can be a laborious and difficult process, but it is also interesting and stimulating, as it gives the respondents scope to embellish their answers. It also enables the researcher to get a better understanding of how the respondents actually feel about the issues being investigated. Interpretation can be difficult, however, and there is a serious danger that early answers may contaminate (that is, influence the coding of) later answers. After reading the answers to the first set of responses, the coder will gain a general impression of the answers the respondent is giving. This may mean that ambiguous answers given to later questions will be coded to confirm this general impression and the answers of the respondent may become more consistent than is actually warranted by the data.

Data analysis

The analysis of data is never as straightforward as might be thought. This is because all researchers will have expectations about the kind of results the project is likely to generate and this may influence their analysis. Even when analysing quantitative data where there are clear conventions that the researcher can follow, the interpretation of the data and the drawing of conclusions can be influenced by the values and disciplinary training of the analyst. Thus we would not be surprised if a psychologist and a sociologist emphasized different findings and drew different conclusions from the same study. The strength of quantitative research is that since the methods of data analysis are well known and open it is easy for other researchers to follow the same procedures, check the statistical tests and, if those have been carefully done, come up with the same results. The interpretations and conclusions may differ but perhaps not by very much.

In qualitative data analysis the challenges of conducting rigorous and objective data analysis are far greater (Punch, 1998, pp.198–238). How are interview transcripts or field notes to be classified and analysed, and conclusions drawn? If confidentiality has been promised to interviewees, then how can other researchers check that the classifying, editing and summarizing of the data has been well done, and that the analysis conducted and conclusions drawn are appropriate?

Analytic induction is often used by qualitative researchers in their efforts to generalize about social behaviour. Concepts are developed inductively from the data, and are then defined, refined and their implications deduced from the data. In a study of international migrants this might involve defining those who can be described as transnationals and those who are settlers and drawing conclusions about their present and future behaviour: for example, how likely they are to send remittances to relations in their country of origin, how likely they are to learn a new language and how likely they are to migrate to a new country. The most important feature of data analysis is that the researcher should enable the reader to follow the analytical procedures and present sufficient evidence to show that the conclusions are strongly supported.

Publication

The final stage of research is the publication of the results. This usually occurs in the form of a report, academic papers or a book. In general academic researchers have freedom to publish the results of their research providing they have the informed consent of those who have provided them with the research data. If the research has been funded by a Foundation, a Research Council or a University, publication is strongly encouraged. If the research is done as part of a contract with a government department or a company, then permission to publish will have to be obtained from the funder. Normally this is negotiated at the beginning of the project when the contract is drawn up, otherwise the researchers may find their publishing ambitions thwarted after the research has been done. However, it is usually researchers directly employed by funders as part of company or government research departments who are the most strictly controlled. Researchers must also ensure that their manuscript complies with relevant legislation such as the laws of libel and data protection.

The linear model: summary

As the above discussion shows, the simple linear model outlined above can easily be amended to include more stages, especially if the research project involves a sample survey. A more complete outline

Figure 2.2   *The main stages of the research process
as a linear progression*

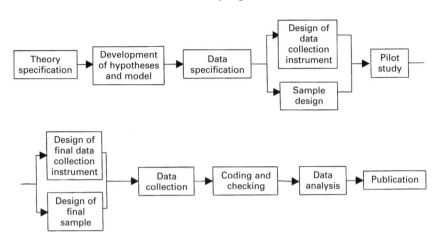

of the linear model of the research process as described above is shown in Figure 2.2.

The linear model has the great advantage of clarity. It specifies the various steps or stages in the research process in a logical and coherent way, but scientific research rarely involves logical sequences. Research rarely goes according to plan, although this is not an argument against having a plan! Burgess notes a study by James Watson which gave a personal account of the discovery of DNA (Burgess, 1993). This showed that science seldom involves a straightforward logical sequence. Instead, in this case it involved some guesswork, competition, rivalry and lucky breaks (Watson, 1968).

A good example of a study which appears to follow the linear model is the classic study of political opinion in Northern Ireland, *Governing Without Consensus,* by Richard Rose (Rose 1971). Rose sets the scene with a detailed historical introduction to the establishment of Northern Ireland as a self-governing province of the UK. He poses what he considers to be the fundamental political problem which is the lack of consensus in Northern Ireland over the legitimacy of the regime and formulates the research problem in terms of the dynamics of political authority. He develops a typology of the authority of regimes based on the degree of diffuse support for the regime among its intended subjects in terms of their support for the regime and compliance with its basic laws, and in

Figure 2.3 *The typology of the authority of regimes*

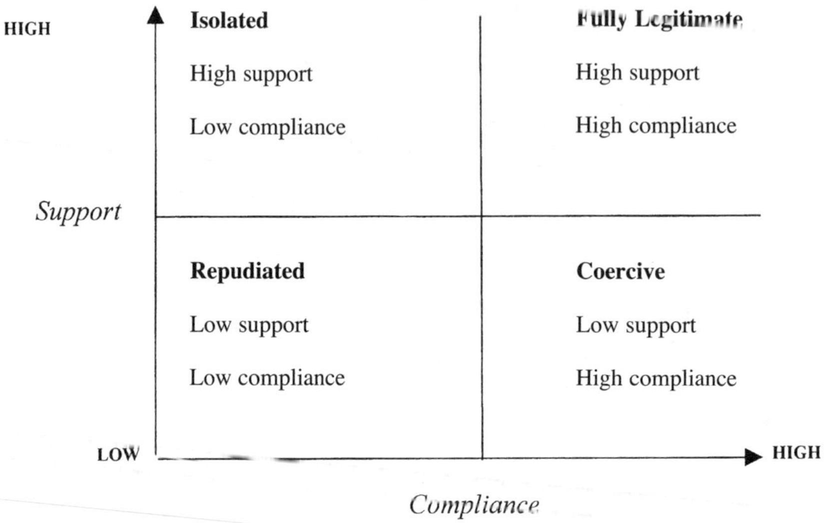

HIGH	**Isolated** High support Low compliance	**Fully Legitimate** High support High compliance
Support		
	Repudiated Low support Low compliance	**Coercive** Low support High compliance
LOW		HIGH

Compliance

Source: adapted from Rose (1971).

particular those laws concerned with political violence, as every state claims a monopoly of the use of legitimate violence (see Figure 2.3).

After a careful discussion of the concept of a regime and related concepts such as nation, state and multi-national regime, Rose develops a questionnaire to measure the dynamics of political authority and the degree of legitimacy the population accord to the Northern Ireland regime. Rose was so concerned to develop a series of questions that would provide valid data from members of both major communities that he piloted his questionnaire seven times. He also used a robust sampling procedure and over-sampled the Northern Ireland population so that he could not only make generalizations about the whole population but also about subgroups such as Catholics and Protestants, working class and middle class, city and rural dwellers.

Surprisingly, Rose found that only a minority of the population (25 per cent) were fully allegiant citizens both loyal to the Northern Ireland regime and willing to accept democratic decisions. A significantly larger proportion (37 per cent) were willing to condone or support the use of violence to achieve or maintain the kind of regime they wanted. These findings about the high level of support for violence were found before the period of the 'troubles' began in 1969, and were particularly strong among the Protestant population.

In general, the description of the research process outlined in *Governing Without Consensus* seems to follow the classic stages of the linear model. Many researchers feel that in practice it is rare for research to follow this step-by-step progression. Mann, for example argues that research is a seamless web without a clear order and without a defined beginning or end (Mann, 1981).

The research wheel

In the research process as wheel, the researcher follows a not dissimilar set of steps to the linear model but may repeat some of the steps in the light of new data which lead to new hypotheses and further research questions requiring additional research. The research process can thus be shown as a large circle containing internal circles. Researchers may repeat the circles as a result of their empirical findings. The research process thus starts with empirical observation which leads to the development of a research proposal or conceptual framework, described as theory specification in our linear model. This then leads to the development of research questions and hypotheses. These may be changed as a result of data collection which may throw up new hypotheses and refute existing ones. This may result in a new conceptual framework being developed and the abandonment of the stages of data analysis, the drawing of generalizations and the development of theory until further research is accomplished. The research wheel highlights the false starts and re-evaluations that occur in all research projects, but this model of research modifies and extends the linear model rather than conflicting with it.

In practice, many researchers feel that both of these models of research design – linear and wheel – are too neat and tidy, to such an extent that they are misleading (Burgess, 1984). Research is a complicated process involving false starts, negotiations with gatekeepers and subjects, ethical dilemmas and pressures from funders and publishers. The project and methods are often redefined in the course of the research. The process is complex, uncertain and never as straightforward as these ideal typical models of the research process suggest.

Figure 2.4   *The research wheel model of the research process*

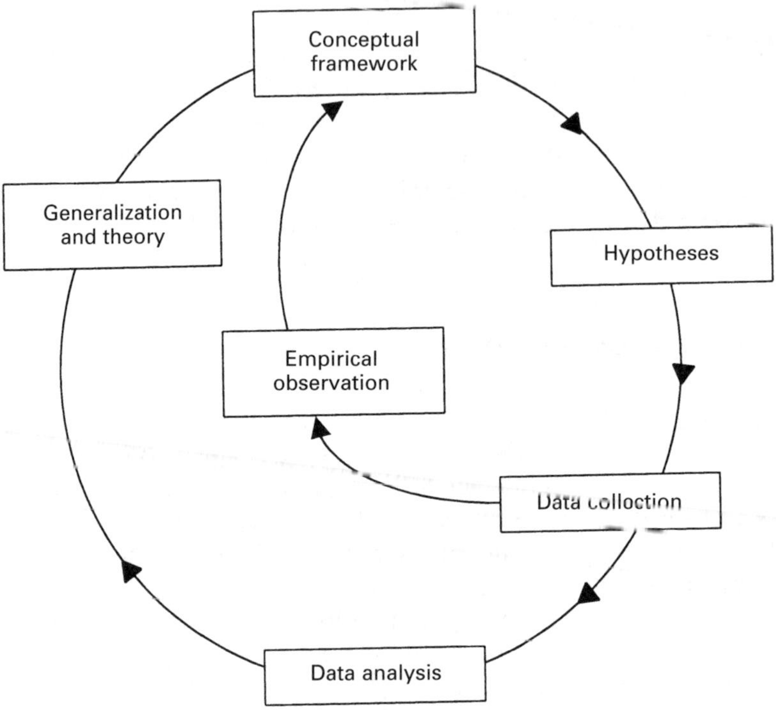

Source: adapted from Burgess (1993), p. 6.

Types of research design

There are five major types of research design, namely experimental design, cross-sectional design, longitudinal design, case study design and comparative design.

Experimental design

Experiments are widely considered to be the best way of determining cause and effect in scientific research. In the laboratory, the scientist is able to control all the variables and, in particular, to manipulate the independent variable and measure its effects, if there are any, on the dependent variable. The effect of heat, light and pressure, for example, on chemical compounds can be measured very accurately and their effects recorded with complete accuracy. In the social sciences it is very difficult to carry out experiments, first because it is extremely difficult to control all the variables, and second because of ethical difficulties involved in experimenting on human beings.

In the early development of sociology, experimental designs were used by researchers interested in the interactions between individuals in small groups. In particular, they were interested in how different leadership styles affected group cohesion and problem-solving capabilities. Groups would be established and the leaders told to act in democratic or dictatorial styles and given tasks to perform. The behaviour of the groups would be observed through two-way mirrors by the researchers in an adjoining room. The impact of these different leadership styles would then be analysed. The smallness of the groups and the use of two-way mirrors enabled the experiments to be conducted, more or less, under laboratory conditions (Bales, 1951). This kind of research is relatively expensive and time-consuming to establish and the results are rather limited.

A famous example of experimental design was an experiment carried out by Milgram to test how far people can be induced to inflict extreme pain and harm on others, when they are ordered to do this (Milgram, 1974). How much pain would they be prepared to inflict before refusing to obey the orders? Milgram recruited volunteers to act out the role of teachers who were instructed to punish learners when they gave incorrect responses to questions. The punishment was in the form of electric shocks which were not, of course, real. The learners were instructed by the researchers on how to act in response to the supposed intensity of the shocks (for example, by howling in simulated pain). The level of the electric shocks was increased until the teacher volunteers refused to administer more shocks. One of the researchers remained in the room with the volunteer teachers encouraging them to continue to administer shocks, arguing that this was part of the experiment and suggesting that the pain was not as bad as the howls from the volunteer learners suggested. To the surprise of the experimenters, some volunteers were willing to continue administering electric shocks even when the learners were exhibiting extreme pain and some even administered (supposedly) lethal doses.

This experiment highlights some of the problems of experimental design in the social sciences. First, how far can this experiment be used to explain 'real life' examples of brutality such as occurred in Nazi concentration camps or in situations such as Rwanda or Bosnia? Second, did the volunteers who participated in the experiment really believe that they were inflicting extreme pain on their supposed victims or did they believe, perhaps subconsciously, that the researchers would not allow the experiment to go so far? This raises the issue of whether experiments involving people can illuminate real-life situations. Third, is it ethical to induce people to inflict pain on others even when this is simulated and in the interests of scientific research?

Events may occur in the real world, as opposed to the laboratory, where something close to an experimental situation happens. In the mid-1990s, television was introduced to the isolated island of St Helena in the South Atlantic. This was seen by some researchers as an ideal opportunity to measure the impact of television (the independent variable) on the local community (the dependent variable) and in particular to assess the impact of television violence on the behaviour of children and young people. A key research question was whether television causes anti-social behaviour. The initial results from the research programme suggest that it does not (Charlton, Gunter and Coles, 1998; Charlton, Coles and Hannan, 1999). However, even in this unique situation it is impossible for the researchers to control all the variables and so measuring the impact of television will be very difficult. It is, for example, impossible to know how the community would have developed without television.

An excellent piece of research was carried out by Daniel into racial discrimination Britain in the 1960s. Daniel employed African-Caribbean, Hungarian and English actors, all claiming the same qualifications and references, to apply for jobs and accommodation. He found that frequently the Caribbean actor was told that the job or accommodation was taken when it was later offered to one of the other candidates. By controlling ethnicity, Daniel was able to prove without any doubt that high levels of racial discrimination existed in the employment and housing markets (Daniel, 1968).

Cross-sectional design

As experiments are so difficult to carry out in real life, social scientists have adopted cross-sectional design as one of their most popular research designs. Cross-sectional design involves the collection of information on a large number of cases at a single point in time, in order to accumulate a body of quantitative or qualitative data in relation to a number of variables in order to discover patterns of association (Bryman, 2001).

Cross-sectional design is strongly associated with quantitative analysis due to the large number of cases on which data is collected and the ease of carrying out statistical tests on these. The data is collected over a short period of time and then analysed for patterns of association between the variables. The variables are not controlled and manipulated by the researcher. This means that it can be very difficult to prove the direction of causality. It is well known, for example, that people upwardly mobile from the working class are more likely to vote Conservative than those who are not upwardly mobile, but is this Conservative voting a result of upward mobility or a precondition in the sense that working-class people with conservative predispositions are more likely to strive for upward mobility?

In political science, social surveys are used with great frequency to explain voting behaviour. In America, Australia and European countries, research funders provide considerable finance for surveys which attempt to explain the reasons why voters have supported particular parties in general elections. The reasons may be short term, such as their policy priorities, their assessments of the party leader, their impression of the economic competence of the party, or manifesto promises. Longer-term factors such as the social environment of the voter – for example, working in the public or private sectors, their class identification and housing tenure – may also be important. Sophisticated statistical analysis is necessary to determine the relative importance of each of these variables.

In Australia in the late 1990s there was considerable concern at the rapid rise and then sharp decline of Pauline Hanson's One Nation Party. In 1998, the One Nation Party gained nearly a quarter of the votes in the Queensland state elections and in the federal elections in October won almost 10 per cent of the votes. Gibson and her colleagues (Gibson, McAllister and Swenson 2002) used data from the Australian Election Study survey to try to explain the bases of support for the One Nation Party. This survey was based on a random sample of the electorate and was conducted by means of a self-completion questionnaire, filled in and returned shortly after the federal elections in October 1998. The response rate was 58 per cent.

The One Nation Party's platform was based on socio-economic populism combining economic protection subsidies for farmers and small businessmen with opposition to Asian immigration, subsidies for Aborigines and gun control. The researchers wished to determine whether racial prejudice formed the basis of support for the One Nation Party, or whether it was based on economic insecurity and fear of unemployment. The data from the 1998 Australian Election Study showed clearly that strong dissatisfaction with Australian democracy and resentment against immigrants and Aborigines made voters more likely to support the One Nation Party. The findings indicated that a voter who was dissatisfied with Australian democracy, viewed immigration as an important issue, resided in the most rural areas and was very hostile to immigrants and Aborigines had a 78 per cent probability of voting for the One Nation Party in the 1998 election for the Australian House of Representatives (Gibson, McAllister and Swenson, 2002, pp.836–7). The authors concluded that race and immigration issues have the potential to mobilize voters and that the decline of the One Nation Party after 1998 did not mean that this issue would not recur in Australian politics.

A major limitation of this kind of cross-sectional design is that the information is collected at a particular point in time and so quickly becomes out of date and is overtaken by new events. In order to overcome the time limitations of cross-sectional design, social scientists often use longitudinal design.

Longitudinal design

The major limitation of cross-sectional design is that it is unable to explain change over time. Social surveys provide a snapshot of facts and opinion at the time the survey was carried out. It is thus impossible to make generalizations over time and to explain the changes that may have taken place. Longitudinal design is one way of overcoming this difficulty. Usually longitudinal design is an extension of survey research. A sample is selected and interviewed at a particular time, $t1$, and the identical sample, as far as possible, is re-interviewed at subsequent intervals, perhaps a year later, $t2$, and then a year after that, $t3$. The researcher can then compare the data from different periods and discover what changes have taken place in, for example, the attitudes and opinions of the sample. He or she will then attempt to explain why the changes have taken place.

Two main types of longitudinal design are often used. The first is the panel study which has already been described. A sample is drawn from a population and interviewed on a topic or series of topics, and then at a later time the identical sample is reinterviewed. It is difficult in practice to reinterview the whole sample as some may have moved, may refuse to be interviewed a second or third time, or may be ill. Those most interested in the research topic are most likely to stay in the panel and these may become more knowledgeable as a result of the interviews.

The second method is to select a group which forms a 'cohort': that is, they are people with a similar characteristic or experience. They may have all been born on the same day, or belong to the same class at school, or belong to the same church, or have been married on the same day. The researcher may wish to interview the cohort about, for example, their education experiences, their health over the years, their occupations, or their experience of family life. This data may be related to their parents' background, the area they come from, and other factors.

A good example of longitudinal analysis in political science was the panel study carried out by David Butler and Donald Stokes called *Political Change in Britain* (Butler and Stokes 1969). Butler and Stokes wished to explain electoral change in Britain and, in particular, why voters switched between the major parties from election to election. They examined some long-term factors influencing electoral change, such as demographic factors, the decline of religion, and immigration, but they were mainly concerned about short-term factors such as changes in attitudes and opinion. They assumed that a national random sample of the electorate reinterviewed several times would provide the best data to explain short-term electoral changes.

Butler and Stokes chose a sample size of 2,560, of whom 2,009 were interviewed in 1963. These people in the panel were re-interviewed in 1964 and 1966. A wealth of detailed information was collected on attitudes to policies, parties, the media, class affiliation, trade union membership and the influence of the local political environment. They were able to begin a popular article on the book with five hypotheses:

H1 People tend to become more Conservative as they grow older.

H2 Trade union membership and activity increase the disposition to vote Labour.

H3 The number of people voting on class lines has been decreasing.

H4 The terms 'left' and 'right' are familiar to most of the electorate.

H5 Within the lifetime of a single Parliament, deaths and coming-of-age among the electorate have only a negligible effect on party fortunes compared with all the switches due to political moods and events.

They were able to claim on the basis of their data that all these hypotheses were false (Butler, 1969).

When it was published, *Political Change in Britain* provided by far the most detailed analysis of voting behaviour in Britain. The authors made some notable findings on the volatility of political opinion, the lack of political sophistication of the electorate and the importance of local environmental effects. They were criticizsed for having a narrow definition of electoral change which focused on the two main parties, and neglected both turnout decline and increasing support for minor parties. However, the book greatly increased the sophistication of British voting research.

Several disadvantages of longitudinal design were evident in the study. First, people in the panel proved increasingly hard to reinterview and so the panel's size declined over time. Second, those most interested in politics stayed in so, for example, the proportion who knew the name of their MP rose from 50.3 per cent in 1963 to 56.3 per cent in 1966. This could partly have been due to the fact that the interviews had an educative effect.

The timing of the interviews can have a big impact on cross-sectional design, but this is also true of longitudinal design. The timing of the interviews in 1963, 1964 and 1966 coincided with times of Labour Party ascendancy in the opinion polls. If the timing had been different, the Conservative Party would have done much better.

In the USA the major example of a longitudinal study is the Panel Study of Income Dynamics which is carried out by the Institute for Social Research at the University of Michigan. The study began in the 1960s with a representative sample of over 5,000 families who are interviewed each year about their income, employment, health, changes in family composition and standard of living. When family members leave to create new households and families, these are included in the panel to compensate for families that drop out of the study. Care is taken to ensure that the panel is as representative of American families as possible. The result of this research is a rich source of data on the employment, income, health and mobility of American families (Hakim, 2000, pp.114–15).

Cohort studies are frequently based on age cohorts: that is, groups of people born at around the same time. A major example is the National Child Development Study in Britain, which focuses on all people born in a single week in March 1958. Information has been collected on this cohort at birth, then at the ages of 7, 11, 16, 23, 33 and 42 years. The data collected has been used to research child development, health, educational progress and attainment, the transition from school to work, family formation, participation in the housing market, and income. Important comparative research has been done on the impact of type of school attended, of an unemployed father, of physical disability and of unequal pay (Hakim, 2000).

Case study design

Case studies are an extremely popular form of research design and are widely used throughout the social sciences. Case studies enable researchers to focus on a single individual, group, community, event, policy area or institution, and study it in depth, perhaps over an extended period of time. The researcher will usually have a number of research questions or hypotheses to give focus to the research and organize the data collection, analysis and presentation of the material. This approach is closely associated with historical study and with anthropology, especially the study of tribal groups, each of which is assumed to be unique, although some of the rituals and milestone events – such as the transition from adolescence to adulthood – may provide interesting comparisons with similar events in other communities.

While both quantitative and qualitative data can be generated by case study design, the approach has more of a qualitative feel to it as it generates a wealth of data relating to one specific case. The data cannot be used to generalize about the population as a whole as the case study is unique and not a representative sample of a tribal group, institution or policy area. Some researchers therefore argue that case studies should be used only to generate hypotheses and theories which then require testing by generating data through other forms of research design which then may lead to wider generalizations.

Despite the limitations of case study design, this approach has had considerable influence in social science research. Whyte's study of a street corner gang in a Boston slum (Whyte 1993) generated considerable insight into the life of the community and fierce debates over the appropriateness of his methodology (Boelen 1992). Similarly, Pettigrew's study of Imperial Chemical Industries (Pettigrew, 1985) and Pryce's study of African-Caribbeans in Bristol (Pryce 1979) both generated considerable discussion about their wider importance and applicability. In political science, the theoretical debates which surrounded community power studies in the 1960s were illuminated by case studies of the organization and operation of power in such local communities such as New Haven (Dahl, 1961) and Baltimore (Bachrach and Baratz, 1970).

In order to have a wider impact than that of merely being a detailed account of a unique case, a strong theoretical dimension is often incorporated into case study design. A good example of this approach is the critical case study. Here the researcher has a clearly defined hypothesis or theory to test and the case study is designed so that wider generalizations can be drawn. A good example of a critical case study is the research by Goldthorpe and his colleagues, *The Affluent Worker: Political Attitudes and Behaviour* (Goldthorpe *et al.*, 1968). In the 1960s the theory developed that rising living standards and higher pay were causing some manual workers to adopt middle-class values and lifestyles, including changing their political allegiances from Labour to Conservative. This became known as the 'embourgeoisement thesis'.

Goldthorpe and his colleagues were highly sceptical of this thesis and decided to test it using a critical case study design. They selected a town and three groups of affluent workers whom they thought fitted the affluent worker thesis. They thus gave the embourgeoisement thesis the most favourable conditions for being proved. They then interviewed random samples of these affluent workers about their lifestyles, voting behaviour and political attitudes. They found no evidence to support the embourgeoisement thesis but they did argue that traditional forms of working-class solidarity were being replaced by more instrumental forms of behaviour. They then argued that as the embourgeoisement thesis was disproved under these most favourable conditions, the thesis was unlikely to exist anywhere else. It was widely agreed that Goldthorpe and his colleagues had convincingly supported their case. As a result of the study, the embourgeoisement thesis was discredited and new theories had to be developed to explain Conservative voting among manual workers.

Subsequent research challenged some of the conclusions of the affluent worker case study, in particular the argument that more instrumental forms of lifestyle were being adopted. Devine suggested that lifestyles and attitudes had not changed as much as Goldthorpe and his colleagues had supposed (Devine, 1992).

Even in descriptive case studies there must be a focus for the research so that it does not become a haphazard collection of material about the selected case study. In Seyd and Whiteley's study of British Labour Party membership, the focus is on the importance of ordinary Party members, their functions in the Party and reasons for joining. Seyd and Whiteley then develop a theory of selective incentives to explain why people join the party (Seyd and Whiteley, 1992).

A case study design can be based on single or multiple cases.

Carefully selected multiple cases will provide a much more robust test of a theory and can specify the conditions under which hypotheses and theories may or may not hold. Thus Seyd and Whiteley followed up their study of Labour Party membership with a similar study of Conservative Party membership to see whether their theory of party membership could be confirmed or modified (Whiteley, Seyd and Richardson, 1994).

The attractiveness of case studies is that data on a wide range of variables can be collected on a single group, institution or policy area. A relatively complete account of the phenomenon can thus be achieved. This enables the researcher to argue convincingly about the relationships between the variables and present causal explanations for events and processes. These explanations and generalizations are limited to the particular case study at the particular time of the investigation so a wealth of detailed information is collected which is specific to the particular case study. It may be possible to replicate the research at a later date but it may be impossible to know whether changes in an institution, for example, are due to changes in personnel or external developments such as new government policies.

Comparative design

Comparative design is one of the most important research designs in political science. If we wish to understand the conditions under which democracies develop and thrive, or the conditions under which revolutions occur or under which wars break out, there is no alternative but to compare these events. Other forms of research design would be impracticable or less appropriate. The more cases or examples that are studied, the more likely that common causes can be found and generalizations made. Political events and processes are often clarified and illuminated by comparison with similar events and processes in other contexts. Thus it is impossible to judge how successful British democracy is without a benchmark for comparison. The benchmark may be an idealized model of a modern democratic system or existing democratic systems which are felt to make fair and appropriate comparators, perhaps because they have similar levels of education, wealth and industrialization. Thus Butler and Stokes argue that 'Comparisons of political systems can extend our understanding of British politics and lead to still more general formulations of the process of change' (Butler and Stokes, 1969, p.533).

The major difficulty with comparative design is in finding comparable cases: that is, examples which are similar in a large number of respects to the case which the researchers want to treat as constant, but dissimilar in the variables that they wish to compare to each other. The researchers can never be certain that the two or more political systems being compared agree or differ in all respects save the ones under investigation (Lijphart, 1971).

Comparative design has thus grown out of the desire both to understand better one's own political system by comparing it with others, and also to make generalizations about political practices and processes, such as what are the conditions under which territorial minorities prefer integration, or autonomy in a federal state, or complete independence? Does proportional representation ensure greater parliamentary representation for minorities and women?

A classic study using comparative design in political science was *The Civic Culture* by Almond and Verba (Almond and Verba, 1963). They wished to investigate the political cultures of western democracies in order to understand the basis on which democracy was sustained. They decided to interview random samples of the electorates in five democracies, namely Britain, the USA, Germany, Italy and Mexico. They endeavoured to build up a picture of the political culture of each country by interviewing voters about their knowledge of the political system and its operation, their feeling about political roles and institutions and their judgements about the effectiveness of government, the wider political system and the role of democracy. They were particularly interested in what voters felt about their own rights and duties as citizens and their own political role in the democratic process. Almond and Verba developed three typologies of political culture, namely the parochial, subject and participant political cultures. They then analysed the effectiveness of democracy in each of these cultural contexts and classified each of the countries they had investigated. They concluded that a mixed political culture, which they called the Civic Culture, showed the best degree of congruence between democratic political institutions and types of political culture.

Armer argues that a major methodological task in comparative research is to devise and select theoretical problems, conceptual schemes, samples and measurement and analysis strategies that are comparable or equivalent across the societies involved in a particular study (Armer, 1973, p.51). *The Civic Culture* was a hugely ambitious comparative study which generated considerable information and stimulating ideas about political culture, but failed some of Armer's tests. The countries were too diverse, particularly Mexico and the USA, to make appropriate comparators and it proved impossible to standardize the samples and questionnaires. There thus developed considerable scepticism about the concept of political culture used by Almond and Verba and the value of some of their findings.

Comparative design thus presents the researcher with considerable challenges, especially when different countries are being compared. The researcher must select a theoretical problem that is best illuminated by comparative research: for example, why women are included in the political elite in Denmark but excluded in Britain and France (Siim, 2000). Relevant and equivalent data should then be collected and hypotheses tested, such as the impact of the electoral system or diverse traditions of citizenship in the various countries, and appropriate conclusions drawn. Comparative analysis sharpens our understanding of the context in which theoretical problems occur and enables causal inferences to be drawn. However, as comparative analysis usually involves only a relatively limited number of cases, caution has to be maintained about the levels of generalisation that can be made.

Conclusion

The planning and execution of a research project are critical to its success. This plan or research design involves determining the objectives of the research, developing research questions, transforming these questions into hypotheses, and deciding on the appropriate research strategy to test the hypotheses and convince a sceptical audience that the evidence is appropriate and valid and that the conclusions drawn from the analysis are accurate. This chapter has contrasted the linear model of the research process with that of the research wheel. It has been argued that both of these models are valuable in describing the research process but that neither fully captures the complexity of carrying out research. In practice, research is a highly complicated process involving the development of ideas, raising funds to finance the testing of these ideas, negotiating with the funders, employing researchers or managing co-researchers, negotiating with gatekeepers and subjects, collecting data, resolving ethical dilemmas and writing up the material for publication. This chapter has described five major types of research design including their advantages and limitations. The issues raised in this chapter are discussed in greater detail in the following chapters, beginning with the comparative method.

Chapter 3

Comparative Methodology

To make comparisons is a natural way of putting information in a context where it can be assessed and interpreted. This is especially true when we encounter new information about some issue and begin to integrate it with previous knowledge. For example, we might know that in Germany, Denmark and the Netherlands the political executive is based in the legislature and can only survive with support from the legislature; this is what makes these countries so-called parliamentary political systems. Then, turning to France, it is striking that its political executive is linked to the legislature in quite a different way: the French President is a directly elected Head of Government (and Head of State) whose survival does not depend on the support of the legislature. To understand fully the significant political consequences of the French semi-presidential political system, it is quite instinctive to compare it to the already familiar parliamentary systems, and in this way to integrate old and new knowledge. By comparing parliamentary and presidential systems, it is possible to acquire a greater understanding of each; as Rudyard Kipling said in his poem, 'The English Flag': 'what should they know of England who only England know?' Research from virtually all political science research traditions and sub-fields of study can (and does) fit under the label 'comparative'. There are examples of quantitative and qualitative comparative research, large-n, small-n and even single-n comparative research, inductive and deductive comparative research, spanning every conceivable substantive topic (see Rogowski, 1993, for an extensive survey of comparative research).

In order to gauge what the comparative method can and cannot achieve, it will be placed alongside the experimental and statistical methods in the first section of this chapter. The subsequent section details some basic comparative research designs, while the advantages and disadvantages of this type of research are spelt out in the next two sections. Case selection is the topic of the final section. Case selection merits some special attention because the quality of a piece of comparative research depends very largely on what cases are

58

included. Applying the comparative method in a rigorous attempt to test some proposition is only possible if the cases are comparable. This is the sort of comparison that this chapter addresses. In contrast, comparisons of cases as a means of persuasion without a clearly thought out case selection and analysis are not, strictly speaking, using the comparative method.

Comparative political science: substance and method

Calling oneself a comparativist, or saying that one is studying comparative political science, can mean at least three different things (Mair, 1996, pp.309–10). First, comparative political science can refer to the study of foreign countries. This type of comparative political science often consists of single-country studies (such as Italian politics, New Zealand politics, Canadian politics, etc.) which can be considered as implicitly comparative if they draw on more widely applied theories or models of politics. If so, then case studies can be seen as part of a larger, comparative body of research. Nevertheless, this type of comparative research tends to be more focused on collecting and presenting facts about a single case than on making a sustained contribution to the development of theories and hypotheses. Second, there is a significant body of explicitly comparative research: that is, research covering more than one case. Systematic comparisons of some aspect of the political systems of two or more countries often provide the empirical basis for building and refining general political science theories. The third meaning of comparative political science refers to the methods used to carry out comparative research, and this is the focus of the remainder of this chapter.

In a seminal article from 1971, Arend Lijphart placed the comparative method, which he defined as 'a broad-gauge, general method, not a narrow, specialized technique' (1971, p.683), alongside experimental and statistical methods in political science (see also Ragin, 1987, pp.61–4, on the relationship between comparative and statistical control). The article posited that these three methods aim to establish scientific explanations consisting of two elements: first, a specified empirical relationship between two or more variables, and second, the potential effects of all other variables on that relationship are held constant (that is, they are somehow eliminated or controlled for in the research design). It is, strictly speaking, not necessary to include the second element since it follows automatically from the first element: unless 'all other variables' are controlled for, it would not be possible to specify an empirical relationship between two or more variables. The experimental method normally has a better ability to generate this type of explanation than the statistic and comparative methods. However, in political science such explanations are rare because the research environment is impossible to control fully. Take the example of some political scientists who are studying an election because they want to learn about the impact of the particular electoral system used in that election. In order to be certain that it was the electoral system and not something else that had a particular consequence, it would be necessary to turn back time, change the electoral system in some major respect, and then rerun the election. The observed differences between the first and second time the election took place could then safely be put down to the electoral system. The impossibility of controlling the research environment leads to what King, Keohane and Verba (1994) call the fundamental problem of causal inference, and it is a very fundamental problem because without experimental control it is impossible to say with complete certainty that one's conclusions are correct (causal inference is discussed in more detail in Chapter 6).

The experimental method is the best known way of establishing explanations that fulfil the criteria of, first, having a specified empirical relationship between two or more variables, and, second, controlling for possible effects of other variables. When experiments are not possible, the statistical method is often available to political scientists. This method 'entails the conceptual (mathematical) manipulation of empirically observed data – which cannot be manipulated situationally as in experimental design – in order to discover controlled relationships among variables' (Lijphart, 1971, p.684). That is, when it is not possible to manipulate a research setting as in an experiment, then the statistical method can be a useful way to assess the relationship between two or more variables. The statistical method does not have as strong a control function as the experimental method, and thus statistically established empirical relationships cannot be viewed with the same level of confidence. However, there are techniques for assessing how much confidence one can have in a given statistical relationship (see Chapter 6).

The comparative method is about observing and comparing carefully selected cases on the basis of some stimulus being absent or present. The comparative method operates on the same logic as the experimental method, which has been described as 'nothing but the comparative method where the cases to be compared are produced to order and under controlled conditions' (Parsons, 1949, p.743). For example, we might like to know whether and how decreases in trade union membership (a phenomenon that occurred in many western European countries in the last decades of the twentieth century) affect class-based voting. In order to assess the impact of trade union membership on class-based voting, then, it is useful to compare levels of trade union membership and class-based voting in different countries (or over time). However, since the ability to control the political environment is so limited, these comparisons do not reach experimental standards. The conclusions are drawn from comparisons, not experiments. As a consequence, the comparative method (and the statistical method) makes claims about empirically observed relationships without rigorous controls for other variables, and here the comparative method is even weaker than the statistical method. Quantitative comparative research bridges the two research methods. If a comparison involved enough cases for statistical control to be possible, then, as Lijphart points out (1971, p.684), there would be no real difference between the statistical and comparative methods. In fact, the only thing that prevents (much) comparative analysis from being statistical is the number of cases included. The number of comparable cases available seldom satisfies the assumptions of statistical control techniques.

Political science proceeds by imposing some sort of order on processes, events and phenomena that do not easily conform to any sort of order. The real difficulty of political science is to make 'convincing statements about the causation of political phenomena, given the complexity of interactions among the whole range of social phenomena and the number of external sources of variance' (Peters 1998, p.28). Researching politics can be seen as a process of shifting focus from the level of *particular* pieces of information to the *general* level of theory and hypotheses. If, for instance, we are interested in the fairly recent electoral successes of far right parties across Western Europe, we might decide to study the rise of the Austrian Freedom Party and the Vlaams Blok in Belgium. The reason to study these *particular* cases is to formulate *general* conclusions about far-right parties. A general theory of far-right parties is the 'order' we want to impose on flourishing far-right parties.

The comparative method can help alleviate but rarely, if ever, resolve the fundamental problem of causal inference inasmuch as it can emulate the experimental method. A chemist might, for example, pour a measure of a chemical into two bowls, and then add a second chemical to one of the bowls and observe what happens. The chemist can safely attribute the reaction between the two chemicals to the addition of the second chemical, because in the bowl containing only one chemical no reaction at all took place. In a similar vein, in political science the comparative method can facilitate the isolation of certain factors of interest, if the cases that are selected for study have been carefully chosen with this in mind. This is the logic of making comparisons. Exploiting the logic of comparison means choosing cases that isolate one or a small number of factors that appear relevant in producing a particular political outcome.

Designing comparative research

There are two basic comparative research designs: most similar research designs, and most different research designs. The most important aspect of formulating either a most similar or a most different research design is to select cases that make it possible to conclude something interesting about one's research question. Comparative case selection should take place on the basis of three selection principles: cases should 'maximise experimental variance, minimise error variance, and control extraneous variance' (Peters, 1998, p.31). In less technical language, by choosing cases that isolate the effect of the factor or factors that is being investigated, we exploit the logic of comparison as much as possible (we 'maximise experimental variance'). To do so, it is necessary to choose cases that are representative, not one-off or unusual ('minimise error variance') and to minimize the effect of all other factors ('control extraneous variance').

Variables (or factors) can be divided into three categories: dependent variables, independent variables, and other variables, which we can call spurious or intervening variables. Dependent variables are the phenomena that we want to explain in the research. Independent variables are the things we suspect influence the dependent variable. Everything else (that is, everything that makes up the social, economic and political context and backdrop of the dependent and independent variables) fits into the third category. Such variables might be spurious (that is, falsely appear to have some bearing on the relationship between the dependent and independent variables) or intervening (that is, actually having some bearing on the relationship between the dependent and independent variables).

The simplest way to understand what most similar and most different research designs are, and how they differ from each other, is to keep these three categories of variables in mind. The first point to note is that the dependent variable is irrelevant at the research design stage, in the sense that cases should not be included or excluded on the basis of their values on the dependent variable. This can be called 'the principle of not selecting on the dependent variable', and there is an example of this in the final section of this chapter (see also Geddes, 1990, pp.134–41). The second point to note applies to most similar research designs (see Box 3.1). They compare two or more cases that are as different as possible in terms of the independent variable(s) and as similar as possible on all the spurious and intervening variables ('backdrop variables'). In contrast, a most different research design compares two or more cases that are as similar as possible in terms of the independent variable(s) and as different as possible on all the spurious and intervening variables.

The logic behind most similar research designs is that by a basic process of elimination all the variables in the 'other' category can be ruled out of the research. If they do have an effect on the dependent variable, they have the same effect on the dependent variable across all cases. This leaves the independent variable, which has a differential effect on the dependent variable in the two or more cases (which is the reason why the cases were selected in the first place). This means that any observed differences between cases with respect to the dependent variable can be associated with the only variable that makes the cases different: the independent variable. In brief, 'the more circumstances the selected cases have in common, the easier it is to locate the variables that do differ and which may thus be considered as the first candidates for investigation as causal or explanatory variables' (Castles, cited in Pennings, Keman and Kleinnijenhuis, 1999, p.12).

For example, the well-known hypothesis about economic voting holds that voters judge government performance on the basis of the state of the economy and vote to return or replace the government on the basis of this performance indicator (Kinder and Kiewiet, 1979; Lewis-Beck, 1988; Lewis-Beck and Lockerbie, 1989; Markus, 1993; Gavin and Sanders, 1997). Here, 'the state of the economy' is the independent variable, which is hypothesized to generate a specified political outcome on the dependent variable, 'government popularity'.

The logic of comparison in a most similar research design is consequently to isolate the effect of an independent variable by controlling

Box 3.1   Research design: most similar electoral systems and gender balances in Parliament (I)

This type of research design compares two or more cases that have as much in common as possible, except the independent variable. Trying to answer the research question 'Do electoral systems that are more proportional generate a more even gender balance in Parliament?', these variables might be deemed relevant:

Dependent variable:	Gender balance in Parliament (%)
Independent variable:	Electoral system
Spurious/intervening:	Gender balance in the workforce (%)
	Equality legislation
	Political culture
	Parties' candidate selection procedures

The cases in a most similar research design should have different electoral systems but be as similar as possible in all other respects. On this basis it is reasonable to compare the UK to any of the West European proportional representation (PR) countries. However, an even better idea would be to break down the UK case into several cases. General elections in the UK (Westminster elections) use the Single Member Plurality (SMP) system. However, elections to the UK's three devolved assemblies take place by other electoral systems: the Northern Ireland Assembly is elected by proportional representation by the single transferable vote (PR-STV), while the Scottish Parliament and the Welsh Assembly are elected by a mixed (e.g., mixing elements of SMP and PR) electoral system.

→

for the effects of spurious and intervening variables. For an illustration of some of the difficulties of case selection, see Box 3.2.

The third point to note is that most different research designs use the logic of comparison in a reverse manner (see Box 3.3). Case selection proceeds on the basis that the cases must not differ from each other with respect to the independent variable, but must be as different as possible from each other in terms of spurious and intervening variables. The logic behind this type of research design is that if the independent variable has an effect on the dependent variable, then it should have the same effect despite the cases being so different when it comes to the spurious and intervening variables. To continue with the example of economic voting, a most different research design would be based on the assumption that if the 'state of the economy' strongly influences 'government popularity', then

→

By breaking the UK case into many cases that can be compared to each other, many (if not all) spurious and intervening variables are held constant: the electoral system changes depending on what body is being elected, but political culture, proportions of women in the workforce, etc., remain relatively unchanged. To test the effect of electoral systems on gender balance, the following four cases could be compared:

- Westminster elections
- Northern Ireland Assembly elections
- Scottish Parliament elections
- Welsh Assembly elections.

If the proportionality of an electoral system really impacts on gender balance, then election results should show the following (if they do not, then there are intervening variables that have not been, but should be, taken into account):

- the Northern Ireland Assembly is the most gender balanced Assembly in the UK
- the Scottish Parliament and the Welsh Assembly have intermediate levels of gender balance
- Westminster is the least gender balanced Assembly in the UK
- within Northern Ireland, Scotland and Wales, the gender balance among returned representatives to the devolved assembly should be greater than among returned representatives to Westminster.

Sources: Farrell (2001); Gallagher, Laver and Mair (2001).

we would expect to see governments win elections in cases where the economy is doing well, and lose elections in cases with poor economic performance, regardless of all other circumstances. Francis Castles has summarized the most different approach as one that involves 'a comparison on the basis of dissimilarity in as many respects as possible in the hope that after all the differing circumstances have been discounted as explanations, there will remain one alone in which all the instances agree' (cited in Pennings, Keman and Kleinnijenhuis, 1999, p.12). If the economic voting hypothesis were true, then the variable that remained would be 'the state of the economy'. Comparing two or more cases with similar economic performance in the year or so prior to an election, but which were different in terms of party systems, electoral systems, single party/coalition government, (and so on) should ideally establish

Box 3.2   The Difficulties of Case Selection: Almond and Verba's The Civic Culture

Gabriel Almond and Sidney Verba's *The Civic Culture: Political Attitudes and Democracy in Five Nations* (1963; later complemented with *The Civic Culture Revisited* first published in 1980) remains a landmark text in the study of political culture. The authors' hypothesis was that democracy is more stable in countries with a particular kind of political culture, which they labelled a 'civic culture'. (Note that the cases were selected on the dependent variable.)

Almond and Verba's criteria for case selection:

- the selected cases had to be democratic countries
- the selected cases had to be countries with different historical experiences with respect to democracy.

Selected cases:

- USA and Britain: examples of stable democracies
- Germany: had a 'broken' democratic record
- Italy and Mexico: had less developed societies whose political systems were in transition to democracy.

Points to note about this case selection:

- selection on the dependent variable: this is suitable for a small *n* study
- failure to include any non-democracies: Almond and Verba forwent the possibility of examining their hypothesis as rigorously as possible. If their hypothesis about political culture and stable democracy were true, then the political cultures of non-democracies would presumably be in some key respect fundamentally different from the political cultures of stable democracies. Due to their case selection, however, Almond and Verba were not able to answer this key question.

whether 'the state of the economy' has a constant effect on 'government popularity'.

Both the most different and the most similar research designs can 'result in the confirmation of theoretical statements' (Przeworski and Teune, 1970, p.35). In theory both types of comparative research design make the assumption that it is possible to reach the level of experimental control. In actual political science research designs this is highly unusual, but the comparative method remains one of the most widely used forms of research because it is often the best available alternative to experimental research.

Box 3.3   Research design: most different electoral systems and gender balances in Parliament (II)

This type of research design compares two or more cases that are as different as possible except on the independent variable. For simplicity's sake, let's stay with the research question from Box 3.1: 'Is there a connection between a country's electoral system and the gender balance in Parliament?' To recap, the all the relevant variables are as follows:

Dependent variable:	Gender balance in Parliament (%)
Independent variable:	Electoral system
Other variables:	Gender balance in the workforce (%)
	Equality legislation
	Political culture
	Parties' candidate selection procedures

In a most different research design the independent variable should be the same across all cases. Referring back to Box 3.1, elections to the Scottish Parliament and Welsh Assembly might seem the ideal cases to compare here, since they use the same mixed electoral system. However, the other requirement of a most different research design is that the cases should be as different as possible in terms of all the other variables. Scotland and Wales are clearly not wisely selected cases from this perspective.

The 'devil is in the detail' when it comes to electoral systems: there is almost endless variation between electoral systems in different countries, even ones that can be broadly categorized as belonging to the same general category of electoral systems (e.g., although both France and Australia have majority systems, France operates a two ballot system, while in Australia the system has a single round of preferential voting where voters are obliged to rank all candidates on the ballot paper, or else their vote is declared invalid).

Since there is so much variety it is often necessary to select the 'least bad' cases: for example, two countries with List-PR electoral systems even if it is well known that they differ in the detail. Sweden and Portugal, for example, have List-PR electoral systems, but have different constituency-level seats allocation formulae; in Sweden there is a higher tier but not in Portugal; and in Sweden voters can choose candidates within a party on the party list, but Portugese voters are not able to do this.

A Swedish–Portugese comparison in a most different research design would also be useful in that these countries are quite different generally in terms of gender roles. Therefore, if it is really the electoral system that determines the gender balance in Parliament, then the Swedish and Portugese Parliaments (and all other Parliaments elected by List-PR) would be expected to have similar gender balances despite all the other differences between these countries.

Why compare? The advantages

The primary advantages of the comparative method can be summa rized under four headings: it allows us to contextualize knowledge; to improve classifications; to formulate and test hypotheses; and to make predictions (Hague and Harrop 2001).

We make comparisons to contextualize knowledge almost without thinking about it in everyday life as well as in more formal political analysis, to integrate and make sense of newly acquired knowledge. Even if the primary interest and concern is with one particular case or event, considering it in the context of other, similar cases or events advances our understanding of the one of primary interest. Dogan and Pelassy (1990) add that this enables us to overcome implicit ethnocentrism, in that comparisons force the recognition that not all countries have the same political system as the one with which we might be most familiar. This point applied more broadly tells us that the comparative method advances a heightened, comprehensive awareness of the diversity of the political world.

A related advantage of approaching a research question comparatively is that doing so has the potential to improve the classifications we use to impose some sort of order on the diversity of the political world. Classification is the 'basic type of concept formation ... neither comparison (non-metric ordering) nor measurement proper can take place without it' (Kalleberg, 1966, p.73): that is, classification is prior to comparison in the sense that typically we choose cases to compare because they belong to a particular classification. Consequently, a comparative analysis is only ever as good as the classification behind it. However, since the research process is a dynamic between theoretical level (that is, the classification) and the empirical level (the measurements we use), the comparison will then feed back into the classification and improve it by refining it on the basis of additional empirical information. The concept of the nation-state is a good example of how comparisons can improve classifications. Since the Treaty of Westphalia (1648) the sovereign nation-state has been the basic political unit in Europe and, later, elsewhere, too. The concept of the nation-state suggests that a nation and its state coincide with each other perfectly, and that within its state a nation exercises its right to self-determination. This is more or less the case with highly homogeneous countries such as Denmark, where the Danish nation is co-terminus with the Danish state. However, it is also routinely assumed that, for example, Ireland is a nation-state, although the

Irish nation is not co-terminous with the Irish state. A significant proportion of the Irish nation in fact live in Northern Ireland which is in the jurisdiction of the UK. The UK itself provides another example of how mistaken the assumption can be that a nation and a state coincide: here, several nations (English, Irish, Scottish and Welsh) live within the same state. Comparing Finland, Denmark, Ireland, the UK and additional nation-states reveals how varied and layered a seemingly straightforward and commonplace concept such as the nation-state is, and points up the need to refine it into a number of classifications of different types of nation-states on the basis of how nation and state relate to each other.

In a similar vein, taking a comparative perspective on a research question also enables hypothesis testing and development. As we have already seen, in investigating a supposed empirical relationship between two or more variables, a comparative research design can test hypotheses through isolating the effect of one variable on another. Inasmuch as doing so throws up new ideas and possibilities, it can also suggest how the hypothesis might be usefully refined or reformulated. Having a hypothesis about the effect of the electoral system on the nature of the party system (a much-debated matter: see Duverger, 1954; Harrop and Miller, 1984; Lijphart, 1994; Sartori, 1994; Farrrell, 2001) to the effect that a plurality electoral system has a tendency to generate two-party systems and proportional representation electoral systems tend to generate multi-party systems, simply studying one country will not reveal enough. It is only by taking a comparative perspective that the differential effect (or lack thereof) on party systems of different electoral systems may be identified. In the process of testing this hypothesis, some cases might seem to offer confirmation whereas other cases might seem contrary to it (and there is of course the question of how to classify cases such as Germany and Italy, whose electoral systems combine elements of plurality and proportional representation). As an example of a country with a plurality electoral system, the domination of two parties (the Conservative and Labour parties) in British politics ostensibly confirms the hypothesis although there are other parties, too. Similarly, the Netherlands, Belgium, the Scandinavian countries, Spain and many others confirm the hypothesized relationship between proportional representation and multi-party systems. In contrast, Malta has proportional representation but Maltese politics is highly dominated by two parties (the National and Labour parties), possibly even more so than British politics. This might be taken to suggest that the original hypothesis might be too simplistic, and that there are other relevant variables that influence the extent to which electoral systems shape party systems.

Finally, the comparative method can enable predictions about politics. If an empirical relationship between two or more variables has been observed in one temporal or spatial setting, then it can be inferred that the same relationship would hold in another temporal or spatial setting. We can take the example of how EU membership has affected the ability of the four traditionally neutral member states – Austria, Finland, Ireland and Sweden – to make independent foreign policy. Since in the post-Cold War era the EU has started to develop its own foreign, security and defence capability and identity, commensurate with its global economic standing, it might reasonably be assumed that these four member states would find their independent policy-making capacity (a minimum requirement of neutrality) restricted through EU membership. Meanwhile, Switzerland is an additional neutral country standing outside the EU although membership has been on the Swiss political agenda. Concerned Swiss observers might study Austria, Finland, Ireland and Sweden to find out how Swiss neutrality might be affected by EU membership at some future point in time and on that basis make a prediction based on taking a comparative approach.

These advantages of the comparative method make it a very valuable tool in the political scientist's toolkit. However, assuming that any one of these advantages automatically accrues through comparative research is a flawed assumption: comparative research involves a significant risk of turning into a 'wonderful, creative exercise of comparison that ultimately is meaningless' (Peters, 1998, p.85).

The limits of comparison

Just as the comparative method can have a number of advantages, there are a number of reasons why comparisons can turn out to be meaningless. Most famously, the condition known as 'too many variables, not enough cases' is the reason why experimental control is rarely an option in political science. Additionally, comparative research is affected by two manifestations of the so-called travelling problem: that is, that neither theoretical concepts nor empirical measurements are consistent (they do not 'travel') across temporal and/or spatial settings. This diminishes the possibility of controlling for the effect of variables other than those that are of primary interest.

The comparative method also contends with the issue of value-free interpretations, and with the so-called 'Galton's problem'. All these issues are elaborated below.

The 'too many variables, not enough cases' problem of comparison arises because the political world that is the research environment of political science is too rich and varied (that is, it consists of too many variables) for the researcher to be able to find enough cases to control for all the effects of these variables; it thus becomes impossible to isolate the dynamics of the relationship of primary interest (Ragin, 1987, pp.23–6). As an illustration, consider the case of even the simplest possible hypothesised empirical relationship: that is, a relationship between one independent and one dependent variable. For example, the emergence of a Green Party as a political force might be expected to affect other parties' positions on environmental policy; the hypothesis might be that other parties will develop their own environmental policies to counter the Green Party's electoral appeal. In this bivariate relationship 'presence of Green Party' is the independent variable and 'other parties developing their environmental policies' is the dependent variable. Examining the relationship between these two variables comparatively requires at a minimum two cases.

Let's suppose a two-case most similar research design was developed, covering the same party system at two points in time: before and after a Green Party became a force in electoral politics. If the hypothesis was correct, then the other parties would pay more attention to environmental issues after the arrival of the Green Party than before. However, in addition to the two variables involved in this hypothesized relationship ('presence/absence of Green Party'; 'environmental policy of other parties'), other variables in the political environment might impact on this relationship. For example, if the Chernobyl nuclear disaster occurred in between the two points in time of measurement, then this rather than competition from the Green Party might have focused party minds on the environment. Of course, environmental disasters of that magnitude might have had the consequence of upgrading the salience of environmental policy generally, as well as generating public support for Green parties. In this case the hypothesized relationship between 'presence/absence of Green Party' and 'environmental policy of other parties' is at least partially spurious (that is, the two variables are linked to each other through some third, unidentified variable; here, 'environmental disaster'). But there is no way to test how this additional variable is related to the original two variables without additional cases that have all the attributes of the two original cases but which were somehow not exposed to Chernobyl; given the global repercussions of this event, it is difficult to imagine that such a case exists. Accordingly, there are not enough cases to facilitate controls for all possible variables. As a general rule, a research design requires at least one more case than it needs variables.

The so-called travelling problem is not entirely unrelated to the 'too many variables, not enough cases' problem, insofar as both have a bearing on the possibility of isolating a hypothesized empirical relationship between two or more variables from other variables. The first manifestation of the travelling problem is conceptual: does the meaning of a concept stay constant across time and space? The significance of this was discussed above (definitions of nation-states) in terms of how the comparative method can improve classifications, and it follows from that discussion that mistaken assumptions about concepts and their meanings lead to confusion about what it is that is being compared. The second manifestation of the travelling problem concerns empirical measurement, the concern being that even if the meaning of a concept is constant across cases, if it is operationalized differently for different cases, then there is measurement inconsistency.

A well-known example of this is the measurement of the so-called party identification model of voting behaviour (Budge, Crewe and Fairlie, 1976; Harrop and Miller, 1984; Heath and McDonald, 1988; MacKuen, Erikson and Stimson, 1993; Niemi and Jennings, 1993; Norris, 1997; Todal Jenssen, 1999). This model attempts to explain voting behaviour with reference to voters developing an affinity with a party relatively early in life, and then voting for that party for more or less the rest of their lives. Increased volatility in voting behaviour across the western world (a combination of realignment and dealignment) has diminished the perceived value of this explanation of voting behaviour, but the value of the model here is that it was developed with respect to understanding voting behaviour in the USA, where voters are required to register as supporters of a particular party to vote in primary elections. Political scientists have used this registration as evidence of party identification, and compared it against actual voting behaviour in a presidential race. For a long time they found that few people voted against their party identification, and concluded that party identification was a strongly predictive indicator of voting behaviour. In Western Europe, however, there are no primary elections and there is thus no need for voters to register as supporters of any party. Consequently, there was no obvious measurement of party identification against which to compare voting behaviour. Researchers attempted to overcome this problem by formulating survey questions that distinguished between what party a voter or survey respondent usually sympathized with most closely, and which party they had voted for in a recent election. While this was a reasonable solution to a measurement problem, it did mean that transatlantic comparisons were based on different measurements of party identification. The measurement did not travel well (see Box 3.4).

Box 3.4   Does the measurement travel? Comparative Manifesto Research

The so-called Comparative Manifesto Research group has used all post-war election manifestos in 25 democracies around the world to develop comparable measurements of party positions (see, for example, Budge, Robertson and Hearl, 1987, Budge and Laver, 1992; Klingemann *et al.*, 1994; Pennings, *et al.*, 1999; Budge *et al.*, 2001; Laver, 2001). They have coded each sentence in every manifesto to a category or categories to which the sentence refers, such as 'regulate capitalism' or 'law and order'.

The measurement

- interparty comparisons: the coded text makes it possible to compare party positions at a given point in time, on one or more issues in one or more countries
- intraparty comparisons: the coded text makes it possible to track changes in party positions over time, on one or more issues in one or more countries.

Travel issues

1   Cross-sectional (e.g., county, region, unit) comparisons: the same word/phrase can have different connotations in different political systems. 'State' means something different in western Europe and the USA. There are many forms of democracy, so when Dutch parties refer to their consociational democracy they refer to something quite different compared with when Austrian parties refer to their, until recently highly corporatist, democracy.
2   Language issues: a subcategory of cross-country comparisons. Although it is of course possible to translate manifestos, the act of translation may subtly alter the connotations and symbolism of specific words and phrases.
3   Cross-time comparisons: over time, the meaning of a word or phrase within a country can change. Some may disappear altogether while others are new additions to the political discourse. When party positions are tracked over time, the meaning and usage of words and phrases used may subtly change.

The question of whether value-free interpretations are possible is not unique to the comparative method, but it can be particularly troublesome here because this type of research frequently requires researchers to consider unfamiliar political systems or phenomena. The difficulty is that the values of the researcher and the values embodied in the political system under observation may lead the researcher to misinterpret the unfamiliar political system. While complete objectivity is probably never possible, it is worthwhile for comparative researchers to be explicit about how their values might influence the way they approach an unfamiliar political system as a case.

Finally, 'Galton's problem' occurs when the expectation is not met that political outcomes are due to processes internal to each case in the research design. If some hypothesized empirical relationship under examination is really the result of an external or even global process, then studying more than one case will not in truth provide a comparative perspective because the cases will not be independent from each other. In this vein, studying economic policy developments in EU member states represents a clear instance of Galton's problem, since the EU's influence on the economic policy of all member states is undeniable, especially in the era of the single currency and in the period preceding its introduction when member states planning to adopt the Euro were also required to adhere to the so-called stability pact. Similarly, the fact that many former British colonies have adopted the Westminster model of government belies any assumption that this choice of government in post-colonial states is the result of internal processes. Comparative researchers are, in other words, stuck between Galton's problem and the need to find cases that are comparable, the problem being that cases that are comparable often are comparable precisely because of being affected by some external process; that is, they are similar because of a Galton's problem.

Cases: how many, and which?

Comparative political science is usually concerned with some abstract and generic theory, such as the relationship between class voting and industrialization, to use Ragin's example (1987, pp.9–12). However, the research question derived from a theory and asked of a number of cases is typically in itself much more historically and socially circumscribed than the theory. This is at least partly because comparative studies often do not include enough cases to allow the research question to be generically formulated. As indicated in Chapter 2, and as Chapter 6 discusses in detail, sampling occurs when a researcher selects a number of cases for study rather than including the whole universe (or population) of possible cases in a study, and comparative research is typically based on a sample of cases. Quantitative research often deals very explicitly with sampling issues, but in qualitative research it is common that sampling does not receive the attention it deserves (given its potentially crucial impact on the conclusions drawn from the research; see Chapter 6). Typically, qualitative research designs are small-n and quantitative research designs large-n. Qualitative data is typically too rich and complex to make it possible to manage more than a few cases, whereas contemporary computer technology makes it easy to handle very large amounts of quantitative data.

The number of cases to be included in a comparative research design depends essentially on how many suitable cases (given the particular research question) are available. Normally comparative researchers are not lucky enough to find themselves in the 'predicament' of having too many suitable cases; having to make do with what is available is more common. Even the study of a single case can be considered implicitly comparative (if it applies some widely used theory or model); at the other end of the scale the demands of inferential statistics can make 1,000 or more cases desirable. Whatever the number of cases in a comparative study, some criterion for case selection must be employed, and here the 'most similar' and 'most different' research designs provide guidance, but only to a point. In addition to the selection criteria set out by these two types of research design it is also important that cases are not selected on the dependent variable. To select cases on the dependent variable (see Box 3.5) means that cases are chosen because they belong to a specific classification category (e.g., have a particular value) on the dependent variable, and this can become a particular problem in small-n research designs. The problem with selecting cases on the dependent variable is that it becomes impossible to find out about the effect of the independent variable on the dependent variable because there is not even a theoretical possibility of variance on the dependent variable.

Whether a study is large- or small-n makes an important difference in terms of how one might select cases for comparison.

Box 3.5 Selecting cases on the dependent variable: the European Union as an international actor

The member states of the European Union (EU) have been making increasing efforts to act coherently in international politics in general, and in specific conflicts in particular. The rationale behind this is that by acting in a unified manner the EU member states increase their influence, compared to if they acted as 15 (or 25) individual countries.

Students of European and regional security might wonder under what conditions the EU member states manage to maintain a unified position, and under what conditions unity breaks down. Since all EU member states are also members of the UN, one way to investigate this is to study how EU governments have voted in the UN General Assembly, on resolutions referring to a particular conflict or issue.

Take Kosovo as an example of a conflict in geographical proximity to the EU, and therefore of immediate significance to the EU. In the 1990s the General Assembly adopted six resolutions about Kosovo by voting. The EU15 voted as follows:

Date of Vote	EU Bloc Vote	Comment
23/12/1994	EU14	Abstention (Greece)
22/12/1995	EU14	Abstention (Greece)
12/12/1996	EU14	Non-voting (Greece)
12/12/1997	EU15	
09/12/1998	EU15	
17/12/1999	EU15	

To select *either* exclusively votes where EU bloc voting broke down, *or* exclusively votes where it was maintained, is to select cases on the dependent variable. Selecting on the dependent variable means that there is no variance on the dependent variable. The practical implication of this is that it becomes impossible to reveal under what conditions the EU15 do (or do not) succeed in adopting unified positions on international politics.

For example, if two or more of the successful votes are selected and compared, the researcher might be able to say something about what these cases had in common. Equally, if two or more unsuccessful votes are selected and compared, then the researcher will be able to say something about what those cases had in common.

However, unless cases are included that are *different with respect to the dependent variable*, it will not be possible to draw any conclusions that specify whether particular conditions make it possible/impossible for the EU15 to maintain a unified position.

Source: UN (October 2002).

Specifically, random selection is usually the preferred way of deciding what to observe in large-*n* studies (especially the selection of respondents in opinion polls). In small-*n* research cases are typically not randomly selected – and in fact doing so might not be at all appropriate – but are selected precisely because they belong to a particular classification category on the independent variable. We have seen that this is the case in both 'most similar' and 'most different' research designs. In most similar research designs cases are selected according to difference on the independent variable (and similarity on other backdrop variables), and vice versa for most different research designs. However, non-randomly selected cases must not be selected on the dependent variable: that is, if the objective of a research design is to investigate whether mixed-gender units of the armed forces perform differently from all-male units, then 'performance' (poor, medium, good) is the dependent variable. If the units selected for comparison all performed equally (whether they were uniformly poor, or all medium, or good across the board), nothing would be revealed about the research question. The selection on the dependent variable prevents the observation of, even in theory, any difference between mixed-gender and all-male units becoming evident. The consequence of this extreme selection bias is that nothing is learnt about the performance effects of men and women serving alongside each other in the armed forces.

Selecting on the dependent variable may seem like an easy mistake to avoid, but sometimes it is not. Political scientists (especially those researching sensitive topics, and the presence of women in the armed forces may be one such topic) are often forced to use whatever data is available, or made available by 'gatekeepers'. Such 'gatekeepers' may have reasons to give and withhold certain information precisely on the basis of how it relates to the dependent variable. For example, in the above example, a 'gatekeeper' may only provide information on mixed-gender units which performed very poorly; or if the political agenda was different, might withhold that information and only reveal information about excelling mixed-gender units. The consequence for the research project would be a serious source of selection bias that the researcher may only suspect but never overcome. Box 3.6 provides an overview of the points made in this chapter through a check list.

Box 3.6   Research design check list

1. The Research Question
    *   What is the research question?
    *   What is the dependent variable in this research question?
    *   What is the independent variable(s) in this research question?
    *   In addition to the independent variable(s), what other variables might also be related to the dependent variable?

2. Case Selection
    *   Can you list all/several cases that would be appropriate in a study of your research question?
    *   Are you sure you the cases on the list have not been selected on the dependent variable? *(All comparative research projects need to contain at least a theoretical chance of variance on the dependent variable. Selecting on the dependent variable is a particularly easy mistake to make in small-n projects.)*
    *   Are the cases on your list 'typical' examples of the problem/ tension/issue contained in your research question? *('Typical' examples maximize experimental variance. 'Deviant' cases do not minimize error variance, because it is impossible to extrapolate from unusual cases; see Chapter 6 for more on inference-making.)*

3. Most Similar or Most Different Research Design
    *   Are there cases on the list that would form a solid most similar research design? *(For example, cases that are different on the independent variable but 'the same' on other variables. This controls extraneous variance.)*
    *   Are there cases on the list that would form a solid most different research design? *(For example, cases that are 'the same' on the independent variable but different on other variables? This combination also controls extraneous variance.)*

Conclusion

Most political science is comparative, even if not explicitly so. Comparativists 'examine a case to reveal what it tells us about a larger set of political phenomena' (Lichbach and Zuckerman, 1997, p.4), and 'perhaps the only circumstance in which a political scientist is not also at least implicitly a comparative political scientist is when he or she remains consistently and exclusively concerned with his or her own national system' (Pennings, Keman and Kleinnijnehuis, 1999, p.70). Even then, it is questionable whether such a consistent and exclusive focus on a single system is not at least implicitly comparative because it is likely to make use of the same concepts, models and theories that have been applied elsewhere; if it does not, then it can hardly be said to constitute a part of a wider political science body of knowledge.

This chapter has approached the comparative methodology as the way to obtain as many of the advantages as possible of experimental control in research, but has also acknowledged some common problems which make full experimental control almost impossible to achieve. By careful case selection some of these problems can sometimes be alleviated or even avoided, but even where this is not possible the comparative methodology can be the best alternative available for political scientists.

Chapter 4

Surveys and Opinion Polls

Introduction

The importance of social surveys and opinion polls in contemporary life is hard to over-estimate. A great deal of what we know about our society, such as its social composition, the attitudes and priorities of its citizens, information about such important areas as employment, health, education and crime, are obtained from surveys and opinion polls. In the USA, the Survey Research Center, affiliated to the Institute for Social Research at the University of Michigan, is the leading survey institution and is responsible for the American National Household Survey and the panel study of Income Dynamics, and it is also famous for its studies of national elections. Each year in Britain the National Centre for Social Research carries out the *British Social Attitudes Survey* which provides a detailed map of contemporary British values and shows how these have changed over the 20 years that these surveys have been carried out (Park *et al.*, 2002). These surveys are invaluable resources for researchers. The conducting of surveys and market research has thus become a major industry and an accepted part of everyday life in all democracies. In the USA and Britain, organizations such as Gallup and MORI have become household names.

This chapter will examine the importance of opinion polls and surveys for political scientists and describe how they developed. It will consider the problems associated with the administration of surveys and describe the main types of survey design. Problems associated with questionnaire design and the administration of questionnaires will be analysed and the importance of interviewer effects will be considered. Finally the increasing use of focus groups as a supplement to surveys or as an alternative means of gaining similar information will be discussed.

Surveys, opinion polls and politics

Is there a difference between a survey and an opinion poll? A survey, or more precisely a sample survey, attempts to obtain accurate information about a population by obtaining a representative sample of that population and using the information from the sample to make generalizations about the whole population (see Chapter 6). The information could be descriptive, outlining the age or class or family composition of the population, or it could describe their values, opinions or behaviour. Opinion polls are surveys concerned to measure the opinions of the population and, in particular, the political opinions of the electorate. Opinion polls receive the most attention in the run-up to general elections or presidential elections when they are used to predict which political party or presidential candidate will win the election.

Every month polling organizations publish a wide range of information of interest to political scientists, politicians and the politically aware public. They publish data on the popular standing of leading politicians such as the President of the United States or the Prime Minister of Britain. They measure the popularity of the parties, the views of the electorate on key issues such as the state of the economy, the crisis in the Middle East, or the inadequacies of health treatment. The timing of referenda such as on the Maastricht Treaty or the Nice Treaty are influenced by poll findings. As elections approach, the importance of the polls greatly increases. Politicians look to them for information to guide and inform their campaigns; newspapers and television news programmes compete to publish the latest findings and to predict the result; potential tactical voters seek information to cast the most effective votes. Even apathetic voters may get caught up in the competition to predict which party will win the election and form the next government. Butler and Kavanagh argue that

> opinion pollsters are now major players on the electoral scene. Their findings shape the mood of protagonists and of voters. In a competitive world, their commercial success in the market research trade depends significantly upon their accuracy in indicating the likely division of the vote. Election forecasting is not their main source of income, but it is their most publicised activity. (Butler and Kavanagh, 2002, p.121)

In recent election campaigns in Britain, hardly a day has gone by without the publication of a national opinion poll (Moon, 1999).

Despite the fact that polling organizations have occasionally made major mistakes in predicting the results of elections, as in the British General Election of 1992, they are widely regarded as reliable and accurate sources of information on public opinion. Moreover, those experts who can provide evidence to back their assertions are in a strong position to convince others of the value of their analysis, particularly if their audience lacks the skills to challenge the basis of the data that is presented to them. Moon cites Peggy Newman, a speechwriter for Presidents Reagan and Bush, saying, 'In every political meeting I have ever been to, if there was a pollster there, his words carried the most weight because he was the only one with hard data . . . I felt that polls were driving more than politics. They were driving history' (Moon 1999, p. 183).

Political scientists have been avid users of surveys and opinion polls in their research into voting behaviour, political participation, and other aspects of multi-party democracies. They are, of course,

---

Box 4.1   Survey of public and elite opinions on ethical standards among Australian politicians

The 1996 Australian Election Study investigated voters' confidence in the ethical standards they expected from the politicians. At the same time a sample of elected representatives were also asked about the importance they attached to eight principles set out in the Federal Parliament's ethical guide. The results of the survey showed that voters, especially if they grew up in a democratic culture and had higher education, expected high standards from their legislators. The legislators did not expect such high standards from themselves, though legislators with more experience of national institutions, such as membership of the cabinet or shadow cabinet, did have high ethical expectations. The gap between voters' expectations and legislators' expectations could contribute to growing voter disillusionment with politicians, and has the potential to undermine public confidence in Australian democracy. The author argues that it highlights a dilemma for those charged with enforcing ethical standards when legislators and voters have such different expectations.

The Australian Election Study 1996 was a nationally representative self-completion survey of voters held after the March 1996 federal election. The sample of 1,788 was drawn from the electoral register and the response rate was 61.5 per cent. The survey of election candidates was also based on a self-completed questionnaire and resulted in 427 cases, a response rate of 63.5 per cent. Of these, 105 were elected and they form the basis for the data from elected representatives (McAllister, 2000).

more interested in explaining relationships between variables than in the distribution of the vote between parties or the standing of candidates in the polls. They want to discover, for example, the reasons for the rise and fall of the Lijst Pim Fortuyn in the Netherlands, or to know why popular interest in participating in elections and political parties has been diminishing whilst participation in demonstrations and single issue groups has been growing in importance. Considerable research has been done on, for example, the health of democracy and public attitudes towards, and confidence in, their politicians. A good example of this is research on the ethical conduct voters expect from Australian politicans (McAllister, 2000; see also Box 4.1).

History of opinion polls and surveys

Political opinion polling began in the USA (Teer and Spence, 1973, p.13). Journalists often took soundings to try to forecast who would win Presidential elections and this activity developed into more systematic efforts by newspapers to predict election results. By 1916 the *Literary Digest* was sending out huge numbers of postal ballots to voters in an effort to predict Presidential election results accurately, names and addresses being obtained from lists of telephone subscribers and from state records of car registrations (Moon, 1999, p.8). This was the first systematic effort to use opinion polls to predict election results. By the Presidential election of 1936 the Literary Digest was sending postal ballots to 10 million people and receiving 2 million completed ballots back. By this time the *Literary Digest* had a string of successes behind it, having correctly predicted the results of the four Presidential elections between 1920 and 1932. However, it failed badly in 1936 when it predicted a large majority for the Republican candidate, Landon, who was easily defeated by Roosevelt. The embarrassment was even greater for the *Literary Digest* in that George Gallup, who had set up the American Institute of Public Opinion in 1935, had not only predicted the result correctly, but had predicted the extent of the *Literary Digest*'s error.

It is easy to explain, with hindsight, how the *Literary Digest* got the result so badly wrong. The 1936 election was fought very much over social issues with Roosevelt campaigning for his New Deal and high levels of government spending to reduce unemployment and lift America out of the Depression. His campaign was thus highly attractive to the unemployed and the less affluent, who were very under-represented in the *Literary Digest*'s address lists, based as they were on ownership of cars and telephones, both of which were at that time far less widespread than is the case today. Previous Presidential elections had not been so polarized on class lines, so the biased nature of the *Literary Digest*'s samples had not undermined its ability to predict previous winners of Presidential contests. Shortly after the major embarrassment of this inaccurate prediction, the *Literary Digest* ceased publication.

Early survey work in Britain was concerned with poverty. Rich philanthropists such as Charles Booth and Seebohm Rowntree were concerned to explain the causes of poverty: Booth initiated the use of the interview survey to investigate social issues, while Rowntree carried out his famous survey of poverty in York in 1899 and decided to repeat it in 1936. Both times he attempted to interview all working-class people in the city, even though by this time sampling theory was being developed, particularly by A. L. Bowley, a statistician, at the London School of Economics (Bowley, 1913). Rowntree was very sceptical of sampling as a method of collecting data and decided on a complete enumeration of working-class households. However, he decided to test the reliability of sampling against his complete results. He listed all the working-class poor by streets and sampled 1 in 10, 1 in 20, 1 in 30, 1 in 40 and 1 in 50. His results, classified by income classes A to E, are shown in Table 4.1.

The sample results, on the whole, were good and were probably better than Rowntree could ever have imagined. Nevertheless he felt he was justified in carrying out the complete survey or, more accurately, a census. He was unwilling to admit that he could have saved himself a large amount of money, without too much loss of accuracy, if he had carried out interviews based on a sample survey rather than a complete enumeration. This example shows that,

Table 4.1   *Survey of Working-Class Households in York, 1936*

	Complete survey	1 in 10	1 in 20	1 in 30	1 in 40	1 in 50
AB	31.1	30.9	32.6	30.1	33.1	31.7
C	18.9	17.7	15.3	20.3	13.9	18.2
D	13.9	13.7	12.4	15.0	14.1	12.3
E	36.1	37.7	39.7	34.6	38.9	37.8

Source: Rowntree (1941), p.481, with the permission of the Joseph Rowntree Charitable Trust.

depending on the degree of accuracy desired, there may be no need to carry out a complete census. The costs today of a complete enumeration would in any case be enormous and impossibly expensive for most researchers. Also, given that sampling techniques have greatly improved since Rowntree's day, the value of a complete enumeration is even lower. In fact, since a census is such a huge task to carry out, the possibility of mistakes and 'missed cases' is great and there is usually no way to estimate how flawed a census might be. In contrast, in a well-designed, randomly drawn sample, it is possible to estimate error (Schofield, 1996, p.29) and for this reason a sample can actually yield more accurate information than a census.

Rowntree's belief in the importance and value of a complete enumeration and his scepticism of the value of sampling procedures have largely disappeared. Sample surveys are so much quicker, more efficient and economic compared with censuses. Complete enumerations involve huge expense, considerable preparation and extensive organization. The scale of the decennial censuses in Britain and the USA shows that only governments can undertake such huge tasks. In Britain the census involves collecting information on nearly 60 million people and in the USA on 280 million. The preparation, collection and analysis of such vast quantities of data is a mammoth task.

Censuses have always suffered from a number of deficiencies and these seem to be getting worse. A census should be a complete enumeration, especially as it is a legal obligation to participate. In practice, many people are omitted. The homeless, travellers, young single people, non-citizens and people in multi-occupied dwellings are for various reasons inadequately covered. Second, only a limited amount of information can be demanded in the census form and the questions are usually concerned with family structure and housing issues, never politics. This limits the value of the census for political scientists. The scale of the data from the census means that there are significant delays before the results are published. In Britain, this delay can be as long as 18 months, so the results are out of date by the time the findings become widely available. In the USA with its continental size, large population and high rates of geographical mobility, the expenses and practical problems of carrying out censuses are much greater than in Britain. The value and attraction of opinion polls and sample surveys is thus even greater.

Sampling procedures

There are two types of sampling procedure: probability (or random) sampling, and non-probability (or non-random) sampling. There are five main types of sample design based on random sampling: (1) simple random sampling; (2) systematic random sampling; (3) stratified random sampling; (4) multi-stage sampling; and (5) cluster sampling. There are two main types of non-random sampling: (1) quota sampling and (2) snowball sampling.

In sampling theory a population is defined as an aggregate of elements. It is the universe of units from which the sample is to be selected. It could be a population of tea, marbles, wheat, voters, towns or cities. The target population is the one the researcher wishes to sample, but certain areas may be left out to save resources. For example, in Britain the Highlands and islands of Scotland may be omitted because the population is very small and spread over a large geographical area and so it may be considered too expensive to interview the tiny number from those locations who would fall into a national sample. In the USA, Alaska and Hawaii may be left out for similar reasons. The survey population may thus be slightly different from the target population. Generalizations drawn from a survey relate, of course, only to the survey population, not to the target population. The sampling frame is the list of units from which the sample is to be drawn. The choice of sampling frame will depend on what lists of the population are available and how accurate they are. The choice will also depend on the subject of the research. In studies of voting behaviour in Britain, the appropriate sampling frame would be the register of electors, which is fairly accurate as it is updated on a regular basis. In studies of voting behaviour in the USA, where many people register to vote at the last minute or are registered in another place because of geographical mobility or other reasons, a register of households, or the telephone directory, may be more appropriate. Researchers may need permission to use specialized sampling frames such as party membership lists, for example, when surveying party activists.

Types of sample design

Random sampling

Random sampling is a mechanical and rigid procedure which eliminates bias in choosing the members of the population who will be selected for the sample. Randomness means that each case in a population has an equal and independent chance of being included in the sample. One way to do this would be to allocate numbered papers to everyone in the population to be surveyed, put the papers into a drum, churn them around numerous times and then draw out a sample of numbered papers equal to the sample size that has been selected. However, once a piece of paper had been drawn, it would have to be replaced in the drum prior to the next draw, otherwise it would not have an equal and independent chance of being selected (Schofield, 1996, p.31). In reality, however, once a person has been selected to answer a survey, they are usually not replaced in the population so that they can be sampled again. In any case, a more usual procedure is to use computer-generated random numbers to select the sample, either by using random number tables or by preparing a simple computer programme that will select the numbers at random. In practice the simple random sampling procedure is rarely used as it is time-consuming to organize, and expensive. There are a number of variations on simple random sampling which are described below.

Systematic random sampling

This is a convenient and straightforward variation of simple random sampling. Here the researcher chooses a random starting place on his sampling frame and then interviews every tenth, fiftieth, hundredth or whatever interval will provide the appropriate size of sample. If, for example, the population to be sampled is 110,000 and a sample size of 1,000 is required, then by interviewing every 110th person the researcher will achieve the appropriate sample size. Providing that there is no systematic variation in the population, this sampling procedure is very close to simple random sampling. A systematic bias that could occur would be if every 110th person were female or lived on a corner plot, making them different from the sample members as a whole, but such a bias is unlikely and should quickly become apparent to those carrying out the survey.

Stratified random sampling

Stratification is a procedure by which the accuracy of simple random sampling can be improved because the investigators already have relevant information about the population they wish to survey. They divide the sample into homogeneous groups or *strata* on the basis of this information and take random samples from within these groups or strata. For example, a research project on the political attitudes and behaviour of university students might hypothesize that gender and academic discipline were important explanatory variables. The university authorities might be willing to provide general information on the numbers of male and female students and the numbers studying arts, social sciences, natural sciences and engineering. If the investigator took a simple random sample of all the students, then the proportions of male and female students and of those in different academic disciplines would be subject to sampling error, but because accurate information is available from the university, the correct data can be used and sampling errors reduced. Stratification is thus a procedure which improves the accuracy of simple random sampling but which can only be employed when investigators have accurate and relevant information on the population they wish to sample. Often access to relevant information may be hard to obtain or too difficult to use, so it may be quicker and easier not to try to stratify the sample.

Multi-stage sampling
Multi-stage sampling is often used by researchers undertaking large national samples. In this case, the population is divided into groups or areas and the samples are drawn from within these. For example, in carrying out national voting studies, it is common practice to divide the country into constituencies and to draw a sample of constituencies and then a sample of voters within the selected constituencies. Unlike stratified random sampling, the stages are chosen for convenience and not because they are homogeneous and detailed information is known about them. Multi-stage sampling thus increases the sampling errors.

A multi-stage sample design was used by Whiteley, Seyd and Richardson in their study of British Conservative Party activists (see Box 4.2). First they drew a 5 per cent sample of constituencies at random from the regional lists contained in the 1990 Conservative Party *Conference Handbook*. The use of a sampling frame stratified by Conservative Party regions ensured that a representative regional distribution of constituency associations was obtained. The investigators then approached local Conservative Associations within each selected constituency to obtain membership lists of party members in order to draw a sample of individual members (Whiteley, Seyd and Richardson 1994, p.239).

Box 4.2 Multi-stage sampling

Whiteley, Seyd and Richardson used a two-stage sampling design in their study of Conservative Party members, *True Blues*. The first stage was a 5 per cent sample of constituencies which was drawn at random from the regional lists contained in the 1990 Conservative Handbook. This sampling frame was stratified by Conservative Party regions, which helped to ensure that a regional distribution of constituency associations was obtained.

Each Conservative association in the sample was then approached to access their membership lists as there was no national membership list at this time. A one-in-ten systematic random sample of party members was then selected from the membership of 34 Conservative associations. In the West Midlands region, where an above-average number of associations refused to participate in the survey, a large sample of one-in-seven was drawn to compensate.

The researchers decided on a postal survey and despatched 3,919 questionnaires. In order to improve the response rate, a letter endorsing the research, signed by the Conservative Party Chairman, was sent to each member in the sample a week before the questionnaires were posted. A letter explaining the purpose of the research and the bona fides of the researchers was enclosed with the questionnaires. A telephone hotline was also set up so that those in the sample could have any questions about the research answered. Two reminders were also sent to those who failed to reply. These efforts resulted in an excellent response rate, for a postal survey, of 63 per cent. In all, 2,466 usable replies were returned (Whiteley, Seyd and Richardson, 1994).

Cluster sampling

This is similar to multi-stage sampling except that the last stage in the sampling procedure is a group of individuals (that is, a cluster) rather than a single person. The reason for this procedure is to reduce costs by bunching the interviews. Thus the researcher might take a sample of administrative regions and within of them select a sample of villages and then interview every person in the selected villages. This saves on transport costs but increases sampling error as people living in the same village are likely to have some characteristics in common such as employment and housing, and may not be representative of people living in other villages. They key point about cluster sampling is that the clusters must be both *comprehensive* in the sense that they collectively must cover the entire population, and *mutually exclusive* so that all cases belong to one but not more than one cluster.

Panel study design
A major limitation of surveys is that they provide investigators with a snapshot of opinions and other data at a single point in time. In order to discover information about changes over time it is possible, resources permitting, to re-interview a sample of the population at a later date. This sample procedure is known as a *panel study design*. The classic example of panel study design is the study of voting behaviour by Butler and Stokes, *Political Change in Britain*. They interviewed a random sample of the British electorate in the summer of 1963, re-interviewed them following the General Election of October 1964, and re-interviewed them after the General Election of 1966 (Butler and Stokes, 1974, p.14). The limitations of panel studies are that people may be lost to the panel because they move, become ill or refuse to be re-interviewed. Second, the panel may become less representative over time as those most interested in the subject of the survey remain in the panel. However, this study did throw considerable light on British voting behaviour and one finding thrown up by the panel design was the high degree of volatility of the electorate which was concealed by the overall figures.

Non-random sample designs

Quota sampling
Quota sampling is widely used by market research organizations, especially when carrying out research for commercial clients, but also for more academic research into voting behaviour, for example, when quick results are required. A company may have designed a new product, such as a perfume, and may then commission a market research organization to interview a sample of potential customers to assess their reactions to the product, especially its price, quality and packaging. They can thus assess its market viability. The market research organization may decide to interview a sample of women of varying ages, backgrounds and localities. The interviewers are given quotas of people to interview, such as x number of working-class/middle-class women within various age groups. The aim is to include the key characteristics of the population in the quotas so as to obtain a representative sample of potential customers.

The key differences between quota sampling and random sampling are that in random sampling an objective procedure is followed in choosing the sample and members of the sample cannot be replaced. The representativeness of the sample can then be calculated. In quota sampling key variables such as age, gender, occupation and ethnicity can be specified, but the interviewer is free to choose any person who fits the criteria; and, if they refuse to be interviewed replacements are allowed. It is thus impossible to calculate how representative the final quota sample is, and the problem of non-response is circumvented.

It is clear that the time of day and place where the quota sample interviews are carried out will affect their representativeness. Thus interviews during the day in a public place will result in the under-representation of full-time workers and especially factory workers. Homeworkers and public service workers will be over-represented. The interviewers may have more success with people similar to themselves in terms of gender, race, age and perceived social class, and thus bias the results unconsciously. However, market researchers claim that quota sampling can be nearly as reliable as random sampling, provided that the quotas are carefully chosen and implemented. Quota samples have the great advantage of being quicker, less expensive and more efficient than random samples, but the non-random nature of quota samples means that drawing inferences from quota samples is questionable (see Chapter 6).

Snowball samples

Snowball sampling is another very popular form of non-random sampling. In this procedure investigators use their initial contacts to recommend people in similar circumstances to be interviewed. This is a valuable strategy for generating a sample of people or groups which otherwise would be impossible to access. The classic example of this approach is with drug users. Becker used his contacts with marijuana users to generate a snowball sample of 50 people whom he interviewed (Becker, 1963). A more recent example is a study by McCarville of second-generation Irish young people in Birmingham. McCarville found that not only was snowball sampling useful in generating a large number of people to be interviewed, who could not be easily contacted any other way, but the fact that he was recommended by someone they knew made those whom he approached much more willing to be interviewed (McCarville, 2002).

The weakness of snowball sampling is that the sample generated is very unlikely to be representative of the group under investigation. However, it may be the only way of generating a sample of members of particular groups, such as homeless people, drug users or travellers. The information collected can then be used to generate hypotheses for further research or used to develop tentative generalizations which again would need to be confirmed by additional studies. On the whole, snowball sampling is more suited to in-depth interview research than to survey research, as conventionally understood.

Administering surveys

It is often assumed that the most important source of inaccuracies in surveys is sampling error: the possibility that the sample that has been selected is unrepresentative of the population from which it has been so carefully drawn. In fact, the organization and administration of surveys can be a much greater source of bias and inaccuracy. The major sources of bias that occur for organizational reasons are problems with the sampling frame, the size of the sample, the questionnaire, interviewing, non-response, coding, and analysing the results.

The sampling frame

As has already been discussed, the sampling frame is the list of the population that you wish to survey. In the UK, the closest to a complete list of the adult population is the electoral register, which used to be the sampling frame of choice. Now the preferred sampling frame is the Postcode Address File (PAF), which is a list of addresses (or postal delivery points) compiled by the Post Office. People living in institutions, though not in private households at such institutions, are often excluded, as are households whose addresses are not included in the PAF. Once a sample of households is drawn from the PAF an individual is randomly selected from the household for interview (see Box 4.3). There are other national lists that are published and therefore easily accessible, such as telephone directories, but again these are not completely accurate as some people have no telephone, while a significant number (nearly one-third) prefer to be ex-directory. Those people not in the telephone directory may well have characteristics in common, such as low incomes or sensitive occupations: for example many medical doctors prefer to be ex-directory. Surveys using the telephone directory would therefore under-represent these groups.

Obtaining a sampling frame of particular groups can involve a lot of preparatory work. Whiteley, Seyd and Richardson's study of British Conservative Party activists showed that there were considerable ambiguities over what constituted a Conservative Party member. Was it someone who supported Conservative Party ideals

---

Box 4.3 Sample design of the 19th British Social Attitudes Survey

The sampling method consisted of a multi-stage design in three parts.

1. A sample of 200 postcode sectors was drawn by systematic random sampling from the Postcode Address File. (For practical reasons only those in private households were included and Scotland north of the Caledonian Canal was excluded due to the high costs of interviewing there.) Before the sample was drawn the postcode sectors were stratified by geography (into 37 subregions), population density and owner occupation in England and Wales, and non-manual heads of household in Scotland. The sample was selected with probability proportional to the number of addresses in each sector.
2. Thirty-one addresses were selected in each of the postcode sectors by systematic random sampling. In all 6,200 addresses were selected.
3. Interviewers called at each selected address and made a list of individuals eligible for inclusion in the sample. These were all persons over 18 years resident at the address. The interviewer then selected one respondent to be interviewed using a computer-generated random selection procedure. Where there was more than one household at the address the random procedure was used first to select a household.

Source: Park *et al.*, (2002), pp.231–2.

---

and worked for the Party, but did not contribute financially? Was it someone who paid an annual subscription but did not participate in other ways? Was it a person who belonged to an affiliated organization such as a Conservative Club? Or was it all of these? A major initial problem facing the researchers was thus obtaining and preparing an accurate sampling frame of party members. This had to be drawn up in co-operation with local Conservative Associations as there was no central Party list of members at this time (Whiteley, Seyd and Richardson, 1994, pp.22–5).

The size of the sample

The size of the sample needed for statistical analysis depends on the degree of accuracy required, and can be calculated mathematically. However, gains in accuracy from increasing sample size become very limited after a quickly-reached point (see Chapter 6). In statistical theory a sample size of 300 is large enough for most analytical purposes, though in practice researchers and opinion pollsters use much larger samples. The reason for this is partly to inspire confidence in the results but it is the sample size of important subgroups or categories in the survey population that is important, rather than the size of the overall sample. Researchers, for example, may wish to analyse the behaviour of floating voters, women, trade unionists or ethnic minorities, so it is the size of these groups which must be 300 or more in the sample.

If researchers are particularly interested in relatively small groups in the population such as Catholics, farmers or African-Caribbean people, then these groups may be over-sampled in a general survey to ensure that statistical analysis can be done on their opinions and valid generalizations can be drawn about their behaviour. This is known as a booster sample (see Box 4.4). When generalizations are made about the whole survey population, the size of the groups in the booster samples can be given their correct proportion in the whole population. This is known as reweighting. In the British Election Study of 1997, booster samples were included of Scots, Welsh, Northern Irish and ethnic minority voters. The data based on

---

Box 4.4   Booster samples

An ideal sample is perfectly representative of the population that it was drawn from, and if there are any errors in the sample they should ideally be random (since random errors cancel themselves out). Non-random error, or systematic error, wreaks havoc with a sample. However, sometimes it can be useful purposefully to draw samples that systematically over-sample cases belonging to particular categories. For instance, there may be reasons to over-sample women parliamentarians in surveys of legislators, or members of ethnic minorities in opinion polls, and so on.

The reason for such booster samples is that an analysis which compares, say, opinions within different ethnic groups requires the data set to be divided into categories based on survey respondents' ethnicity. If an ethnic group constitutes only a small proportion of the overall population, then there is a risk that the measurement of opinion within that group will be based on such a small sample that it will undermine the conclusions drawn (see Chapter 6 for an explanation as to why the number of cases matters).

To deliberately over-sample a subgroup of the sample by a known amount enables the researcher to draw more solid conclusions and to take the over-sampling into account when formulating the conclusions.

the booster sample of ethnic minority voters was analysed and published in *Race and Representation: Electoral Politics and Ethnic Pluralism in Britain* (Saggar, 2000).

Designing the questionnaire

It is often believed that question wording is the major source of errors in surveys because small changes in wording or even different emphases put on words by interviewers might lead to large differences in responses which would not otherwise exist (Payne, 1951, p.5; Tourangeau, Rips and Rasinski, 2000, pp.23–61; Gilland, 2001, pp.149–52). This is most likely to occur if the respondents are uninterested in the subject of the survey or are lacking in knowledge about it. Topics on which respondents are knowledgeable and interested are unlikely to be influenced by slight changes in wording or emphasis. Nevertheless, question wording is clearly very important.

The function of a questionnaire is to translate the investigator's hypotheses into a series of questions designed to elicit the information needed to test them rigorously. The questions must be designed so that variations in response reflect real differences between the respondents. The questions must be self-explanatory and concise so that they are easy to understand. This can be quite difficult to achieve as language is often ambiguous and the comprehension of respondents may vary considerably. Questionnaire designers must be alert to such aspects as the status implications of the terms used, the sensitivity of particular issues, and the importance of being careful not to embarrass the persons being interviewed (for example, by exposing their lack of knowledge of current events). Even straightforward factual questions may prove embarrassing: for example, if people are assumed to own equipment they do not have by being asked a question such as 'Do you shop on the Internet?', since this assumes that the respondent has a computer and is capable of using it. An initial probing question such as 'Do you happen to own a computer at present?', may be a better approach.

Ambiguous questions are often those which try to include too much in one question. A good example is a question from the Gallup Poll:

'Do you think it is a strength or a weakness of the Labour Party that it should have a close relationship with the trade unions? In other words, should they stress it as an advantage to be close to the trade unions or keep quiet about it?'

The first part of the questions emphasizes the strength or weakness of the association and the second the value of secrecy. Naturally one could believe it was a strength and that it should be kept quiet.

Hoinville gives another example of an ambiguous question: 'Would you mind telling me whether you and your husband sleep in single beds or a double bed?' He argues the deserved answer is 'Yes' (Hoinville, Jowell *et al.*, 1978, p.31).

Embarrassing or sensitive questions are usually asked towards the end of questionnaires, thus giving the interviewer time to develop a rapport with the interviewee and to build up their confidence. A major aim of the interview is to elicit honest and truthful responses. This is difficult with certain topics. People are naturally very reluctant to divulge details of their income and so it is best to ask them to give a general indication of their income range, perhaps by having a numbered card on which there are a range of income intervals, and inviting them to tick the range which includes their income, as illustrated below:

Would you indicate whether your annual income is:	
£ 0–£10,000	☐
£10,001–£20,000	☐
£20,001–£30,000	☐
£30,001–£40,000	☐
£40,001–£50,000	☐
Above £50,000	☐

A common fault in questionnaires is the length of the questionnaire. There is a great temptation for researchers to ask far too many questions resulting in inconvenience to the interviewees and the risk of alienating them, especially if the interviewer has under-estimated to them the length of time the interview will take.

Generally people who have agreed to be interviewed are very willing to co-operate, especially if the survey is on a topic that is interesting to them and about which they are knowledgeable. Co-operation can be a problem if respondents are so helpful that they allow themselves to agree to leading questions. In their 1963 interviews Butler and Stokes asked the following question:

'There's quite a lot of talk these days about social classes. Most people say they belong either to the middle class or to the working class – do you ever think of yourself as being in one of these classes?' (Butler and Stokes, 1969, p.478)

This question was strongly criticized by Iain Macleod in his review of the book, in which he expressed amazement that only 66 per cent had agreed that they thought of themselves as belonging to a particular class in response to such a loaded question (Macleod, 1969). When the question was rephrased for the follow-up survey in 1964 to the more neutral 'Do you ever think of yourself as belonging to a particular social class?', then only 50 per cent agreed. A large part of this substantial difference was probably due to the rewording of the question (Butler and Stokes, 1969, p.491).

A distinction is often made between 'free answer' or 'open-ended' questions, and 'closed' questions. Open-ended questions are valuable to discover what the respondent really feels. They provide the researcher with richer material, examples of his concerns and valuable quotes to illustrate the findings. The results are thus more interesting. As can be seen in Box 4.5 they are often used in pilot studies to discover the range of answers to a particular question to see if it can be precoded. The disadvantage of open-ended questions is that they are difficult and time-consuming to code. Closed questions have the advantage that they take less time to administer and are quick and easy to code. They provide less information and are thus more superficial.

Question wording depends on what you wish to discover. If you are investigating the intensity of opinion on a particular issue, then the questions should allow respondents to express moderate opinions, otherwise the results will be invalid. It is easy to see when an interviewee has been pushed into particular responses. On the other hand, knowledge about the topic may allow the researcher to improve the accuracy of responses. Thus when it is known that people exaggerate their behaviour, a loaded question may provide more accurate results. Electors often exaggerate their willingness to vote in local government elections, so Butler and Stokes deliberately designed a loaded question to gain a more accurate estimate of turnout than a more neutral question would have achieved. The question they asked was:

'Talking to people around the country, we find a great many people weren't able to vote in the local council elections earlier this spring. How about you? Did you vote in the local elections

---

Box 4.5   Questionnaire design

A classic example of questionnaire design in political science is found in *Governing without Consensus: An Irish Perspective* by Richard Rose. He argues that asking the right questions is the most difficult task in a survey. Three major difficulties were anticipated in designing the questionnaire to discover the political opinions and loyalties of the people of Northern Ireland. These difficulties were:

- theoretically important questions might be irrelevant or incomprehensible to most members of the sample
- using colloquial language might impart sectarian bias or employ words meaning very different things to Protestants and Catholics
- important questions might fail to be asked.

In the event, Rose writes, it took two-and-a-half years to develop a questionnaire that covered all the points of interest to the researcher and to the people being studied. Seven pilot surveys were conducted from June 1966 to November 1967. The questionnaire was rewritten and revised after each pilot study in the light of knowledge gained from previous interviews. By acting as the interviewer for the initial pilot, the author was immediately able to see how individuals responded in conversation to questions that were easy to pose in the abstract. At first nearly all the questions were open-ended: that is, no preconceived list of alternative answers was given to the interviewer or to the respondent.

The replies to each questionnaire in each pilot were carefully read by the author to see to what extent the language of Northern Ireland people could be matched to the concepts of social science. Upon occasion the answers not only revealed ambiguities in the questionnaire, but also ambiguities in social science concepts.

The success of the intense preparation and piloting of the questionnaire can be seen in the very high response rate that the interviewer achieved (87.3 per cent). Rose also found that people were willing to be interviewed at length and were prepared to give frank answers to sensitive questions such as those on the use of violence (Rose, 1971, p.182).

---

this year or did something prevent you from voting?' (Butler and Stokes, 1969, p.490)

The results they obtained (62 per cent and 38 per cent respectively) were still too high compared with actual turnout but closer than a more neutral question would have achieved.

Response rates

In every sample survey a certain proportion of the sample will not be contacted. Response rates can be greatly increased by two or three call-backs to those who are out but there are people who are always out despite repeated calls back to their addresses. Young adults are notoriously difficult to catch at home. Some potential respondents will be on holiday, and some may refuse to be interviewed because they are too old, ill, shy or non-English-speaking. Some may object to the survey.

The problem of non-response for the investigator is that non-respondents are not randomly distributed among members of the sample. It is more likely that they have characteristics in common, such as similar ages, similar leisure pursuits or similar views. There is evidence to suggest that in the 1992 British General Election, Conservative Party supporters were more likely to refuse to be interviewed by pollsters, and this contributed to the failure of the polls to predict the Conservative victory (Moon, 1999, pp.122–7). It is therefore quite common in random sampling for the researchers to try to obtain some information about non-respondents, perhaps from neighbours, to check the characteristics of the non-respondents.

The survey of political opinion in Northern Ireland had an exceptionally high response rate of 87.3 per cent, the non-response rate being only 12.7 per cent (Rose, 1971, p.185). We can thus have a high degree of confidence in the representativeness of the survey. Butler and Stokes in their study of voting behaviour in Britain also achieved an excellent response rate of 79.3 per cent (Butler and Stokes, 1969, p.453) but even so this represented a significantly higher rate of non-response (20.6 per cent) than that achieved by Rose. The classic American study of political culture, *The Civic Culture* (Almond and Verba, 1963), shows a more usual range of non-response rates for social surveys. Almond and Verba organized surveys in five countries: the USA, Britain, Germany, Mexico and Italy. The conditions for survey research varied greatly in each country but the response rates varied surprisingly in at least one respect. The USA had the highest response rate of 83.3 per cent, followed by Germany and Italy, both with 74 per cent. Mexico, where survey research was relatively new and where parts of the country were difficult to survey, had a response rate of 60 per cent. The big surprise was in Britain, where the lowest response rate – only 59 per cent – was achieved. This was partly owing to a high rate of refusal to be interviewed. Also the youngest age group, those between 18 and 25 years of age, proved to be very hard to contact and were heavily under-represented in the British sample. The high rate of non-response of 41 per cent suggests that the British sample was not representative of the British electorate as a whole (Almond and Verba, 1963, pp.509–25).

The ethnic minority booster sample in the British General Election study survey in 1997 obtained a very poor response rate of only 44 per cent. This was due partly to refusals (21 per cent) and partly to non-contacts (14 per cent), but also to a significant proportion being unable to be interviewed owing to inadequate knowledge of English (16 per cent). This poor response rate reduces the value of the careful analysis of the data (Saggar, 2000, p.247).

In general, postal questionnaires have a much lower response rate than face-to-face interviews in people's homes, but sometimes good organization and an interest in the research may increase the response rate considerably (see Box 4.6). Whiteley, Seyd and Richardson achieved a response rate of 63 per cent for their postal questionnaire of Conservative Party members. This is an excellent response rate for this type of survey design. The response rate was increased by the researchers having secured the support of the Conservative Party Chairman, by their giving the promise of anonymity to the respondents, and by their chasing up slow respondents with telephoned reminders. There was also a well-used hotline which respondents could ring for further information about the content of the research, the use to which it would be put, and the bona fides of the researchers (Whiteley, Seyd and Richardson, 1994, pp.240–1).

Interviewing

The success of any survey will depend a great deal on the skill of the interviewer employed to interview the respondents. Increasingly interviewers employed by market research firms are highly trained and skilled people who enjoy their work. In carrying out quota surveys they must ensure that the interviewees fit the criteria and answer each question appropriately. Persuading respondents to co-operate is a skill and in order to fulfil their assignment of, usually, 20 interviews in a day they must have good interpersonal skills. Traditionally women have been employed as interviewers but this is less true today. Because the prestige of market research firms is heavily bound up with their ability to predict election results accurately, these firms use their best and most experienced interviewers for these polls (Moon, 1999, p.81).

Box 4.6   Improving response rates

The response rate is a crucial factor in the success or otherwise of survey research. In postal surveys the response rate can be enhanced substantially by following up the initial survey mailing with further prompts. For example:

Week 1:   Post surveys to all intended respondents, with a cover letter explaining the purpose of the survey, why/how the respondent has been chosen, and how important their individual contribution is to the research project. (A franked, self-addressed envelope may also be included for the convenience of the respondents.)

Week 3:   Send post cards to all intended respondents. The post card should thank those who have already responded, and gently remind those who have not yet responded to do so.

Week 5:   Send surveys and cover letter to intended respondents who have not yet replied. The cover letter should remind them of the importance of their contribution, and thank them for their participation.

Week 7–9:   Make telephone reminders to intended respondents who have not yet replied.

A further useful tip in some situations, such as when surveying party activists, election candidates or any group of people belonging to a particular group or structure, is to obtain the explicit support for your survey from an influential person in the relevant group/structure. This would take the form of a letter on headed notepaper from, say, a party secretary, in a postal survey of that party's activists. This requires contacting the party secretary in advance of sending out the survey to activists, agreeing the contents of a letter to be signed by the party secretary. A copy of the letter is then posted with each survey to the activists. This is a common procedure in different kind of elite surveys, and generally enhances response rates.

There are two major concerns with interview situations: first, there is the issue of interview effects, and second, the issue of interviewer fraud.

Interviewer effects arise when respondents give different responses to interviewers because they are perceived to be more or less empathetic to the respondent. This may be because of gender, ethnicity, accent, demeanour, dress or similar attributes. It is widely assumed that interviewers will be more successful in gaining full and honest answers when they have an understanding of and sympathy for the situation of informants and their point of view. In the USA and Britain there has been a considerable debate over the impact of the ethnicity of the interviewer on the interviewee and in particular whether black people's mistrust of white people in general will be extended to white researchers and interviewers (Twine and Warren, 2000, pp.6–19). The evidence is not clear-cut: some studies have found that the ethnicity of the interviewer does produce significant effects but that these effects are not easily predicted (Phoenix, 1994). In a recent study of African-Caribbean people and citizenship in Britain, which involved questions on discrimination, it was considered sensible to use African-Caribbean interviewers (Layton-Henry, 2003). In his Northern Ireland study, Richard Rose considered matching the religious affiliation of the interviewers to that of the respondents, but the pilot studies showed that this was not an issue raised by the respondents (Rose, 1971).

In spite of the importance of interviewer effects, there has been relatively little research on this. There has, for example, been a considerable debate on the influence of gender and the assumption that women interviewers empathized with women much more than male interviewers and are able to obtain much richer, more detailed and fuller information (Oakley, 1981). In a study of interviewer effects Padfield and Proctor found that in answering the questions gender did not seem to be important in generating noticeable differences between the interviews. However, they did find that the women they interviewed were more likely to volunteer additional information on sensitive topics to the female interviewer (Padfield and Proctor, 1996).

Interviewer fraud is another concern. The fear is that interviewers may run out of time and make up some of the interview reports or else, if they do conduct them, ask only a few of the questions and make up the rest. In order to avoid this, survey managers will arrange for a sample of the respondents to be contacted or even re-interviewed to confirm that they did indeed participate in the survey. These checks may be conducted by post, telephone or even personal visits by supervisory staff (Moon, 1999, p.81). If an interviewer is caught cheating, then that person will not be employed again by the market research company and may find it impossible to find similar work again.

Coding and analysis

Surveys and opinion polls can generate large quantities of data which then have to be coded and analysed. Academic investigators can take more time and care as they are not so client-driven as is usually the case for market research investigators. If a newspaper has commissioned a poll on a 'hot' political topic or an impending election, they will want to publish the results very quickly, perhaps the very next day or the day after that. Market research firms thus prefer closed questions as these can be quickly and accurately coded. The interviewer just has to circle the number relating to the appropriate answer. An example of a closed question would be:

Which party are you most inclined to support?

Conservative	1
Labour	2
Liberal Democrat	3
Scottish National Party	4
Plaid Cymru	5
Other party	6
Would not vote	7
Undecided	8
Refused	9

Source: Moon (1999), p.74.

The data from open-ended questions is much more difficult and time-consuming to code and the coders need clear instructions to avoid miscoding. An example of an open-ended question from Saggar (2000) is: 'Why didn't you vote in 1997?' This open-ended question provided the distribution of responses illustrated in Table 4.2.

This question revealed a large variety of reasons. If a pilot study had revealed a more limited range of answers, it would have been possible at that stage to turn the question into a closed question.

Computers have greatly assisted both the coding and analysis of survey data. Computer-assisted telephone interviewing, for example, has made telephone polls much more attractive to and popular with market research firms. Here the interviewer will have the questionnaire on screen in front of them while they carry out the telephone interview. Instructions to the interviewer such as the question order, when to skip particular questions or when to emphasize particular words, can be built into the programme so that there is less chance of errors. The answers to the questions will be recorded on the computer as the interview progresses, again increasing accuracy and efficiency. The results can be quickly transmitted to the office after the interviews for analysis (Moon, 1999, pp.89–90).

Table 4.2   *Why didn't you vote in 1997?*

	Ethnic group		
	White	Asian	Black
Voted in election	78.9	79.5	68.2
Deliberately abstained	1.2	1.1	2.6
Work prevented me	1.6	1.1	2.2
Sickness prevented me	1.3	2.0	3.6
Away on election day	3.3	4.1	2.2
Other commitments, etc.	2.6	3.9	4.4
Couldn't be bothered/not interested	2.7	1.3	2.6
Couldn't decide between parties	1.4	0.9	0.4
Not affected by who won	0.6	0.2	1.1
Religious reasons	0.2	0.2	0.4
Respondent had moved	1.0	1.3	1.5
Polling card/station problem	2.1	2.2	5.8
Never vote/have never voted in my life	0.5	2.0	2.9
Other reason	2.3	0.0	0.4
Don't know	0.1	0.2	1.5
Not answered	0.1	0.0	0.4
N	3,471	458	274
Total (%)	100.0	100.0	100.0

Source: British Election Study (1997), merged file (weighted data), quoted in Saggar (2000), p. 109, with the permission of Manchester University Press.

The analysis and interpretation of survey results is not straight-forward. The investigators may be tempted to present the findings as if they were concrete and accurate rather than tentative and subject to sampling error. This may be encouraged by the clients. Managers may want hard evidence about the potential market for a product in order to get backing for the decision to invest in production. They may therefore present tentative findings as hard facts. Newspaper editors may wish to predict the election result and may be tempted to ignore poll findings that suggest that the gap between the leading parties is narrow and uncertain. However, the failure of the polls to make the correct predictions in the British general elections of 1970 and 1992 have made even newspaper editors more cautious.

A good example of the problems of analysis and interpretation is presented by the BBC 'Panorama' polls on the responses to Enoch Powell's speeches. In December 1968 the BBC commissioned

Opinion Research Centre (ORC) to carry out the polls. ORC carried out two surveys: (1) a quota sample of 522 white adults, and (2) a quota sample of 466 black adults, who were stopped in the street and interviewed in ten cities with significant black populations. One question asked of the black sample was, 'Would you like to return to your country of origin if you received financial help?' The responses were: yes 38 per cent, no 43 per cent, don't know 11 per cent, British origin 8 per cent. Another question was 'Have you yourself been treated better or worse by white people since Mr Powell's speech?' The responses were: worse 8 per cent, better 5 per cent, no difference 80 per cent, don't know 7 per cent. Enoch Powell used these poll results to acquit himself of harming race relations and to support his proposals to repatriate non-white immigrants.

However, there are major problems with accepting the results of these polls at face value. First, as they are quota samples, there is no indication of the rate of non-response or refusal to answer. In such a controversial survey, these figures could be very high. Second, it is likely that most interviewers were white, which may have had an impact on the replies of black respondents. Third, the question about 'returning to your country of origin' is hypothetical as it is well known that migrants keep open the possibility of return long after they are well settled in their new country. A positive answer therefore is a very poor predictor of future behaviour. The publication of such dubious and controversial data should be done only with a full explanation of the way the data has been generated and of the limitations of the findings (Teer and Spence, 1971, pp.125–8).

Focus groups

The use of focus groups has been very extensive in market research for some time, but they have only recently been accepted as a worthwhile technique in the social sciences. Focus groups have attracted considerable attention in recent years because of their widespread use by the modernizers in New Labour's successful campaign to win the 1997 General Election (Butler and Kavanagh, 1998). New Labour strategists such as Philip Gould have argued that if the Labour leadership in the 1980s had paid attention to the findings of focus groups they would have realized how unelectable they had become (Gould, 1998, pp.327). However, Gould did concede that research, both quantitative and qualitative, had misled Labour in the run-up to the General Election of 1992 and failed to alert the leadership to the size of their impending defeat. None the less, Gould said that he found focus groups a source of enormous insight into the views and opinions of voters, the intensity with which these views are held, and as a means of measuring changes in voters' opinions. Focus groups are now extensively used by the parties to plan electoral strategies, to measure the impact of party leaders, and to assess the impact of new policy proposals. The media also increasingly uses them to assess people's views on such topics as the single European currency and how they would vote in a referendum on the Euro.

Focus groups are groups composed of carefully selected individuals brought together to discuss a specific topic (see Box 4.7). Kitzinger defines them as 'group discussions organised to explore a specific set of issues such as people's views and experiences of contraception, drink driving, nutrition or mental illness'. He argues that what distinguished the focus group technique from the wider set of group interviews is the explicit use of group interaction as research data (Kitzinger 1994). Focus groups may be led by a trained facilitator or one of the researchers managing the project for which the groups will provide the information required. Philip Gould preferred to lead the Labour party's focus groups himself as, he argued, this provided an understanding of the members' feelings and the intensity with which these were held which could not be conveyed by a professional facilitator's report.

Focus groups thus have a specific purpose, an appropriate size (usually considered to be between six and ten people), composition, and method of proceeding. The purpose of the group is to discuss a specific issue, product or service so that the researcher can understand how people react to and feel about the topic or product that they are discussing. Participants are selected because

---

Box 4.7   Definition of focus groups

A focus group study is a carefully planned series of discussions designed to obtain perceptions on a defined area of interest in a permissive, non-threatening environment. Each group is conducted with 6–8 people by a skilled interviewer.

The discussions are relaxed and often participants enjoy sharing their ideas and perceptions. Group members influence each other by responding to the ideas and comments of others (Krueger and Casey, 2000).

thcy have characteristics in common which relate to the issue to be discussed by the group. In their preparations for the 1997 General Election campaign, the Labour Party conducted a large number of focus groups composed of one key group of voters: 1992 Conservative voters who were considering switching to Labour (Gould, 1998, p.204). These were the key group in the electorate that Labour wanted to win over. Focus groups can be composed of a wide variety of individuals such as opinion leaders, voters, lawyers, single mothers, motor cyclists or members of environmental pressure groups. The appropriate mix of age, gender and occupation will depend on the research questions to be investigated.

Some researchers feel that focus groups can be a good strategy for carrying out a large number of interviews very efficiently, perhaps even ten at one time! But focus groups are very different from a series of individual interviews. Focus group discussions can tackle issues in some depth, members of the group can bounce ideas off each other, and can agree or disagree. If the discussion goes well, a relaxed but purposeful atmosphere will be created in which participants are willing to discuss and debate issues which they might not normally reveal to, for example, a survey interviewer at their front door (Box 4.8).

The debate and discussion among members of the group allows issues to be explored in much more depth than a survey, and the interaction between members of the group becomes part of the data which the research needs to take into account. The role of the focus group leader or facilitator is also important. Philip Gould liked to stimulate and challenge his groups to test the strength with which

---

Box 4.8   Functions of focus groups

1. Learning how respondents talk about the topic of interest and especially the strength of their feelings and priorities.
2. Generating new research hypotheses that can be submitted to further research and testing.
3. Stimulating new ideas.
4. Diagnosing the potential for problems with a new service, or programme, or policy initiative.
5. Obtaining background information about a topic of interest.
6. Interpreting previously obtained quantitative data.

Source: adapted from Stewart and Shamdasani (1990).

opinions were held. Members of a focus group may be able to raise issues, with the support of other members of the group, which were not initially a priority of the researcher and so have an impact on the research agenda. In a recent project on citizenship and its meaning for African-Caribbean people in Birmingham, it was found that citizenship was initially defined in terms of the passport the person held. This led to a discussion of the problems created for many Jamaicans and Barbadians when their islands became independent during the 1960s. On independence, people born in Jamaica and Barbados became citizens of these new states, even though they had lived in Britain as British citizens for many years, and even though they had served in the British armed forces. They found that they could retain their entitlement to a British passport only by registering as British citizens and paying the fee. This was greatly resented. The discussion then turned to broader issues such as dual nationality and the rights and duties associated with citizenship (Layton Henry, 2003).

This example illustrates one of the claimed advantages of focus groups, that the participants in the research play a more prominent and empowered role than they do in most research. There is less opportunity for the researcher to control them and manipulate them. The subjects of the research can combine and insist that their concerns are discussed. On the other hand, group moderators must not allow the group to leave the subject entirely and wander off on to other topics. They must also ensure that dominant personalities do not take over the group and suppress the opinions of other members.

The planning of a focus group study involves a number of stages (see Box 4.9). Once the purpose and aims of the research have been decided, then it must be determined whether focus groups are the

---

Box 4.9   Planning a focus group study

1. Determine the purpose.
2. Decide whether focus group interviewing is the right method.
3. Identify information-rich participants.
4. Determine how many groups to conduct.
5. Listen to and record your target audience.
6. Analyse the data.
7. Publish the results.

Source: adapted from Krueger and Casey (2000).

right method. Focus groups are very flexible and can be used to illuminate a wide range of topics, so the crucial decision is whether other methods are more appropriate in this particular case. In researching public attitudes towards New Labour and its policies, it might be considered that a survey of a random sample of the electorate would be more appropriate. A survey would provide more or less accurate information about voters' attitudes at the time of the survey, providing that there was a good response rate and respondents were honest. It would be harder for a survey to provide information in depth from a particular group such as electors thinking of switching from one party to another. Surveys are, of course, relatively expensive and would have to be re-run to provide an estimate of changes over time.

The sensitivity of an issue may be an additional justification for choosing focus groups. If the research topic is potentially embarrassing (for example, research on contraception, sexually transmitted diseases or hereditary diseases), then focus groups may be much more appropriate than other research methods. A survey could result in a high level of non-response which would undermine the representativeness of the data. In a group situation, people's confidence will grow as they find others in the group with similar views and experiences struggling to find solutions to common challenges.

Bryman (2001) argues that the focus group is a much more natural environment for sharing information and contributing to research than situations such as an interview in the street or alone in one's home. He also argues that a different power relationship can be created between the researcher and the subjects of the research. Thus the risk of researcher domination is less in a focus group where respondents can look to others in the group for support when they wish to challenge the moderator or researcher. This may partly depend on the role the moderator adopts. Gould clearly led his groups with a firm hand. He says, 'I do not just sit there and listen. I challenge, I argue back, I force them to confront issues. I confront issues myself. I like to use the group to develop and test ideas' (Gould, 1998, p.238). However, there is more potential in a focus group situation for members of the groups to challenge the research agenda and raise related issues which are of greater concern to themselves. This may change the future direction of the research. The research is thus more of a joint enterprise than is the case with, for example, a survey which usually only involves the respondent in a peripheral way.

According to Bryman, this makes focus groups attractive as a research methodology to feminist researchers (Bryman, 2001, p.348). Sensitively handled, focus groups can create the space for respondents to modify the research agenda and challenge the researcher and so avoid a research situation of researcher dominance. Also they can provide a situation where marginalized groups, which are often female, are able to voice their views and experiences.

The identification of information-rich participants follows from the design of the research. A project on car accidents would focus on those most at risk, such as young, newly-qualified male drivers, perhaps with groups composed of female and more experienced drivers as a contrast. But information from young male drivers would be crucial for the research. In studying the reasons why people take up smoking, the focus would be on young people and, in particular, young girls, as these are the groups causing special concern.

The decision on how many groups to conduct and how many meetings to organize for each group is largely a matter of resources and the added value provided by additional meetings. New Labour organized focus groups all over the country, and particularly in marginal seats (Gould, 1998). They ran the groups intensively in the last year of the election campaign right up to the last few days before the election. This kind of intensive research with focus groups would be far beyond the budget of academic researchers. Social science projects would be more specific and would aim to obtain the information they needed from a small number of meetings. Lunt and Livingstone argue that the researcher should continue to run new groups until the last group has nothing new to add and just repeats previous contributions (Lunt and Livingstone, 1992). This is a counsel which ignores the constraints of time and resources.

A critical issue in focus group research is how to record the data. The ideal method is to video and tape-record the whole discussion. This enables the researcher to identify the contributions of each individual in the group discussions. Just taping the sessions is less satisfactory as problems may arise in identifying the discussants, especially if the debate becomes heated and contributors speak at the same time. A video also enables the researcher to capture the enthusiasm, intensity and dynamics of group interactions. If researchers receive only a report of the focus group meetings, they will have lost much material relating to group dynamics, the use of body language and the intensity of feelings and emotions. However, researchers rarely have the resources to video sessions and so have to rely on tape recordings, which then have to be transcribed and analysed.

The number of groups required depends largely on the socio-demographic variables that need to be controlled to illuminate the phenomenon. The researcher may need to control for (have separate groups for) such variables as age, gender, occupation and religion. If this is the case, then more groups will be needed. The more groups there are, the greater the variety of views, depending on the topic. In practice, the resources available to conduct the research will play a major role in determining how many group sessions can be conducted.

New Labour clearly invested considerable resources in their focus groups between 1992 and 1997. The members were recruited by a market research firm according to such criteria as who they had voted for at the last election, their age, and their occupation. The number in each group was eight, and the discussion took place in the homes of participants. Interestingly, Gould attended some focus groups in Los Angeles organized for President Clinton by Stanley Greenberg. These focus groups also consisted of key groups in the electorate such as women college graduates, blue-collar workers and black voters. Gould is a focus group enthusiast. He argues that focus groups worked because he always learnt something new and surprising. Focus groups show that people do not think in predictable ways or conform to conventional prejudices. It is also possible to test the strength and depth of feelings of the voters in ways that are impossible in social surveys. It is clear that Gould found it invigorating and valuable to have discussions and debates with 'ordinary' voters (Gould, 1998).

The value of focus groups

Focus groups are an extremely valuable technique because they allow topics to be discussed in depth by carefully selected respondents with a stake in the topic, they allow respondents to stimulate one another and to provide information based on a range of personal experiences, and they also allow respondents to interact with the researcher and to modify the research agenda. Rich data can be generated in the respondents' own words. A wide range of topics is suitable for focus group discussion. However, the relatively small numbers involved in focus groups and the haphazard selection procedure limit the generalizations that can be made from focus group research. The results of any particular group can be distorted by one or two over-dominant members. Collecting the data can be difficult if appropriate equipment is not available and the researcher as group leader and facilitator may influence the responses of the group members too much. The impact of the focus group discussions does not depend on the members of the group: it is entirely up to the researcher or the market research consultant how the data will be analysed and presented.

The major weakness of focus groups is that it is impossible to know how representative the groups are of the population being researched. No matter how carefully the participants are selected, representativeness cannot be guaranteed. This means that the results are qualitative and indicative rather than valid for the whole population. They will never, therefore, replace surveys and opinion polls as predictors of election results or as sources of data on the state of public opinion.

On balance, the advantages of focus groups outweigh the disadvantages. The use of focus groups can provide rich and meaningful information and valuable insights and understanding. Moreover, if the discussion and debates go well, the respondents will feel much more positive about their involvement and contribution than is often the case with social science research.

Conclusion

Surveys, opinion polls and focus groups have proved to be of great value to governments, commercial companies, pressure groups and the public. They provide a quick and affordable means for governments and other organizations to obtain information and opinions on a wide range of issues and social processes. Government, for example, can obtain information on housing conditions, employment and the health of the population, and use this information to prioritize their resources or amend their policies. The view of the public on these initiatives can be discovered and again used to amend the policies or change their delivery. Companies can use surveys and focus groups to obtain information on the quality of their products and on how well they are recognized and trusted by the consumers. Politicians avidly use polls and focus groups to assess their popularity, the success of their party, and the priorities of the electorate.

In political science, surveys and the data they generate are a crucial part of political analysis. In the public mind, political science is closely associated with the study of elections and explaining voting behaviour. If political scientists are invited to provide expert opinion on radio or television, the most likely reason is to explain election results. A knowledge of survey techniques and the basis of sampling theory is thus essential to students of political science.

However, the value of surveys and the tremendous interest they generate should not result in our taking them for granted. Despite the scientific basis of sampling theory, surveys do have their limitations. They can provide an accurate snapshot of conditions or opinions at the time the survey was carried out, provided that the sample is carefully drawn, the questionnaire is well designed, the interviews are sensitively managed, and honest answers are obtained. But this is a lot to demand. Surveys are never exact and precise. Their accuracy varies depending on the type of sampling design and the care with which any particular survey is carried out. Moreover, surveys are necessarily superficial. Investigators rarely have the time and resources to research deeply into why people hold the opinions they claim to hold, and people are notoriously bad at predicting their own behaviour in the future. Nevertheless carefully designed and executed surveys can yield interesting and reliable data. They are a vital part of modern society and an essential ingredient in the investigator's armoury, but they are not the only research technique available. Surveys must be supplemented by information and evidence from other sources.

Similar arguments apply to focus groups. These have become extremely popular as an alternative to survey research, especially when representative samples are difficult to obtain. They provide the opportunity to gain detailed information on sensitive topics in a relaxed and natural setting. However, even when care is taken to achieve a cross-section of the relevant population, the researcher can never be sure how representative they are. The information obtained should therefore also be reinforced by evidence from further research.

Chapter 5

Descriptive Statistics

Descriptive statistics is a range of basic statistical tools for describing data. The main appeal of descriptive statistics is that it is a powerful and economical way of measuring, analysing and presenting political phenomena such as voting behaviour, political participation, and social and political attitudes generally. Description of political attitudes is essential not only because it is of interest in itself, but also because it is the basis for explanations and for inference (see Chapter 6) when, as is usually the case, a piece of research only includes a sample rather than an entire population.

Questions such as 'Is there a relationship between voters' age and their voting decision?'; 'How have women's incomes changed in the last 20 years?'; 'Are people without university degrees more opposed to immigration than graduates?'; and 'Is there a correlation between religion and party preference?' can be effectively addressed using descriptive statistics. Note that all these questions ask *either* 'What is x like?' *or* 'Is there a relationship between x and y (and z), and if so, what is it like?' Descriptive statistics can be used to address political science questions that follow this basic model (see Box 5.1).

The chapter opens with three sections that each deal with a basic component of descriptive statistics: levels of measurement, measures of central tendency, and measures of spread. Levels of measurement concern the essential nature of a variable, and it is important to know this because it determines what one can do with a variable. The section about measures of central tendency covers the mean, median and mode. They are three different ways of stating what is a typical value for a variable. The next section discusses spread in three aspects: modality, skewness and kurtosis. In terms of measures of spread, the section covers the standard deviation and quartiles.

A question that quickly arises is how to decide what descriptive statistics to use. As the next section explains, the most important point is that, some measures of central tendency and spread do not

Box 5.1 Addressing research questions with descriptive statistics

Different kinds of questions can be addressed with descriptive statistics (variable names in italics).

1. Univariate questions: focus on a single variable; 'What is *x* like?'

    Example: 'What proportion of *seats* in Parliament does each of the parties hold after the election?'

2. Bivariate questions: focus on the existence and nature of a relationship between two variables; 'Is *x* related to *y*, and if so, how?'

    Example: 'Did parties that attracted more *votes* in the election receive more *seats* in Parliament?'

3. Multi-variate questions: focus on the existence and nature of a relationship between more than two (usually three) variables; 'Taking into account *z*, is *x* related to *y*, and if so, how?'

    Example: 'Taking into account how many *constituencies* each party contested, did parties that attracted more *votes* receive more *seats*?'

4. Comparative perspective: univariate, bivariate and multi-variate questions can be comparative across time and space.

    Temporal comparison: 'What proportion of *seats* in Parliament did each party have before and after the British election that took place in 2001?'

    Spatial comparison: 'Did parties that attracted more *votes* in elections receive more *seats* in their respective parliaments, in the British and Danish elections that took place in 2001?'

'go' with some levels of measurement. An understanding of why this is so is essential before one can start thinking about using descriptive statistics.

The next section deals with presentational issues, since normally the reason for producing descriptive statistics is to share them with others in a report, essay, conference presentation, and so on. There are a number of ways to present descriptive statistics, and the chapter focuses on some of the most common alternatives as well as issues to bear in mind when choosing between them.

The final section is a reminder that the economy of descriptive statistics is not cost-free, since their simplicity means that much of the richness of political phenomena is necessarily excluded. This raises the question of whether the sorts of measurements that are the stock in trade of descriptive statistics are valid indicators of political phenomena, as well as several other issues that make it possible to mislead an audience to a greater or lesser extent. Using descriptive statistics competently includes being aware that seemingly innocuous decisions about how to analyse and present one's data can make the research unintentionally misleading. The chapter's final section offers some advice on how to avoid this.

Levels of measurement, central tendency and spread

'Levels of measurement' is a cumbersome term that means some-thing quite simple. To identify a variable's level of measurement is to ask 'What kind of data is this? Does it make sense to try to add, subtract, multiply and/or divide the values on this variable?' It is necessary to know a variable's level of measurement in order to decide what kind of descriptive statistics to produce: it is not possible to make informed decisions about measures of central tendency and spread without taking into account a variable's level of measurement. In general terms, a useful way of understanding a variable's central tendency is to think of it as the question 'What is a typical value on this variable?' If the variable is 'age', measured simply in terms of some survey respondents' ages, then the question to ask about the central tendency becomes 'What is a fairly typical age among the respondents to this survey?' In contrast, to examine a variable's spread is to ask 'What is the range and distribution of values on this variable?' Applied to 'age', the question becomes 'What are highest and lowest recorded ages, and how are age groups distributed between the highest and lowest ages?'

Levels of measurement

There are four levels of measurement: categorical (or nominal), ordinal, interval and ratio (Harrison, 2001, pp.17–19). These labels give some intuitive clues about the nature of each type of datum.

Table 5.1   *Categorical data: the french*
presidential election, 2002

Bayrou	1
Chevenement	2
Chirac	3
Jospin	4
Laguiller	5
Le Pen	6
Others	7

Notes: Categorical data relating to candidates in the first round.The way the candidates are ordered here (e.g., alphabetically) has no numerical or statistical significance.
Source: Office of the French President (2002).

Categorical data are data which are essentially qualitative, but which have been quantified. As illustrated in Table 5.1, it is possible to assign values 1, 2, 3 and so on to election candidates where numbers are essentially used as labels: category 1, category 2 etc. We could, of course, use letters just as well: category A, B, C or indeed names, e.g., catholic, protestant, muslim etc. However, it is not possible to use these values arithmetically. For example, Jospin is not 'twice as much' as Chevenement; neither is Chirac 'half' of Le Pen. Assigning numbers to qualitative information can nevertheless be useful when one wants to enter the information into quantitative statistical software programmes, typically in order to use the programme to count how many occurrences there are of each category. This kind of frequency count is the only quantitative operation that is meaningful with categorical data.

Ordinal data is quite literally data that can be ordered. As Table 5.2 shows, in the first round of the French presidential election Jacques Chirac attracted the single largest proportion of votes, followed by Jean-Marie Le Pen, Lionel Jospin, and the rest of the candidates. However, although it is possible to order the candidates according to how well they did in this round, the data is rather imprecise: it is incorrect to assume that because Le Pen is between Chirac and Jospin he is equally far from Chirac and Jospin. Ordinal data only reveals the order of categories, not how far, arithmetically, they are from each other, and whether they are equidistant (that is, equally far away from each other arithmetically). Therefore, it is often inappropriate to use ordinal data in mathematical operations, too. However, it often happens that ordinal variables with several categories are treated as if they were ratio variables. Survey scale questions with response categories such as '1: agree very much', '2: agree to some extent', '3: neither agree nor disagree', '4: disagree to some extent' and '5: disagree strongly' are ordinal but are frequently treated as if they were ratio variables. Mean attitudes for men and women might be calculated and compared, to the effect that men might be said to have a mean attitude of 2.0 and women 4.0. In other words, men appear to be more in agreement with the survey question than women, by 2.0 units. However, since the values on ordinal variables are not equidistant, this is not an interpretable figure, and therefore it would also be fallacious to conclude that women disagreed twice as strongly as men with the survey question.

Interval-level measurements have ordered categories and equidistant intervals. A special subset of interval measurements is called ratio data. Ratio data meet the general criteria of interval data (e.g., ordered categories and equidistant intervals), and in addition ratio data have a meaningful zero point, such as for example one's age, counted in years, or one's income, counted in dollars or euro. If a variable has no meaningful zero then it does not belong to this subset of interval variables. Temperature is an example of such a variable: zero degrees Celsius does not mean 'no temperature', it means that the temperature is hovering just about freezing point. In political science ratio variables – for instance income, age, years of education, economic growth, levels of crime, infant mortality – are much more common than interval variables, so the issue of a 'meaningful zero' rarely arises. Nevertheless, it is important to be aware of this distinction, because interval measurements without a meaningful zero point (e.g., non-ratio interval

Table 5.2   *Ordinal data: the French presidential election, 2002*

1	Chirac
2	Le Pen
3	Jospin
4	Bayrou
5	Laguiller
6	Chevenement
7	Others

Note: data relate to the first round.

**Table 5.3   *Ratio data: the French
presidential election, 2002***

Candidate	Vote share (%)
Chirac	19.88
Le Pen	16.86
Jospin	16.18
Bayrou	6.84
Laguiller	5.72
Chevenement	5.33
Others	29.21

Note: ratio data relating to results of the first
round.

measurements) are not suitable for multiplication and division. Consider this example. If someone has £20 and then receives a further £20, then he or she has *twice* the amount of money, because this variable has a meaningful zero point: having £0 means 'having no money'. In contrast, if a pot of food on the stove is 20 degrees Celsius and is then heated to 40 degrees Celsius, then the temperature has *not* doubled. The reason is that as a variable, temperature does not have a meaningful zero point: if the food was 0 degrees, say while defrosting, then it would *not* be correct to say that it 'had no temperature'.

We can tell that Table 5.3 contains ratio data because it has a meaningful zero point: receiving zero votes means, quite simply, receiving no votes, and this is a meaningful statement.

Central tendency

There are three measures of central tendency: the mean, median and mode (Lewis-Beck 1995, p.8–10). By definition, measures of central tendency provide summaries of variables' centres; in different ways they reveal what values are 'typical' about a variable (see Box 5.2 for worked examples).

The mean, also known as the arithmetic average, is simply a variable's average value. The mean of a variable x (which is represented by the symbol x) is obtained by the following formula:

$$\bar{x} = \frac{x_1 + x_2 + x_3 + \ldots x_n}{n}$$

> ## Box 5.2   Measures of central tendency
>
> A variable has these five observations: 0, 1, 2, 3, 3. Its three measures of central tendency are:
>
> Mean: $\dfrac{0 + 1 + 2 + 3 + 3}{5} = \dfrac{9}{5} = 1.8$ (the arithmetic average).
>
> Median: 2 (the 'middle value' in ascending or descending order).
>
> Mode: 3 (the value that occurs most frequently).

where each x represents the value of an individual observation and n is the number of observations that the variable has.

The median summarizes a variable's typical value slightly differently. The median is a variable's 'middle' value. The simplest way of obtaining a variable's median is to line up its values in ascending or descending (it makes no difference) order, and identify the observation that is in the middle; that is, the observation that has as many other observations (i.e. cases) above itself as below itself. The value of this middle observation is the variable's median. If the variable has an even number of observations, in which case there is no single observation that has the same number of observations above and below itself, then the customary way to proceed is to conclude that the median is the halfway point between the two middle observations. That is, in such cases the median is the mean of the two middle observations.

The mode provides yet a different interpretation of what is a typical value for a variable. The mode is the most frequent value among all the variable's observations. Variables whose mean, median and mode are exactly the same have what is known as a normal distribution. The properties of such distributions are fundamental to inferential statistics; which one introduced in Chapter 6.

A point to note about measures of central tendency is that two variables that have the same mean can be very different from each other. Box 5.3 contains an example that shows that this can have important political consequences. The box indicates that people in the Philippines and Samoa seem to have very similar average incomes, yet it also makes clear that the two countries have very different income distributions: that is, the spread of incomes differs greatly in these two countries, so that drawing the conclusion that Filippino people and Samoans are roughly equally well off is to

Box 5.3   Same mean, different distributions: per capita GNP and national income distributions

Two variables that have the same mean can have very different distributions. In such situations the mean can make comparisons between the two variables quite misleading. For example, the level of poverty can be quite different in two countries with very similar average incomes (e.g., per capita gross national product, or GNP). Consider the following figures from 1997:

Country	GNP per capita (US$), 1997	Income ratio of highest 20% to lowest 20%, 1997
Bangladesh	360	8.8
Philippines	1,200	9.0
Samoa	1,140	17.0
Thailand	2,740	9.7

From the GNP figures one would assume that levels of income are rather similar in the Philippines and Samoa: US$1,200 and US$1,140, respectively. However, given that in the Philippines the 20 per cent of the population with highest incomes earned nine times as much money as the people in the lowest 20 per cent income bracket, and that in Samoa the highest earners made 17 times more money than the lowest earners, it would be misleading to conclude that people in these two countries are on average more or less equally well off. (The lower the income ratio, the more equal the country's income distribution.)

Source: Asian Development Bank (October 2002).

ignore the fact that their similar means 'hide' important information. This is one important reason why measures of spread matter: they can reveal how well the mean describes a variable.

Spread

A variable's spread, or distribution (these terms can be used interchangeably), refers to how its observations are spread, or distributed, over the range of possible values. Spread can be broken into three factors: modality, skewness and kurtosis. As the term modality implies, it is related to the mode as a measure of central tendency. Modality refers to how many modes there are in a distribution. Distributions with a single mode such as the normal distribution (see

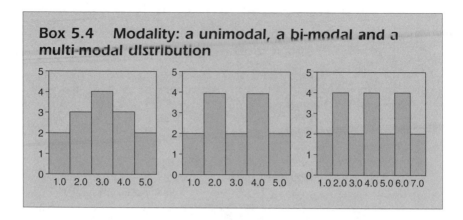

Box 5.4   Modality: a unimodal, a bi-modal and a multi-modal distribution

Chapter 6) are unimodal. Distributions with two modes are bi-modal, whereas the term multi-modal is given to distributions with even more modes (see Box 5.4). Modality impacts differently on different measures of spread: as will become clear, the standard deviation can be strongly affected by bi- or multi-modality, whereas the quartiles measure of spread is quite robust and not greatly affected by bi- or multi-modality. The two variables about mean incomes in the Philippines and Samoa clearly have very different spreads: the Samoan variable would, for example, have a more pronounced bimodal spread than the Filippino variable, due to the greater polarization of incomes between rich and poor people in Samoa.

Skewness is about a distribution's degree of symmetry. A variable has a positive skew if its values are bunched towards the lower end of the variable's range. Vice versa, it has a negative skew if its values

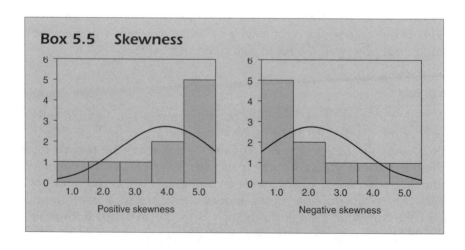

Box 5.5   Skewness

Positive skewness   Negative skewness

are clustered around the top end of the range. As Chapter 6 explains, the perfect symmetry of normal distributions means that they have no skewness, and symmetrical bi- and multi-modal distributions are also non-skewed. Bi-modal distributions are not necessarily more skewed than unimodal ones; in fact, the opposite can be true as often as not.

Kurtosis refers to the peakedness of a distribution. Peaks in distributions with positive kurtosis are tall and the distribution tails are long and thin. Negative kurtosis indicates that peaks are short and the tails are fat and short (Box 5.6).

A variable's standard deviation reveals how far on average the variable's observations are from the variable's mean. (It follows that the standard deviation is more closely associated with the mean – as Box 5.7 illustrates – than it is with the median or the mode). The calculation is expressed in the following equation:

$$\sigma = \sqrt{\frac{\Sigma(x_i - \bar{x})^2}{n - 1}}$$

Box 5.6   Two unimodal distributions

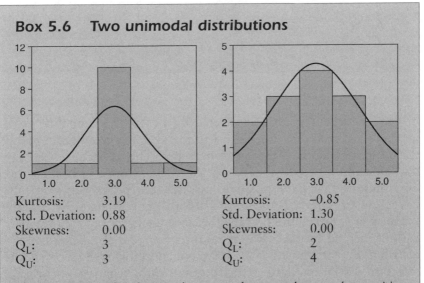

Kurtosis:	3.19	
Std. Deviation:	0.88	
Skewness:	0.00	
Q_L:	3	
Q_U:	3	

Kurtosis:	−0.85	
Std. Deviation:	1.30	
Skewness:	0.00	
Q_L:	2	
Q_U:	4	

Neither of these distributions have any skewness, but one has positive kurtosis and one has negative kurtosis. Because the cases in the distribution with positive kurtosis are closer to the mean than they are in the distribution with negative kurtosis, the standard deviation is smaller in the distribution with a positive kurtosis.

Box 5.7   Calculating the standard deviation: electoral colleges in the US presidential election, 2000

In the election of the United States President, each state's electoral college has a number of votes (based on the state's population size), which are given to the candidate that wins the greatest number of votes in the state. For simplicity's sake, this example of how to calculate a standard deviation only includes the six states that make up New England (Connecticut, Maine, Massachusetts, New Hampshire, Rhode Island and Vermont).

Connecticut	8	New Hampshire	4
Maine	4	Rhode Island	4
Massachusetts	12	Vermont	3

Calculate the mean: $(8 + 4 + 12 + 4 + 4 + 3) / 6 = 5.8$.

Next, subtract the mean from each observation, e.g., obtain the residual for each observation (for simplicity's sake, we round the mean up to its closest integer, from 5.8 to 6).

$$8 - 6 = 2$$
$$4 - 6 = -2$$
$$12 - 6 = 6$$
$$4 - 6 = -2$$
$$4 - 6 = -2$$
$$3 - 6 = -3$$

→

The standard deviation is affected by a variable's modality, skewness and kurtosis. The further a variable deviates from unimodality, the larger its standard deviation becomes. This is because the standard deviation, like the mean, is sensitive to extreme values. Further, distributions that have positive kurtosis (tall peaks and thin tails) have smaller standard deviations than distributions with negative kurtosis (low peaks and fat tails) because the latter have more observations located further away from the mean. All else being equal, a distribution with positive kurtosis will necessarily have a smaller standard deviation than a distribution with negative kurtosis. In contrast, skewness does not affect the standard deviation in a uniform manner: it is not the case that all else being equal, an unskewed distribution has a smaller standard deviation than a skewed one.

A second, common measure of spread is quartiles, which is closely

→
Square the residuals:

$$
\begin{aligned}
2*2 &= 4 \\
-2*-2 &= 4 \\
6*6 &= 36 \\
-2*-2 &= 4 \\
-2*-2 &= 4 \\
-3*-3 &= 9
\end{aligned}
$$

Add the squared residuals and divide the sum by the sample size minus 1 (e.g., $n-1$):

$$(4 + 4 + 36 + 4 + 4 + 9) / (6-1) = 12.2$$

Take the square root of the figure obtained in the previous step:

$$\sqrt{12.2} = 3.49$$

This means that although electoral colleges in New England have on average six votes, this varies from state to state with, on average, 3.49 votes.

The more closely clustered the observations are around their mean, the smaller the standard deviation will be. A small standard deviation is a sign that the mean is an appropriate measure of central tendency in the sense that it is representative of the values on which it is based.

Source: Federal Election Commission (2002).

related to the median (see Box 5.8). Remember that the median is obtained by 'lining up' a variable's observations in ascending or descending order of their values. Quartiles follow a similar pattern. When the observations have been arranged in ascending or descending order they are divided into four sections (hence the label 'quartiles'): the lower quartile, the interquartile range or midspread (the two quartiles in the middle), and the upper quartile. The upper end of the interquartile range is denoted Q_U and the lower end of the interquartile range is denoted Q_L. For reasons that should be obvious (given the definition of the interquartile range), the median is always the middle value in the interquartile range, and if there is an equal number of observations, then the median is the mean of the two middle observations. Similarly, if there are an even number of observations, Q_L and Q_U are the mean of the two values closest to the lower and upper end of the interquartile range, respectively.

Box 5.8   Quartiles: women MPs member states

The proportion of women MPs in the European Union on 1 July 2002 was as follows:

Country	Women MPs (%)	Quartiles
Sweden	42.7	
Denmark	38.0	
Finland	36.5	
Netherlands	34.0	Q_U
Germany	31.7	
Spain	28.3	
Austria	26.8	
Belgium	23.3	Median
Portugal	19.1	
UK	17.9	
Luxembourg	16.7	
Ireland	13.3	Q_L
France	12.3	
Italy	9.8	
Greece	8.7	

1. Median: in ascending (or descending) order, Belgium is the middle value, so the median proportion of women MPs in the European Union is 23.3 per cent.
2. Upper quartile (Q_U): the upper quartile is the middle value of the half of the distribution above the median; here, 34.0 per cent (the Netherlands). It marks the highest value of the interquartile range.
3. Lower quartile (Q_L): the lower quartile is the middle value in the half of the distribution below the median; here, 13.3 per cent (Ireland). It marks the lowest value of the interquartile range.

Source: Inter-Parliamentary Union (2002).

Quartiles are affected by modality, skewness and kurtosis, but in general they are far more robust on all three counts than is the standard deviation. In fact, comparing two variables with the same median, one unimodal variable and one bi-modal variable, it is not by definition the case that they have different Q_L and Q_U. Similarly, the presence and degree of skewness and kurtosis may or may not affect Q_L and Q_U. In contrast, a unimodal and a bi-modal distribution with the same means can be expected to have different standard deviations.

Choosing descriptive statistics

So far, this chapter has introduced four levels of measurement (categorical, ordinal, interval and ratio), three measures of central tendency (the mean, median and mode) and two measures of spread (standard deviation and quartiles). It has also looked closely at modality, skewness and kurtosis. An informed decision about what measures of central tendency and spread to use in a particular situation depends on understanding the relationship between all these things.

Figure 5.1 sets out some rules of thumb for selecting descriptive statistics. The first criterion for selection is a variable's level of measurement. The arithmetic nature of ratio and interval variables makes it possible to obtain mean, median and mode for them; for these types of variables spread is also a factor in selecting descriptive statistics due to the mean's and standard deviation's sensitivity to extreme values. Since the mean and standard deviation are meaningless measures of categorical and ordinal variables, spread is not a relevant selection criterion for them. For ordinal variables it is

Figure 5.1   *Choosing descriptive statistics*

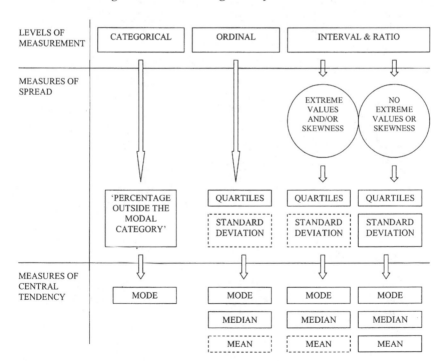

always possible to obtain the median and the mode, and if the ordinal variable has many categories it is also possible to calculate a mean (but this can be a questionable practice, since the categories are not equidistant). The mode is the only measure of central tendency that applies to categorical variables, because the categories of a categorical variable have no arithmetical relationship to one another: the only thing we can do with categorical variables is to count how many observations there are in each category.

A variable's level of measurement and, for interval and ratio variables, their spread, also determine which measure of spread is appropriate. Interval and ratio variables can be described with standard deviations or, if the variable has many outliers, quartiles. Quartiles may also be applied to ordinal variables, and, with the same note of caution as applies to calculating means for ordinal variables, it is also common to apply the standard deviation (see Box 5.9). Neither

---

Box 5.9   The House of Representatives: outlier effects

The House of Representatives has 435 seats, allocated to states on the basis of population size. In the 107th Congress the three states on the Pacific coast, California, Oregon and Washington, had the following number of Representatives:

California   52
Oregon   5
Washington   9

California is a clear outlier here, and it makes a big difference to the mean if California is included or excluded:

Mean, California included: (52+5+9) / 3   = 22
Mean, California excluded: (5+9) / 2   = 7

So, which mean is most representative of the Pacific coast states?
This example also illustrates the relationship between the mean and the standard deviation:

Standard deviation, California included: 26.1
Standard deviation, California excluded: 2.8

The explanation for this is that since including California makes the observations less closely clustered around their mean, the standard deviation becomes larger.

Source: Congressional Directory, 107th Congress (2002).

quartiles nor the standard deviation apply to categorical variables. Quartiles do not apply since this measure of spread requires values on a variable to be arranged in ascending or descending order, and it is not possible to do so with the values on categorical variables. The standard deviation does not apply because, among other things, it requires it to be possible to calculate a variable mean and, again, this is not possible for categorical variables. An alternative way to gauge a categorical variable's spread is to work out what proportion of observations are in the modal category.

Presenting descriptive statistics

There are many ways to present descriptive statistics. The options depend mainly on whether it is a univariate, bi-variate or multi-variate analysis, and what descriptive statistics are to be presented. In addition, there are some rules of thumb to follow but to some extent presentational issues are also a question of personal tastes and preferences.

Pie charts

Pie charts look like a pie that has been sliced but not yet served. Each slice represents one of a variable's observed values, and the relative size of a slice corresponds with its frequency. Pie charts can be used to present categorical, ordinal, interval and ratio data. Pie charts tend to be used to present a single variable, because there are more convenient and informative ways to present relationships between two or more variables. If, however, it is relevant to illustrate two or more variables without making any comments about the relationship between them, then it is of course possible to create one pie chart per variable, and place them beside each other for comparison. (In Box 5.10, for example, it would have been possible to create an additional pie chart for the European Parliament elections that took place in 1994, to see how the party groups fared then.)

Pie charts are quite common despite having a number of weaknesses. The basic premise of a pie chart, that the number of cases in each category of the variable depicted somehow corresponds to the angle of each pie slice (at the pie's centre), is not the easiest way for the human mind to interpret visual information. It is possible of course to add percentages to the pie slices, but even so the pie chart lacks a visually straightforward baseline for comparisons between its categories.

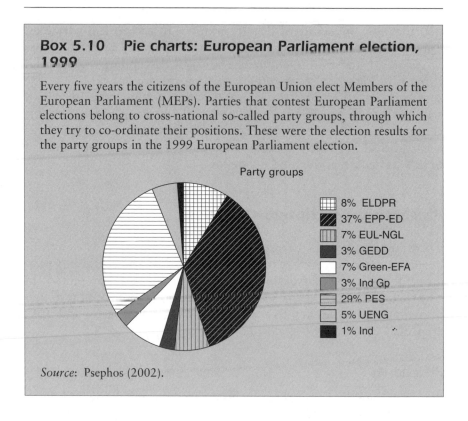

Box 5.10   Pie charts: European Parliament election, 1999

Every five years the citizens of the European Union elect Members of the European Parliament (MEPs). Parties that contest European Parliament elections belong to cross-national so-called party groups, through which they try to co-ordinate their positions. These were the election results for the party groups in the 1999 European Parliament election.

Party groups

8% ELDPR
37% EPP-ED
7% EUL-NGL
3% GEDD
7% Green-EFA
3% Ind Gp
29% PES
5% UENG
1% Ind

Source: Psephos (2002).

Histograms

Like a pie chart, a histogram is a simple illustration of the mode: that is, of how many observations there are of each of a variable's observed values. Each bar is equivalent to a slice of pie in a pie chart, and a bar's height depends on how many observations there were of the value that the bar represents. Histograms can be used to illustrate the mode for variables of all levels of measurement. It is possible to display more than one variable in a histogram (using different colours or patterns on the bars to denote the different variables), but it is not convenient to try to display relationships between variables using a histogram. For example, the histogram in Box 5.11 could have also contained the election results of some previous New Zealand elections.

Since the point of graphs is to offer easily interpretable visual accounts of complex data, histograms are preferable to pie charts because they have a visually straightforward and immediately obvious baseline for comparing categories (that is, the bars) to each

Box 5.11   Histograms: New Zealand election, 2002

On 27 July 2002 the New Zealand electorate returned Ms Helen Clarke and her Labour party to office. The histogram shows that although the National Party was never really a threat to Labour (at least not on its own), Labour's 41.4 per cent of the vote share left it unable to form a single-party majority government.

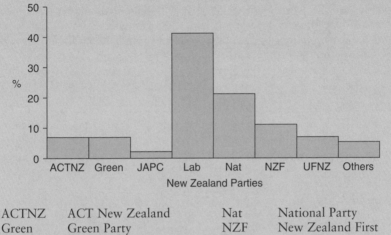

ACTNZ	ACT New Zealand	Nat	National Party
Green	Green Party	NZF	New Zealand First
JAPC	Jim Anderton's	UFNZ	United Future
	Progressive Coalition		for New
Lab	Labour		Zealand

In histograms of interval and ratio variables, such as the one used in this histogram, it is also possible to represent the variable's mean and standard deviation. (The reason why this does not apply to categorical and ordinal variables is of course that they do not have means and standard deviations.)

Source: Psephos (2002).

other. It is immediately clear if one bar is longer or shorter than another, and the vertical axis provides an account of exactly how tall each bar is and what the difference in height is between bars.

Frequency tables and cross-tabulations

A frequency table and a cross-tabulation are the same thing, except a frequency table contains one variable, and a cross-tabulation two.

Box 5.12   Cross-tabulations: the human development index, 2001

The United Nations Development Programme's annual report on human development ranks countries on a human development index (HDI), measuring life expectancy, educational attainment and adjusted real income in different countries. In the 2001 report the 48 highest-ranking countries were classified as having 'high human development'. Among the regions of the world, Europe is heavily represented among the 'high human development' countries. This cross-tabulation shows that it is much more common for European countries to have high human development than it is for non-European countries.

	European Countries	Non-European Countries	Total
High Human Development	28	20	48
Medium Human Development	7	71	78
Low Human Development	0	36	36
Total	35	127	162

Note that the variable with the most number of categories has been placed in the rows, not the columns (although in this example the variables have two and three categories, respectively, so the placement of the variables does not make a great deal of difference).

Note also that the categories of human development have been arranged in descending order; it would have made equal sense to place them in ascending order. There was no intuitive or logical order for the two categories of the column variable, so 'European Countries' and 'Non-European Countries' were ordered alphabetically. The bottom row and right hand column contain column and row totals, and the bottom right hand cell shows the cross-tabulation's total number of cases (e.g., countries). This figure would have been particularly important if the figures were expressed as percentages:

→

Frequency tables and cross-tabulations contain a number of cells, in which there are numbers corresponding to the number of times a variable's value occurs. A frequency table is an alternative to a pie chart or a histogram. Table 5.3 contains a frequency table, showing what percentage of votes cast each of the presidential hopefuls received in the French presidential election of 2002. As Kranzler puts it, frequency tables are 'very useful for providing a pictorial view of a set of data. Although helpful, they often do not provide us with enough

→

	European Countries	Non-European Countries	Total
High Human Development	58.3	41.7	100
Medium Human Development	9.0	91.0	100
Low Human Development	0.0	100.0	100

N: 162

This cross-tabulation contains row percentages, which show what proportion of each level of human development category was European and non-European. The cell in each row containing the highest frequencies (e.g., the most number of observations) are located on a diagonal, insofar as this is possible in a 2 × 3 table. In other words, the cross-tabulation shows a positive correlation between a country's level of human development and its location (in Europe or not).

In contrast, the cross-tabulation with column percentages below reveals the levels of human development in European and non-European countries, respectively. Here, the cells containing the highest frequencies in each column also form a diagonal (e.g., they are not located in the same row). On this basis one can point to a positive correlation between the two variables. Moreover, it is worth noting that the cell frequencies in the 'European Countries' are in perfect descending order (e.g., 80 – 20 – 0 per cent, reading the column from top to bottom). However, the cell frequencies in 'Non-European Countries' are not in perfect descending order (15.7 – 55.9 – 28.3). If they had been, then the correlation between the two variables would have been even stronger.

	European Countries	Non-European Countries
High Human Development	80.0	15.7
Medium Human Development	20.0	55.9
Low Human Development	0.0	28.3
Total	100.0	100.0

N: 162

Source: UN (2002).

or the right kind of information' (Kranzler 2003, p.49). Cross-tabulations are usually more informative, because they cross-reference two variables (see Box 5.12). A cross-tabulation is the most common way to display bi-variate, and sometimes multi-variate, analyses. (In this chapter the word 'correlation' is meant as synonymous to 'relationship' rather than in the more technical sense of being a measure ranging from −1 to 1 of how one variable changes given the nature and magnitude of change in another variable).

Frequency tables and cross-tabulations should state the variable's total number of observations, even if the frequencies (the numbers in the cells) are reported as percentages. It is also a good idea to make an extra column and/or row that contains the row and/or column totals. There is no rule that says whether it is row totals or column totals (or both) that are interesting to include. This varies from table to table, depending on what it is the researcher is trying to show in the table. If the data is interval or ratio (and in some instances ordinal), an additional informative feature is cumulative percentages, so that readers can easily work out what proportion of observations are lower – or higher – than a value of particular interest (for instance, a cut-off point of some kind). Moreover, if a variable has many categories it makes practical sense to place variable categories in the rows of a frequency table, because it is typically easier to deal with a table that has many rows than one that has many columns.

Reading frequency tables is straightforward, simply look at how many frequencies there are in each cell. Reading cross-tabulations can be more complicated. The thing to look for is cells on the diagonal holding very large proportions of the observations, and other cells being almost void of observations. This is evidence of a correlation between two variables. As a rule of thumb, the more highly clustered the observations are in diagonal cells, the stronger the correlation. A positive correlation means that a change on one variable (an increase or a decrease) is associated with a change in the same direction on the other variable. A negative correlation means that a change on one variable (an increase or decrease) is associated with a change in the opposite direction on the other variable. A word of warning: a correlation does *not* involve a statement about the direction of effects, though sometimes the direction of the effect is quite obvious. For example, it is plausible that one's gender influences one's attitude towards abortion, but hard to imagine that it could work the other way round.

Sometimes it is hard to determine whether or not there is a correlation, especially if the variables have so many categories that it is unlikely that a notably large proportion of observations will end up in any one cell. (Even if they do, such observation-rich cells may form a shape that falls well short of a perfect diagonal.) For presentational purposes it can be useful to reduce the number of categories for variables that have a very large number of categories. This is known as 'collapsing' categories, and is done by combining several categories into a smaller number of categories (Sapsford, 1996, pp.201–12). This almost always makes a table or tabulation more convenient and easy to read. For example, on a variable recording people's ages it may be useful to collapse original categories into brackets such as 'up to 14', '15–24', '25–34', and so on. Some information is clearly lost in collapsing categories, and the more detailed data should always be retained even if it is not presented. However, as Chapter 4 discusses in further detail, collapsing categories can bring greater clarity to the results.

Variable categories should be presented in a specific order, for instance from smallest to largest (or vice versa), chronologically or alphabetically. It may also be useful to combine some organizing principle with the alphabetical approach: for example, countries might be presented by continent, as well as alphabetically within each continent subcategory.

Cross-tabulations can also be used to illustrate relationships between more than two variables. If the third variable has more than two categories this quickly gets complicated enough to consider moving on to more sophisticated and powerful forms of analysis, such as multi-variate regression. Adding a third variable to a cross-tabulation between two 'original' variables requires creating one new cross-tabulation for each of the categories on the third variable. For example, if the third variable has two categories, then two new cross-tabulations will be created.

Usually adding a third variable is only considered if the original, bi-variate (two-variable) cross-tabulation showed a correlation. The thing to look for in the three-variable cross-tabulations is whether the original correlation is evident there, too (see Box 5.13). If it is, then the conclusion to draw is that the third variable is irrelevant. In contrast, if the correlation has disappeared (or has been substantially weakened) by the addition of a third variable, then the appropriate conclusion to draw is that in fact the original correlation was (at least partly) spurious. The next step to take is to examine more closely the relationship between the third variable and two original ones.

Box plots

A box plot is a graphical representation of a variable's distrubution, derived from the variable's median and quartiles. As its name suggests, the main feature of a box plot (sometimes also known as a box-and-whisker plot) consists of a box representing the interquartile range (see Box 5.14). In other words, the lower limit of the box is Q_L, and the upper limit of the box is Q_U. There is always a line through the box, representing the variable's median. This line can be anywhere in the box, not necessarily in its middle,

Box 5.13   Cross-tabulations with three variables: the human development index, 2001

This cross-tabulation with a correlation between a country's level of human development and its geographical location (e.g., whether it was a European country) appeared in Box 5.12. The correlations seemed quite strong (e.g., the cells holding a majority of observations in each column were located diagonally *vis-à-vis* each other).

	European Countries	Non-European Countries	Total
High Human Development	58.3	41.7	100
Medium Human Development	9.0	91.0	100
Low Human Development	0.0	100.0	100

N: 162

Below, a third variable has been added: OECD membership. The thinking that motivates this variable's inclusion is the possibility that OECD membership is correlated to a country's having a high level of human development, rather than its geographical location in, or not in, Europe. The OECD variable has two categories, members and non-members. Consequently, two new cross-tabulations are required (Marsh, 1988, pp.240–52).

OECD Members

	European Countries	Non-European Countries	Total
High Human Development	22	6	28
Medium Human Development	1	1	2
Low Human Development	0	0	0
Total	23	7	30

→

since a variable's middle *observation* (which is what the median is) does not necessarily take on a *value* that places it equidistant from Q_L and Q_U.

An additional feature of box plot is that a whisker extends upwards from Q_U, and another whisker extends downwards from Q_L. Just as the line representing the median in the box can be located anywhere in the box, so the lengths of the whiskers depend on the distribution of the variable. There are some alternative ways (differing primarily in the amount of detailed information they convey) of determining how to draw the whiskers. One standard way is to calculate the variable's step (1.5 * the interquartile range), and to

Non-OECD Members

	European Countries	Non-European Countries	Total
High Human Development	6	14	20
Medium Human Development	6	70	76
Low Human Development	0	36	36
Total	12	120	132

What happened to the original correlation? These cross-tabulations show that OECD members, regardless of whether or not they are European OECD members, overwhelmingly have a high level of human development. In other words, the correlation between the two original variables seems to have disappeared in this cross-tabulation. The frequency distribution in the cross-tabulation for non-OECD members shows a substantially weakened correlation between the two original variables, too: among European non-OECD members it is as common to have a high level of human development as it is to have a medium level. Non-European non-OECD members most commonly have a medium level of human development. The conclusion to draw about the three variables is that OECD *membership is more strongly correlated with human development than a country's geographical location.*

That said, remember that these cross-tabulations do not make any statement about the direction of effect: does OECD membership lead to higher level of human development, or does a high level of human development lead to OECD membership?

See also Chapter 6 for chi square tests, which examine whether two variables in a cross-tabulation are correlated or statistically independent.

Sources: UN (2002); OECD (2002).

identify the values that represent Q_U + 1 step and Q_L − 1 step, respectively. The whiskers are then drawn from Q_U and Q_L to the furthest away observations within one step, in either direction. Although one step above Q_U is equidistant to one step below Q_L, this does not mean that the two whiskers will have the same length: this depends on where the observations are located above Q_U and below Q_L. For example, if there are no observations one step above Q_U or below Q_L, respectively, then there will not be an upward or downward, respectively, whisker. Observations that lie further away than one step in either direction from Q_U or Q_L are represented as little dots or stars or some similar symbol.

Box 5.14 Box plots: fatalities in UN peacekeeping operations

The UN has staged 55 peacekeeping operations around the world from 1948 to 2000. UN member states provide military and civilian personnel to these operations, and the UN also hires local civilian personnel. Sometimes UN personnel are among the fatalities in a conflict. As of 1 June 2002, there were 15 UN peacekeeping operations. Fatalities among UN personnel in these operations (again, as of 1 June 2002) ranged from zero (in Prevlaka and East Timor) to 245 (in Lebanon).

East Timor	0	Iraq and Kuwait	16
Prevlaka	0	Bosnia Herzegovina	17
Ethiopia and Eritrea	3	Truce Supervision Organization	38
Georgia	7	Disengagement Observer Force	40
Democratic Republic of the Congo	9	Sierra Leone	82
India and Pakistan	9	Cyprus	170
Western Sahara	10	Lebanon	245
Kosovo	15		

UNMIK, the interim mission to Kosovo which started in June 1999, is the middle value; consequently 15 is the median. The values for Q_I and Q_U are 7 and 40, respectively, making the interquartile range run from 7 to 40. A step then becomes $(1.5 * 33 =) 49.5$. Consequently, the whisker extending from Q_U will stop at the observation closest to but below $(40 + 49.5 =) 89.5$. Outliers (e.g., observations whose values exceed 89.5) will be represented by little dots or some similar symbol. Similarly, the whisker extending from Q_L will stop at $(7 - 49.5 =)$ -42.5, or zero effectively in this example since it is not possible to have less than zero fatalities. For this reason there are of course no outliers below Q_L.

The two small dots in the box plot represent the missions to Cyprus and Lebanon, while the upper whisker's end point represents the mission to Sierra Leone. The median line (Kosovo) is very much closer to Q_L (Georgia) than it is to Q_U (the UN disengagement observer force). The lower whisker's end point, at zero, represents the two missions without fatalities, East Timor and Prevlaka.

More than one box can be shown in the same plot, where it is interesting to compare two or more variables. For example, we might like to compare fatality rates in UN missions in different parts of the world: are African missions perhaps more dangerous for UN personnel than missions elsewhere?

What emerges from this graphical comparison of African and non-African UN missions? The two box plots have similar interquartile ranges, medians, and lower whiskers. They differ primarily in the upper reaches of the plots. Fatalities in African missions are within one step of

→

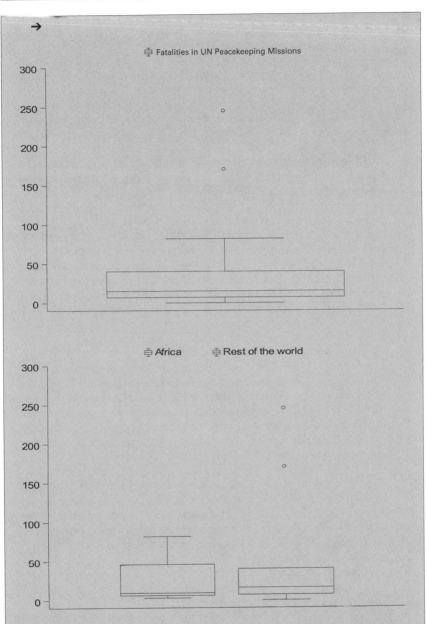

Fatalities in UN Peacekeeping Missions

Africa   Rest of the world

Q_U. Meanwhile, the other box plot is an example of a box with only one whisker: this is because no observations took on a value within one step of that box's Q_U. Instead, there are two outliers beyond the one-step limit.

Source: UN (2002).

Box 5.15 Misleading with descriptive statistics

Descriptive statistics can be a very useful way of analysing interesting hypotheses and presenting data to support or refute them. However, it is also possible to mislead with descriptive statistics. Misleading statistics always undermine research and put conclusions in doubt. Here are some common problems that may occur even if the researcher has no intention to mislead.

1. *Untheorized correlations.* If there is no a priori theoretical reason or plausible a posteriori theoretical reason to expect a relationship between two or more variables, then it is not usually a good idea to carry out any analysis of them. Finding correlations between, let's say, hair colour and voting decision, or between being left handed and being Communist, is not difficult. Less fatuously, there may be correlations between age and church attendance, or income and support for the government. However, if such correlations cannot be theorized a priori or a posteriori then any claim that, for example, age 'explains' church attendance will be rather weak. Untheorized correlations can and do lead to interesting and important new discoveries, but beware of attaching much weight to them until they have been theorized and explored with fresh data.

2. *Poor measurements.* A poor measurement can be invalid (e.g., it measures the wrong thing), unreliable (e.g., it measures something without consistency), or both. Descriptive statistics with poor measurements will be misleading, especially if the researcher does not draw attention to these weaknesses, thereby enabling the reader to assess how they impact on the conclusions. This problem often arises in secondary analysis (e.g., when using data collected by someone else for other purposes). This means the data are not tailor-made for one's own purposes and may therefore not measure exactly what one is interested in analysing. For example, using the opinion poll question 'How well would you say that the government is running the country at the moment? Very well, well, fair, badly, very badly' to examine the government's prospects for re-election is not unreasonable. However, it is quite possible that the question 'How would you vote if there was an election tomorrow?' would give quite a different answer to the question.

3. *Categorisations.* Even if a measurement is valid and reliable, the way its categories are defined can change the apparent meaning of descriptive statistics fundamentally. Variables such as income can be defined to have very many or quite few categories. Each precise income may constitute a category, or they may be collapsed into larger categories. Such decisions are obviously necessary in using the variable, but its categorization can have an effect on the apparent correlation between it and another variable. Choosing one categorization rather than another can make a correlation appear stronger or weaker, or make it disappear.

All that glitters . . .

Descriptive statistics are a resourceful tool in the political scientist's toolkit, either as a preliminary part of subsequent, more sophisticated analysis or as stand-alone research. The economy and precision with which they can enable researchers to analyse and present information nevertheless come at a price. Specifically, while quantitative data of the kind used in descriptive statistics often looks impressive and somehow more 'scientific' than many other kinds of data (especially qualitative ones) that political scientists use, it can never constitute more than a limited aspect of a complex political reality.

The particular criticism that is often made of statistics is that, as a form of information, it fails to capture the richness and complexity of the political world (see Box 5.15). Sceptics argue, with some justification, that the validity of quantitative measurements (that is, the extent to which such measurements manage to capture whatever it is that they are intended to measure) is questionable. It is notable that many sceptics are in fact themselves heavy users of statistical measurements of political processes. The producers of such measurements, meanwhile, are very often official government or political bodies, whose organizational capacity to produce statistics is limited to their organizational responsibility and power. Not even producers of statistics deny that their numbers have limits: 'It is extremely difficult, if not impossible, to make a really radical criticism of society using available statistical sources, which imprison us in the concepts and concerns which dominate official and political and economic life' (Thomas, 1996, pp.125–6). In other words, significant parallels can be drawn between, on the one hand, criticisms of descriptive statistics (and statistics generally) in political science and, on the other hand, concerns in the discipline about behaviouralism more generally, as set out in the introductory chapter.

Conclusion

Descriptive statistics make it possible to summarize large amounts of data for the purposes of data analysis and presentation. This is often a useful way to address questions that are central to political science, sometimes as stand-alone analysis, and sometimes as part of more sophisticated statistical analysis. This chapter has introduced some of the main terminology and concepts in descriptive statistics, and pointed to some of the most common forms of graphic presentation (including their strong and weak points). In addition, there have been some simple tips for enhancing data presentation through careful labelling and categorization. Using descriptive statistics effectively depends largely on being able to present the data effectively.

New researchers often take for granted that the data have a story to tell, but soon realize that it is more complicated than that: using any kind of descriptive statistics means that the researcher makes the data tell a particular story, perhaps while suppressing other possible stories. This is unavoidable, and while it sounds possibly inappropriate there is not necessarily anything wrong with telling one story at the expense of another. However, it behoves researchers to make informed decisions about how to analyse and present their data, and this chapter provides a starting point for that.

Chapter 6

Making Inferences

To make an inference is to ask, 'Are my research results applicable more widely than the specific cases I have used to obtain the results; and if so, how?' For instance, if a research project about proportional representation (PR) electoral systems covers the Netherlands, South Africa, Argentina and Israel, inference-making happens when the researchers ask themselves 'To what extent are these research results about PR in the Netherlands, South Africa, Argentina and Israel also true about other PR countries?' Using more technical terminology, political scientists aim to use a *sample* (e.g., the specific cases included in a research project) to gain knowledge about a particular *population* (in this example, all countries that use a PR electoral system). As Alan Bryman puts it, 'given that it is rarely feasible to send questionnaires or to interview whole populations (such as all members of a town, or the whole population of a country, or all members of an organization), we have to sample' (Bryman, 2001, p.75). However, at some point we will want to generalize from the sample to the population. This is where inference comes into play.

Making inferences is very difficult and very important in both qualitative and quantitative political science, but it is fair to say that it is done more systematically and explicitly in quantitative research. The specialized terminology that goes along with inference-making places it squarely in the quantitative research tradition, and this may be a reason why non-quantitative researchers might feel excused from inference-making. However, inference-making goes on as much in qualitative research as in quantitative: the difference is merely that it is not commonly explicitly done in the qualitative research tradition. Moreover, like all other aspects of research, inference-making must be an explicit act in order to be reasoned and convincing.

The chapter's first section explains why inference matters in political research, and this is followed by a section that distinguishes between descriptive and causal inference. Descriptive inference is the most common form of inference in political science; it is about systematic description of selected cases, and on the basis of that description an inference may then take place in terms of what other cases might look like, or be like. Causal inference is mostly beyond reach for political scientists, who are rarely in a position to identify any causal relationships. Inferring causal relationships is therefore also rare. The chapter then turns to inference in quantitative and qualitative political science. The principle that underpins inference is the same for these two types of research, but the application of that principle differs greatly between them. In quantitative research a whole range of statistical tools are available. The Central Limit Theorem and the known properties of the so-called normal (or Gaussian) distribution enable researchers to attach probability statements to the question 'What is the probability that what the sample shows is also true of the population?' The sample mean is our best guess of the true but unknown population mean. If the sample is perfectly representative of the population, then the sample mean and the population mean will be the same. If there is sampling error, then the sample mean will deviate from the population mean. Since our real interest is in the population, not in the sample, it becomes crucial to be able to answer the question: 'How far away is the sample mean from the population mean?' The chi square test and the t-test can provide answers to this question, and this section of the chapter explains how to use these tests. Tools like these, flawed though they may be, are not available in qualitative research. Qualitative inference is therefore much less developed, although it is based on the same principle as quantitative inference: the principle of linking what we observe in a usually small sample to the usually much greater population that the sample was drawn from.

Why inference matters

Although there is sometimes a conception – or more accurately, a misconception – that figures somehow 'speak for themselves', theories of politics are essential in enabling researchers to interpret data. Theories of politics enable researchers to arrange abstract concepts in some relationship to one another, and then to examine some data to see whether the data seems to lend support to the theory. Usually the data do not include all possible cases, but just a sample. For instance, an opinion poll does not ask all the people in the country for their opinion, but only a small proportion of them. Whether or not the data seem to support the theory, the next step is usually to consider whether the result applies more widely than to the data: if a particular conclusion could be drawn about the thousand or so people in an opinion poll, is it possible to draw the same conclusion about the rest of the population? Differently phrased, is it possible to make an inference from the sample to the population?

Inference-making is often difficult and always uncertain, but avoiding it is normally not an easy option either because non-inferential research is the academic equivalent of navel-gazing. It is only relevant to itself, and is rarely of any importance to anyone else; in the opinion poll illustration above, it would mean that we only learn about 1,000 people, not about public opinion in any broader sense. Therefore, non-inferential research makes no contribution to theory-building or to refining hypotheses about political science and not much even to knowledge itself. Since it is never possible to collect and analyse all pieces of information about any political phenomenon, virtually all general knowledge in political science has emerged through inference-making. We know what we (think we) know about the political world because we have studied a few cases, and from these cases we hopefully extrapolate general knowledge about other, similar cases, and try to determine under what conditions our research conclusions apply to them, too. In this manner inference-making serves to enhance the potential magnitude of the contribution a piece of research can make to theory-building and refining hypotheses. Most things that political scientists study are simultaneously unique cases and parts of general patterns, which means that case studies, even ones that cover only one or two cases, always need to address the questions: to what extent are these conclusions valid beyond the cases from which they were drawn? And to what extent are the conclusions due to the unique features of these cases?

If theory-building and/or hypothesis development are one's purpose, then it often makes sense to deliberately select cases that seem to fit well into a general pattern, and then extend the conclusions from the case to the general pattern. In more technical language, the case as a sample must be representative of the population from which it was drawn (these terms are explained more fully below). Sometimes selecting a case that does not seem to fit well into a general pattern can also contribute to theory-building, by showing precisely how and why certain cases deviate from the norm in some significant way. For instance, Chapter 3 used the rise of far-right parties such as the Belgian Vlaams Blok and the Austrian Freedom Party to illustrate some important aspects of case selection in comparative research, and this example is relevant here, too.

Studying either the Vlaams Blok and/or the Freedom Party in order to learn about a general pattern of far-right parties would be a natural and appropriate choice. In inference-making, cases that are representative of a general pattern are the most useful ones to study. This does not negate the point made in Chapter 1, that unusual or unique cases are sometimes the most interesting to research. Studying a far-right party that has not had an electoral break-through might reveal what it is that makes that party less electorally successful (Chapter 3 introduces some comparative research designs that are useful for research with this type of purpose). Such a case is nevertheless not very useful as basis for inferences, due to it being unrepresentative of the general pattern of successful far-right parties.

Essential terminology

Inference-making has its own terminology. It is derived from statistics and therefore may not only be unfamiliar but also off-putting to qualitative political scientists. However, the terminology is not worse or more difficult to grasp than any other specialist terminology, and having a clear grasp of it helps making it an explicit act.

The data used in a research project is the *sample*. A sample consists of a number of *cases* or *observations* (these two terms are synonymous). In political science cases are often countries, institutions, survey respondents, organizations, interviewees or parties. Sometimes a study deals with just a single case, such as a single Parliament, or a single election. Sometimes there are thousands of cases within a single study, such as in a public opinion survey.

A sample is drawn from a *population*: the total universe of possible cases. The relationship between a sample and the population from which it was drawn is absolutely crucial in inference-making. Inference-making is only possible if the sample is *representative* of the population. Representative how? This depends on the research question. Say the purpose of a research project is to identify whether US citizens of different ethnic backgrounds have different opinions about how well the President is running the country. In terms of inference-making, then, the US population is the population (e.g., the total universe of cases), and the sample must be representative with respect to ethnic groups in the USA: each ethnic group should constitute roughly the same proportion of the sample as they do in the population. However, it does not matter at all if the sample is representative of the population in terms of people's eye colour, height or favourite food. What matters is that the sample is representative of the population in all *research-relevant* aspects. Occasionally, it can make sense to over-sample certain groups deliberately; Chapter 4 discusses this in terms of booster samples.

The more representative the sample is of its population, the greater the certainty of any inference made about the population. Vice versa, the less representative the sample is of its population, the more uncertain the inference. Estimating the *uncertainty* of inferences is a key part of inference-making. This means attaching to the inference some measure of how likely it is that the sample really does teach us something about the population. There are several 'tools' that a researcher can use to manage the sampling process, such as sampling frames and sampling units. Chapter 4 explains what these are and their application.

The divergence or discrepancies between a population and a sample drawn from it is known as *sampling error*. There is always sampling error, and this is the source of uncertainty that is always part and parcel of inference-making. However, not all kinds of sampling error are problematic: in quantitative analysis there is an important distinction between random and non-random sampling error. Random errors (if they truly are random) in the sample will over-estimate and under-estimate the population to the same extent, so on average random errors cancel each other out. This leaves non-random error to worry about, and the label 'non-random' indicates the presence of some systematically distorting influence on the sample that reduces its representativeness. For example, those who are more interested in politics are more likely to answer a survey about politics. Hence, all surveys overestimate things like political interest, voter turnout etc. Because this type of error is systematic, it does not cancel itself out. The implication is that inferences to the population are more uncertain.

Descriptive and causal inference

King, Keohane and Verba (who view inference as 'the ultimate goal of all good social science': 1994, p.34) distinguish between two broad kinds of inference: descriptive and causal. Both kinds of inference involve making a 'leap' from a sample to its population. This leap essentially boils down to distinguishing two kinds of features of the sample: first, what aspects of it are representative of the population; and second, what features of it are not representative of the population?

Descriptive inferences are not mere descriptions: they are an attempt to use available data to create a systematic description about political phenomena about which there are no available facts (see Box 6.1). An accurate, factual description is obviously one *sine qua non* of descriptive inference, but the second integral of descriptive inferences is to make a leap from the systematic description to some account of cases not studied (e.g., the population).

Box 6.1   Descriptive inference: the failed coup of August 1991 in the USSR

A handful of Communist hard-liners calling themselves the State Emergency Committee sought to halt and reverse Mikhail Gorbachev's reforms – *glasnost* and *perestroika* – by staging a coup against him in August 1991. The coup failed, and Gorbachev proceeded with his reform projects, which reached a kind of culmination on 25 December 1991, when he, as President of the USSR, dissolved the Union and by the same token resigned as its President.

Students of transitions to democracy around the world (the former USSR bloc, Africa, Latin America, Asia) might study the August 1991 coup in great detail, to understand what makes anti-reform coups fail. (Ideally, as Chapter 3 explains, such a research design should also include a case of a successful coup.)

Differently phrased, this means drawing an inference from the particular case of the August 1991 coup to coups in general. To do this, all the details of the August 1991 coup must be sorted into two categories:

(a)   details unique to the August 1991 coup (these details are the non-random error); and
(b)   details that are generic to failed coups (these details are the aspects of the sample that are representative of the population).

Inference-making depends on being able to distinguish between these two types of details. Omitting to do so means that there is no attempt to 'leap' from the sample to the population. Failing to do so correctly means that the inference is false.

Causal inferences differ from descriptive ones in one very significant way: they take a 'leap' not only in terms of description, but in terms of some specific causal process. Causality is a fraught topic in political science, but the notion of causality developed by the thinker David Hume (1711–76) has survived relatively unscathed (see Box 6.2). This notion holds that causality occurs if the presence (or absence) of a given factor generates a particular outcome with law-like regularity.

Box 6.2 Causality and political science: the philosophy of David Hume

In *A Treatise of Human Nature*, David Hume (1711–76) ambitiously attempted to set out a complete system of the sciences. He saw all sciences as relating to human nature. Most importantly for the ideas of causality and causal inferences, he argued for a science of man: that is, explaining human behaviour and action, 'from the simplest and fewest causes'. He accepted that if it is possible to observe a 'constant conjunction' between two events or variables then it may be concluded that there is a process of causality at play, a process whereby one event causes another, subsequent event.

Since the political world is so complex and political scientists are rarely in a position to run experiments (see Chapter 3 for more details about the experimental method), political science tends strongly to be about probabilities rather than law-like regularities. Therefore, causal claims are rare in the discipline as political scientists are more comfortable with correlations than with causality. A correlation is weaker than causal mechanisms in two ways. First, a correlation does not assume any law-like regularity. In this respect correlations are probabilities. A strong, positive correlation between two variables means that a change on one variable tends to 'go with' a change in the same direction on the other variable. A weak correlation means that there is no pattern of change between the two variables. A strong, negative correlation means that a change on one variable tends to 'go with' a change in the opposite direction on the other variable. Second, a correlation between two variables leaves unspecified the direction of the effect. In contrast, in a causal relationship it is clear the causal direction is clear and constant. Keeping this in mind, causal inferences are naturally difficult to make, and always uncertain since it can rarely be known whether the variable we think is causing a given political outcome is actually the cause of that outcome.

Since causality is so difficult to establish in political science, inference-making usually pertains to descriptive rather than causal inferences. A causal process will not simply reveal itself even when a researcher has data on all possible cases (the only situation that makes a nonsense of inferring from a sample to a population).

Box 6.3   Causality and correlation: public opinion in Central and Eastern Europe

In a 2001 opinion poll people in 13 Central and Eastern European countries applying to join the European Union were asked these two questions:

'Do you think that becoming a member of the European Union would bring (COUNTRY) . . .'
  Much more disadvantages/More disadvantages;
  As many advantages as disadvantages;
  More advantages/Many more advantages;
  Don't know/No answer.

'Generally speaking, do you think that (COUNTRY'S) membership of the European Union would be . . .'
  A good thing;
  Neither good nor bad;
  A bad thing.

This cross-tabulation shows that people who thought that EU membership would bring advantages also tended to think that EU membership would be a good thing. Equally, people who felt EU membership would be a bad thing by and large tended to hold the view that EU membership would bring disadvantages to their country (and people who were undecided about one question were also in the main undecided about the other question).

	A Good Thing (%)	Neither Good Nor Bad (%)	A Bad Thing (%)
More/Many more advantages	81	20	6
As many advantages as disadvantages	13	46	14
Much more/More disadvantages	2	20	76
Don't know/No answer	4	14	4
Total	100	100	100

→

Therefore, inferences in research about politics are usually about what unknown cases might look like or be like. The next section shows that even in quantitative political science, where inference-making is a far more established practice than it is in qualitative research, all that the statistics can normally achieve is to suggest the strength of some theorized relationship or the absence of such a relationship but statistics-based inference-making does not in itself bring to light a causal process (see Box 6.3).

→

However, does this cross-tabulation show a causal relationship, or a correlation? Two criteria help making the distinction: directionality and regularity.

Directionality: Causal relationships have clear cause(s) and effect(s)

Question: *In the cross-tabulation, is the direction of effect clear?*

Answer: *No. There is no way of telling if people's views on membership being 'a good/bad/neither-nor' thing informs their opinion on advantages and disadvantages, or the other way round.*

Regularity: The cause(s) have the same effect(s) at all times, all else being equal.

Question: *In the cross-tabulation, do all people with the same attitude on one variable have the same attitude as each other on the other variable?*

Answer: *No. There are cases in all cells of the cross-tabulation. If the relationship was causal, only one cell in each column ('A good thing-Many more/More advantages'; 'Neither nor-As many advantages as disadvantages', and 'A bad thing-More/Many more disadvantages') would have observations. All other cells would be '0'.*

The cross-tabulation does not display a causal relationship, but it does display a positive correlation: the more positive someone's view of the EU, the more advantages that person is likely to perceive membership to bring. (A negative correlation would have meant that the more positive someone's view of the EU, the more likely the person would be to perceive EU membership as disadvantageous. No correlation would mean no particular pattern between the two opinions.)

Source: http://europa.eu.int, October 2002.

Inferences in quantitative political science

There are statistical 'tools' for inference-making in quantitative political science. The Central Limit Theorem and the properties of the normal distribution make it possible to estimate how likely it is (e.g., the probability) that a particular event takes place. In inference-making the key event of interest is whether some interesting finding in a sample is also true of the population that the sample was drawn from. This section explains the Central Limit Theorem and the normal distribution, which form the basis for tests such as the chi square test and the t-test. These, and other probability tests, provide answers to key questions such as 'Does the correlation observed in this sample exist in the population, too?' and 'How well does the sample mean measure the population mean?'

However, none of this will work unless samples are random, because it is the randomness of the sample that enables the link between the sample and its population. The definition of 'random' is that every case in the population has an equal and independent chance of becoming part of the sample. To take a simple example, this would mean that if 50 people wrote their names on pieces of paper and put them in a hat from which five names were to be drawn, then each name would have the same chance of being drawn in all five draws. This means that each piece of paper pulled out would have to be put back in the hat, so that it would have an equal and independent chance of being drawn again. The important point about random sampling is that it allows the sampling error to be estimated statistically with respect to both known and unknown sources of influence: this means that it is possible to establish the uncertainty of inferences.

The normal distribution is actually a whole range of distributions, a 'family' of normal distributions. They share some key features that make them, by definition, normal distributions. Normal distributions are symmetric, smooth, and bell-shaped. It follows from this that they are unimodal and have no skewness. What distinguishes different normal distributions is their means and standard deviations. That is, although two normal distributions are very alike in that they are unimodal and unskewed, they may have different degrees of kurtosis (see Chapter 5 for an explanation of modality, skewness and kurtosis).

As the variables that political scientists use are typically samples rather than populations, these variables can be seen as attempts to capture some essential aspects of an unknown population. What is more, each observation on a variable can be seen as a measure of the population, and consequently the sample mean (e.g., the variable mean) represents an estimate of the true population mean. However, this begs the question of how accurately the sample mean estimates the population mean? The particular significance of the normal distribution is that due to its symmetric, smooth and bell-shaped nature it is possible to attach a probability to the sample mean being within a certain distance of the true but

Box 6.4   Calculating the sample mean

A sample mean is obtained by adding up the value of each case in the sample, and dividing the sum by the number of cases in the sample. This sounds far more complicated than it is, not least because statistics computing software packages will do it at the touch of a button. For small samples it is also very simple to calculate the mean manually. The formula is:

$$\bar{x} = \frac{x_1 + x_2 + x_3 + \ldots x_n}{n}$$

where x_1, x_2 (etc.) are all the cases in a sample, and n is the number of cases in the sample.

unknown population mean (see Box 6.4). This distance is expressed in standard deviations, a concept that was discussed in Chapter 5, and again below (briefly, the standard deviation measures how far, on average, observations in a sample are from the sample mean: see also Box 6.5).

For example, in a normally distributed sample, we can say with 90 per cent certainty that the true population mean will be within 1.645 standard deviations above or below the sample mean (see Box 6.6). If we want to be even more certain than 90 per cent, we can say with 95 per cent certainty that the true population mean will be within 1.96 standard deviations above or below the sample mean. Similarly, the true population mean will be within 2.576 standard deviations above or below the sample mean with 99 per cent certainty. The actual distance that, say, 1.96 standard deviations represents depends of course on the size of a sample's standard deviation: if it is small, cases are tightly clustered around the sample mean and 1.96 or even 2.576 standard deviations may not be very much. However, if the standard deviation is large, then 1.96 standard deviations may cover a very large range. The value of a small standard deviation compared to a large one, then, is that it allows for a more precise estimate of the true population mean, at the same level of certainty. These rules of thumb are known as the 90, 95 and 99 per cent confidence intervals. As an illustration, to say that we have 95 per cent confidence in an inference really means that if 100 samples were drawn from the population, in 95 of those samples the population mean would be located somewhere within 1.96 standard deviations on either side of the sample mean. The phrase '90 per cent confidence' means that in 90

Box 6.5   Calculating the sample standard deviation

A sample's standard deviation is obtained by calculating mean squared residuals, and then taking the square root of that mean. This sounds far more complicated than it is, not least because statistics computing software packages will do it at the touch of a button. For small samples it is also very simple to calculate the standard deviation manually. The formula is:

$$\sigma = \sqrt{\frac{\Sigma(x_i - \bar{x})^2}{n - 1}}$$

where Σ is 'the sum of', x_i is the value of a case $_i$, $\bar{x}$ is the sample mean and n is the sample size.

Follow these five easy steps:

1. Calculate the sample mean.
    See equation in Box 6.4

2. Obtain the residual for each case.
    Subtract the sample mean from the value of each case; what you have left are the residuals

3. Square all residuals.
    Multiply each residual by its own value

4. Add the squared residuals and divide the sum by n-1.
    Add up the value of all squared residuals, and divide the sum by the number cases in the sample MINUS 1 (there are statistical reasons to use n-1 rather than n)

5. Take the square root of the figure obtained.
    This is because the figure obtained in step 4 is not in the same units as the sample, due to the fact that the residuals were squared in step 3. Taking the square root here in step 5 simply transforms the standard deviation into the same unit as the sample. If this is not done then it becomes very complicated to interpret the standard deviation – is it large, small . . .?

---

out of 100 samples from the same population the population mean will be located within 1.645 standard deviations on either side of the sample mean, whereas 99 per cent confidence means that in 99 out of 100 samples from the same population the population mean will be located within 2.576 standard deviations either side of the sample mean (Upton and Cook, 2002, pp.76–8). Note that the higher the confidence, the lower the precision.

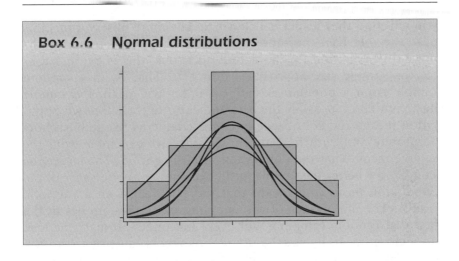

Box 6.6   Normal distributions

This is clearly extremely useful when a distribution is normal, but what about variables that do not have a normal distribution, and populations whose distributions are unknown? Needless to say, most variables that political scientists use are not normally distributed, and population distributions are hardly ever known; if the nature of the population was known, there would be no reason to draw a sample. However, the Central Limit Theorem holds that if repeated random samples are drawn from a population then the means of those samples will always produce a normal distribution (Daly *et al.*, 1995, pp.205–10). More formally, 'The sample mean $\bar{x}$, drawn from a population with mean μ and variance σ^2, has a sampling distribution which approaches a Normal distribution with mean μ and variance σ^2/n, as the sample size approaches infinity' (Barrow, 1996, p.122; note that variance is simply the standard deviation squared).

Since time and other resources usually only allow a researcher to draw one sample, with one sample mean, we typically do not see how this Theorem works. However, a simple demonstration in SPSS or any other statistics software is easy to set up: take any variable with, say, at least 1,000 observations. For the purpose of the demonstration, the variable is treated as if it were a population, and the computer will draw random samples from it (the more samples the better, but 100 should be enough, each consisting of 5 or 10 per cent of the 'population'). Each sample has its own mean, and these means form a normal distribution irrespective of whether the 'population' itself is normally distributed. If you enter each sample mean as an observation on a new variable you will find that its curve is normal. The more observations this new variable has, the more closely its shape will resemble the normal distribution (in the definition above, this is expressed as 'as the sample size approaches infinity'). That is, in a random sample from a population with an unknown mean, the sample mean is a good (possibly the best) indicator of the unknown population mean, and confidence intervals enable us to establish how accurately and with how much certainty we can infer from the sample mean what the population mean might be. The larger the sample, the better the sample mean becomes as an indicator of the population mean (this means that the Theorem is an asymptotic result). The importance of the sampling being random lies in the fact that random sampling will over- and under-estimate the true population mean by equal amounts. As a consequence of this the distribution of the new variable of sample means will take on the symmetric shape of a normal curve, e.g., there will be as many inaccurate estimates above the true population mean as below it. It is surprisingly unimportant what proportion of the population is included in a sample. It is the size of the sample itself that matters in determining the accuracy of how well it measures the population, not the proportion of the population included in the sample. See Box 6.7 and 6.8 for examples.

In normal distributions and under the Central Limit Theorem, it is possible to determine with a specified degree of certainty how close to the sample mean the true population mean is located. What is more, using confidence intervals, we can assess whether two variables that have different means measure two population means that are in fact different from each other. If a survey showed that 50 per cent of people in Italy and 45 per cent in France supported the Euro, we could not be sure whether Italians really were more positive about the single currency than the French, as both results are subject to sampling error. That is, if the 95 per cent confidence interval for each distribution overlaps substantially, there is a possibility that the two true population means (Italian attitudes toward the Euro; French attitudes toward the Euro) might be exactly the same as each other. We can test the probability of these two means really being different from each other with a t-test (Box 6.9). Alternatively, it is possible to use the chi square test to test the association between two variables (Box 6.10). Both tests are based in the idea of a null hypothesis of no association between two variables, and an alternative hypothesis that involves some kind of association between two variables. Moreover, the result of both tests is expressed in terms of the odds, or the probability, that the association between two variables is true not only of the sample, but also of the population from which the sample was drawn. The question is what odds are acceptable. The 90, 95 and 99 per cent confidence interval are frequently used. To use, say, the 95 per cent level means that if the *p*-value (probability value) is 0.05 of below, we can reject the null hypothesis of no association and accept the alternative hypothesis, that there is some association between the two variables. Equally, at the 99 per cent level a *p*-value of 0.01 is necessary in order to reject the null hypothesis, and at the 90 per cent level a *p*-value of 0.1 is sufficient.

Inferences in qualitative political science

The possibility and quality of inferences is very closely connected to the sampling process, which is often (mistakenly) thought to be an issue in quantitative research only. Because the sampling process has such a crucial impact on inference-making, it is necessary to think about inferences at the very start of a research project, although inference-making is typically the very last part of the research.

Qualitative sampling processes are often deliberately not random; in fact, random sampling is often inappropriate in qualitative research. Instead, it is often appropriate to select cases with known relevance to the research question. This can make qualitative sampling seem like a non-issue: instead, the researcher simply selects the cases (e.g., interviewees, official documents, newspapers, pictures, etc.) that it makes sense to select.

However, sampling is an issue in qualitative research except for researchers who are happy to be unable to make any comment beyond their case(s). For example, in public policy research relevant interviewees might include the policy-makers (politicians and civil servants) and the people directly affected by the policy (e.g., in social welfare policy research the people who receive benefits). Interviewing a random sample of people on street corners or by telephone (some of whom may be policy-makers and benefit recipients) does not generate a very useful sample in this type of situation. Yet, unless every single social welfare policy-maker and every single benefit recipient are interviewed (e.g., a census), there *is* a process of sampling. In other words, having a non-random selection criterion does not mean that there is no sampling. In the welfare policy example, the selection of interviewees may, for instance, introduce non-random error, such that the conclusions eventually drawn would not reflect the views of the relevant population.

Box 6.7   The Central Limit Theorem I: British Army bases in Northern Ireland

This example demonstrates the Central Limit Theorem by showing that over repeated random samples from a population, the means of the samples will form a distribution that approximates a normal distribution, even if the population's distribution itself is not a normal distribution. As a consequence of this, the Central Limit Theorem applies even samples whose distributions are not normal, in large-size samples.

In this example, the population is the respondents to the *Northern Ireland Life & Times* survey 2001. Some 1,800 people responded to this survey. One of the questions they answered was:

'Shutting down British army bases is extremely important for peace in Northern Ireland':

Agree strongly	161
Agree	492
Neither agree nor disagree	317
Disagree	433
Disagree strongly	272
Total (N)	1,675
Mean	3.0973
Standard deviation	1.2561

A histogram of the distribution shows that it is not smooth, bell-shaped or symmetric:

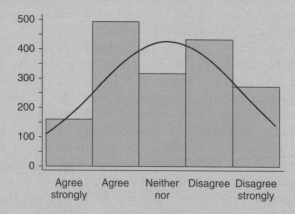

Drawing 20 random samples from this population (each sample consisting of approximately 5 per cent of the population size) generates 20 sample means:

→

→

3.1884	2.9615	3.0161	3.0345
3.3041	3.03	3.0872	2.9894
3.1847	3.0694	3.2241	2.952
2.7904	2.8767	3.0811	3.1069
3.1889	3.122	3.1824	3.2153

The 20 sample means can be conceived of as a sample of 20 observations, with a mean of 3.0802 and a standard deviation of 0.1276. The distribution of the 20 observations in this sample is roughly normal:

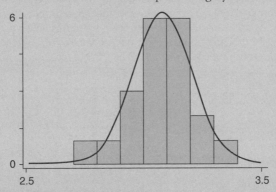

Consequently, random samples drawn from the population can be analysed on the basis of the Central Limit Theorem, because over repeated samples the sample means form a normal distribution. In this example, the population mean is known (3.0973), so it is possible to check whether the data set consisting of 20 sample means does indeed tell us anything useful about the population. Let's look at three levels of confidence.

1. *90 per cent confidence*: this level holds if the true population mean (3.0973) is within 1.645 standard deviations of the sample mean (3.0802). In real figures, this means that with 90 per cent confidence the population mean is within the 2.8702–3.2902 range:

   3.0802 ± (1.645 * 0.1276) =
   3.0802 ± 0.21 = 2.8702 to 3.2902

2. *95 per cent confidence*: this level holds if the true population mean (3.0973) is within 1.96 standard deviations of the sample mean (3.0802). In real figures, this means within the 2.8301–3.3303 range:

   3.0802 ± (1.96 * 0.1276) =
   3.0802 ± 0.2501 = 2.8301 to 3.3303

3. *99 per cent confidence*: this level holds if the true population mean (3.0973) is within 2.576 standard deviations of the sample mean (3.0802). In real figures, this means within the 2.7515–3.4089 range:

   3.0802 ± (2.576 * 0.1276) =
   3.0802 ± 0.3287 = 2.7515 to 3.4089

Note that as the level of confidence increases, the wider the range of precision becomes. This illustrates the trade-off between precision and confidence.

Source: Northern Ireland Social and Political Archive (2002).

Box 6.8   The Central Limit Theorem II: Political Activists

Suppose we have a population (N) of six activists who partake in demonstrations. They have been on this many demonstrations, respectively: 2, 4, 4, 6, 8, and 12. On average, then, they have been on six demonstrations each. If a sample of $n = 2$ is drawn from the population of $N = 6$ people (the population size being designated by N, the sample size by n), then our sampling fraction is one-third (n/N or $2/6$): that is, each observation has a one in three chance of being randomly selected. In all, 15 different random samples of $n = 2$ can be drawn from this small population. If each activist is allocated a letter, so that A has been on 2 demonstrations, B on 4, C on 4, D on 6, E on 8, and F on 12, then we can confirm this as follows:

Sample no:	1	2	3	4	5	6	7	8	9	10	11	12	13	14	15
Observation 1:	A	A	A	A	A	B	B	B	B	C	C	C	D	D	E
Observation 2:	B	C	D	E	F	C	D	E	F	D	E	F	E	F	F
Sample values:	2	2	2	2	2	4	4	4	4	4	4	4	6	6	8
	4	4	6	8	12	4	6	8	12	6	8	12	8	12	12
Average demos:	3	3	4	5	7	4	5	6	8	5	6	8	7	9	10

Normally we draw only one random sample from a population, and if we were to draw only one of the 15 possible random samples from the population of six activists each of the 15 samples would have an equal chance of being drawn (this is the definition of randomness). Consequently, in the long run (that is, by repeated sampling), each of these samples will be

Chapter 9 shows that sampling in qualitative research often depends on access: sampling when it comes to interviews with policy-makers is, for example, often determined by those to whom the researchers manage to secure access. It is possible that potential interviewees are 'not available for an interview' for particular reasons; if so, this introduces systematic error into the sample of interviewees. Similarly, archival research (Chapter 7) depends not only on what documents have survived over time, but also on what documents the government decides to release. Withheld documents are almost certainly not released for particular reasons, which is also a source of non-random sampling error. Since non-random errors do not cancel themselves out, the sample becomes unrepresentative of its population.

It is possible to construct qualitative research designs that allow attempts at inference. For example, Chapter 3 on comparative

→

selected equally often. This being so, it is possible to construct a distrib
ution showing the relative frequency with which, in the long run, different sample averages will occur. This is known as the sampling
distribution of the mean:

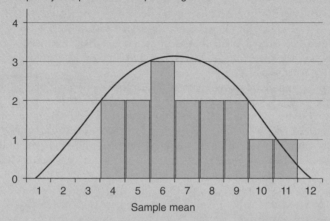

Frequency of a particular sample being drawn

Sample mean

If sample size is increased, then the sampling distribution of the mean
will be reduced. Observations will cluster around the true population
mean in the shape of a normal curve. That is, in the activist example, the
more repeated random samples we draw from our population of six
activists, the more accurately the distribution of means will estimate the
population mean of having taken part in six demonstrations.

research sets out some research designs that can be used to make
inferences from qualitative research: the most similar and most
different research designs are specifically aimed at facilitating inference-making. Research design is not the real problem with inferences
in qualitative political science; the problem is to determine the uncertainty of those inferences. Inferences are always more or less uncertain, but within qualitative political science estimating the
uncertainty of inferences has not been a central issue, quite probably
because of a combination of two factors: first, many qualitative
researchers view their task as describing unique cases without
attempting to make inferences and consequently they perceive no
need to assess uncertainty. Of course, reluctance to make inferences
may simply signal a healthy realization that inferences made would
be so uncertain that they would be misleading. Second, qualitative
sampling processes are typically non-random, and are not effective

Box 6.9   T-tests

T-tests are a class of hypothesis tests that examine whether the means of two distributions (μ_1, μ_2) are the same or different from each other. The hypothesis that there is no difference between the two means is the null hypothesis ($H_{0:}$ $\mu1 = \mu2$). The alternative hypothesis holds that there is some difference between the two means. H_A often does not specify anything more than that the two means are different (H_A: $\mu_1 \neq \mu_2$): that is, H_A is two-sided. In these instances a two-tailed t-test is necessary. Sometimes H_A is one-sided: that is, it specifies which mean is larger or smaller than the other mean (H_A: $\mu_1 > \mu_2$; H_A: $\mu_1 < \mu$). In these instances one-tailed t-tests suffice.

The outcome of a t-test is to reject one of the hypotheses, and to accept the other one. Having determined the two variables' distribution (e.g., normal, Poisson, Bernoulli, etc.) it is possible to decide which hypothesis to accept and which to reject on the basis of the test statistic, t. The likelihood of obtaining a t-value that is as extreme or more extreme than the one that has been obtained is expressed in a p-value (probability value). If we apply 95 per cent confidence intervals, then we look for the p-value to be below 0.05 to reject H_0; if we apply 99 per cent confidence intervals, then we look for the p-value to be below 0.01 to reject H_0.

Two types of mistake are possible in hypothesis-testing: rejecting H_0 when it should be accepted (Type I error), and accepting H_0 when it should be rejected (Type II error). At the 95 per cent level of confidence, an error of either type will occur 5 per cent of the time, or 1 time in 20; at the 99 per cent level of confidence an error will happen 1 per cent of the time, or 1 time in 100, etc.

'tools' for assessing uncertainty under such circumstances. It may often be that awareness of the inadequacies and strengths of a sample is the only way that qualitative research can assess uncertainty. It may allow us to 'compensate' intelligently in the interpretation, for example knowing that the uninterested are likely to refuse an interview we can infer that survey estimates of interest are overestimates, maxima etc.

Conclusion

Inference-making should be a central aim of all forms of political science research because it increases the value and potential audience of a research contribution. Although in some ways inferences and inference-making are very different in qualitative and quantitative political science, in other ways inferences and inference-making unite

Box 6.10   Chi square test (Pearson goodness-of-fit test)

Chi square is denoted x^2. A chi square test is a goodness-of-fit test that can be used to examine if two variables in a cross-tabulation are independent of each other (often called the null hypothesis, H_0), or whether there is a correlation between them (the alternative hypothesis, H_A). The variables can be categorical or ordinal (see Chapter 5 for definitions of level of measurement, as well as for an explanation of how to read cross-tabulations). A chi square test tests H_0, a null hypothesis of no correlation between the two variables, and H_A, an alternative hypothesis of correlation between the two variables. The null hypothesis is either rejected or accepted on the basis of how different the cross-tabulation's frequencies (e.g., the observed frequencies in the test) are from the frequencies that would be expected if there were no correlation between the two variables. The comparison of observed and expected frequencies yields a chi square value with an associated *p*-value. At a chosen level of confidence (usually 95 or 99 per cent), H_0 is either accepted or rejected. If it is accepted, then the conclusion is that the two variables are statistically independent; if it is rejected, then the two variables are correlated to each other (subject to not making a Type I or Type II error; see Box 6.9).

If H_0 is rejected, we want to know something about the strength and direction of the correlation. Computing software programmes typically give (or can be programmed to give) a correlation coefficient that ranges from −1 to 1. The closer the coefficient is to either extreme of the −1 to 1 range, the stronger the correlation is. Vice versa, a coefficient of zero or close to zero indicates a non-existent or very weak correlation. Furthermore, a positive coefficient indicates a positive correlation: that is, as the values on one variable increase, so do the values on the other variable. A negative coefficient indicates that the variables move in opposite directions: as the values on one variable increase, the values on the other variable decrease. This is described by a negative correlation coefficient. There is a *p*-value associated with the correlation coefficient, too, indicating at what level of confidence the correlation can be inferred from the sample to the population. Following the usual conventions, the correlation coefficient may be accepted if its *p*-value is, say, below 0.01 or 0.05.

rather than divide these two branches of research. That is, although there are many more established tools for quantitative inference-making (e.g., random sampling, the normal distribution and the Central Limit Theorem) than for the qualitative equivalent, in both cases making inferences is about acknowledging that one's sample is not the main focus of interest, and that 'the researcher should always keep in mind that the results of research are only as good as the quality of the data' (Gujarati, 1995, p.27). In this context, 'quality' refers primarily to randomness and representativeness. What matters is what the sample reveals about the population from which it was drawn, and with what degree of confidence it is possible to say that what is observed in the sample is also true of the population.

Chapter 7

Documentary and Archival Analysis

This chapter provides an introduction to the range of documentary sources available to the political scientist and assesses the merits of different types of documentary material. Special attention is paid to researching archival material at the most internationally important archive repositories, the Public Record Office (recently renamed the National Archives) in the UK and the National Archives in the USA.

The sheer range and diversity of documentary sources can appear bewildering to the inexperienced researcher. From newspapers to research reports, government records to personal diaries, documentary material constitutes a vast daunting resource which can leave the political researcher feeling very much the second rate historian. The first step to becoming a competent user of documentary material is to employ a system of classification to decide which sources are of most use for specific research purposes. The most common distinction made by historians is that between 'primary', 'secondary' and 'tertiary' sources (Lichtman and French, 1978, p.18). This often involves the use of a simple timescale categorization in which 'primary sources' consist only of evidence that was actually part of or produced by the event in question; 'secondary sources' consist of other evidence relating to and produced soon after the event; and 'tertiary sources' of material written afterward to reconstruct the event (Lichtman and French, 1978, p.18). This system of classification can be made more precise by combining the timescale criterion with the 'intended audience' of the document to yield the following categories: 'primary sources' consist of evidence that was part of the event in question and which was intended for internal or restricted circulation only; 'secondary sources' include material circulated at the time or soon after and which was available to the public at the time of the event in question; 'tertiary sources' consist of all later work in the public domain offering a reconstruction. No system of classification can neatly accommodate all types of document, and in many cases certain types of documentary material (diaries and memoirs, for instance) may cross these artificial divides. Nevertheless, this system provides the essential outer framework for a researcher new to documentary analysis. Box 7.1 illustrates how it can be employed to good effect in relation to tracking down material on the Bretton Woods negotiations of 1942–4.

Once equipped with a rudimentary understanding of how documentary sources are classified, the aim of the serious researcher will be to attempt to work with as many primary documents as possible. Sydney and Beatrice Webb, the founders of the London School of Economics, took a particularly purist view that the aim of the investigator must be to consult original sources as distinguished from writings based on such sources (Webb and Webb, 1932, p.98). They offer a distinction between 'documents' and 'literature' in which a 'document' is 'an instrument in language which has, as its origin and for its deliberate and express purpose to become the basis of, or to assist, the activities of an individual, an organisation or a community' (Webb and Webb, 1932, p.100). The essence of a primary document in this view is that it is not written with a view to inform historians or political scientists, instead, primary documents are 'secreted exclusively for the purpose of action' (Webb and Webb, 1932, p.100). For the Webbs, primary documents are 'facts in themselves' not merely the representation of facts, and in this sense are to be distinguished from 'literature' which constitutes all other writings yielding information as to what purport to be 'facts'.

There can, in this purist view, be no substitute for actually handling the primary documents themselves and for the Webbs no summary or abstract of a document is of any use: 'what the social investigator must always insist on is the original document or an exact verbatim copy' (Webb and Webb, 1932, p.107). In fact, if primary documents are inaccessible, the Webbs conclude that the subject (and any research of it) is impracticable. Taken literally this can severely restrict the use of documentary analysis in political science since the most useful primary documents, government public records, fall under various closure regulations, usually of 30 years' duration. In the UK, for instance, the Public Records Act 1967 ensures a 30-year closure period for most public records and some remain closed for 50 years. Similarly in the USA, despite the Freedom of Information Act, the National Archives and Records Administration generally releases records after a 30-year closure period. In the face of such strictures political scientists often tend to

Box 7.1 Primary, secondary and tertiary sources in relation to the Bretton Woods negotiations, 1942–4

Primary sources

British government documents lodged in the Public Record Office, London
Cabinet documents
Treasury documents
Foreign Office documents
Prime Minister's Office documents
Personal collections such as Keynes' papers

US government documents lodged in the National Archives, Washington, DC
Treasury Department documents
State Department documents
National Security Council papers
Personal collections such as White's papers

Bank of England and Federal Reserve Bank documents

Private papers

Unpublished diaries and letters

Secondary sources

Government Command Papers: Economic Surveys; the Bretton Woods Agreement
Hansard: Parliamentary Debates (House of Commons and Lords)
US Government publications and debates in Congress
British and US newspapers, periodicals and reports

Tertiary sources

Books
Academic journal articles
Published diaries, memoirs, biographies and autobiographies
Unpublished MA, MPhil and PhD theses
All material which offers a reconstruction of the Bretton Woods negotiations

minimize the use of primary documents and opt instead for careful use of secondary and tertiary documentary sources buttressed by elite interviewing. However, as this chapter will indicate, there is a wide range of primary documents that is not subject to extended closure rules and that offers much to the student of politics and international relations. Moreover, as John Scott (1990, p.12) indicates, there are a number of problematic features in the purist argument. Whilst the Webbs identify possible sources of inaccuracy and bias in 'literature', they fail to see that similar problems may beset the analysis of primary documents. A more adequate approach to documentary sources must therefore adopt a more flexible view of the value and use of documents than that used by the Webbs. Accordingly, we will begin our review of documentary material by first assessing the diversity and merits of secondary and tertiary sources before looking in depth at private papers and public records.

Use and abuse of secondary and tertiary documentary sources in political science

All forms of bureaucracy, whether public or private, national or global, produce documentation. Much of this documentation will be of interest to the political science community. It is therefore somewhat surprising that most social science research methods texts fail to give documentary materials more than a passing reference (J. Scott, 1990, p.ix). One reason for this neglect is that traditionally this area has been seen as the prerogative of the academic historian, and the majority of researchers in political science wish to distinguish themselves from contemporary historians. On the relationship between the disciplines of history and politics there are three basic positions. Whilst some pluralists, structuralists and functionalists would maintain that there is an absolute separation between history and politics, the majority view is well represented by Dennis Kavanagh who sees politics as a field of study to which history can make a contribution (Kavanagh, 1991). Historians can do this by providing material for political research; by making political researchers more aware of historical context; by providing a resource for comparative study and by providing lessons from the past for policy-makers today. At the farthest end of the continuum are those who hold the view that there are no differences logically, methodologically or theoretically between history and politics. Those who share the separatist and under-labourer conceptions will rarely, if ever, sully their hands with primary documents. However the fundamental question posed by the interdisciplinary group is whether research in politics can be conducted adequately using only secondary and tertiary documentary material?

The range of documents considered to be of value by the classical school of historians was, as Scott (1990, p.11) points out, remarkably narrow. However in the last 30 years the scope of acceptable secondary and tertiary material has widened significantly. In addition to published diaries, memoirs and biographies it is becoming increasingly common to research photography, film, novels, art, cartoons, maps, architecture, life history and oral history (Plummer, 1983, pp.36–7; J. Scott, 1990, p.13; Catterall and Jones, 1994). However, in politics and international relations, which retains by and large a 'top-down' methodological focus, the principal secondary and tertiary material remains published diaries, memoirs, letters, biographies and parliamentary papers and debates.

One of the most reliable guides to the use of traditional secondary material such as biographies, published diaries, and memoirs is the renowned British historian, Charles Mowat (1971). These sources, Mowat writes, are a way into the closed period before the 30-year rule has opened the archives, and each of these forms of personal record has its pitfalls and something to offer the researcher under one of three headings (Mowat, 1971, p.86). First, they will reveal information about personalities and the role of individuals in major events. In this sense they may help us guard against overtly structuralist and deterministic forms of explanation. Second, they may assist the researcher in understanding the mood of the times, the feel of events. Finally, they may help establish the 'facts', such as a key date, event or meeting. Even the sceptical Mowat concludes, 'somewhere along the line, from personal trivia and impressions on the one hand to invaluable historical evidence on the other, any book in the biographical genre may prove helpful to the historian' (Mowat, 1971, p.86). However, any historical reconstruction in which this type of material plays a significant role is, he judges, at best provisional and is 'not likely to be very reliable' (Mowat, 1971, p.132). It is worth considering some of the pitfalls of the use of secondary data in more depth.

There can be no questioning the popularity of biographies and the size of the market in political biographies that has developed in the last few decades (see, for instance, Short, 1999; Sampson, 2000; Service, 2000; Campbell, 2001; Jenkins, 2001; Clarke,

2002). Even the most dubious autobiographies (Beckham, 2001) may contain information about the context of an event or at least reveal ambitions at play and wire-pulling behind the scenes. However, as a research resource in politics, biographies tend to suffer from three main problems. First, it is worth considering the relationship between the biographer and the individual concerned. To what extent is the biographer a 'friend' of the subject and how sympathetic is the treatment offered? Biographies in this way, cautions Mowat, have the virtues and defects of the old saint's lives: they reveal much personal and inner detail that might otherwise be lost but, as a consequence, 'consistently turn the hero's face to the sun. If there were shadows, they will have to be described by another hand' (Mowat, 1971, p.90). Second, they are by definition an account of the individual's life and not an examination of policy-making. Events therefore will be covered only to the extent that they impinge on the career or personal development of the individual under scrutiny. As Gamble (2002, p.150) notes, biographies and autobiographies are valuable sources on the inside story but often have less to say on the outside story, the wider context in which government operates, and in particular the structures of power that shape society and the state. In addition, since there are few biographies of top civil servants, it is almost impossible to trace the evolution of policy-making through the use of biographies alone.

Finally, they raise one of the fundamental problems of secondary and tertiary sources: the question of reliability. Although many of the best biographies are now written using primary sources which are available to all, those dealing with more recent events are often based on private papers that are unavailable for general inspection. This is not to impugn the integrity of the biographer but rather to recognize that access to private documents will often only be granted to researchers on condition that the 'family' has the right to veto sections of the finished product or withhold publication *in toto*. This rule also governs biographies and autobiographies that may be based partly on public records that are yet to be released. Examples here include the Earl of Birkenhead's study of the life of Lord Cherwell (former Paymaster-General) which for the first time revealed details of secret post-war currency plans, and the recent autobiography of Stella Rimington, the former Director-General of MI5 (Birkenhead, 1961, and Bank of England file G1/123, 'Birkenhead's chapter on Robot' Frank Lee, 10 May, 1961; Rimington, 2001).

Similar problems dog the use of published diaries as a major resource in politics and international studies. Without doubt much valuable material can be found in published political diaries such as R. Hall (1989 and 1992); Shuckburgh (1986); Benn (1989); Clark (1994); Lamont (2000); Colville (1987); and even Moran (1966). However, to assess their reliability as sources, we need answers to the following questions: was the diary written up each day, or days, weeks or months later? Have the entries been altered when hindsight changed an impression? Had the diarist any intention of publishing the diary at the time it was being compiled? In addition, no diary has ever been published in full and so we need to know the criteria which the editor used to select final published entries. In this regard it will always repay the researcher to consult, if possible, the full version rather than the published highlights. Finally, it is worth recalling Mowat's 'cardinal rule': 'the evidence from a diary must if possible be supported by evidence from other sources' (Mowat, 1971, p.99). Without recourse to primary documents such supporting evidence can be difficult to obtain. For this reason, diaries are most effectively used in conjunction with public records to fill in gaps and reveal what may not have been recorded in official documents. Diaries, as Gamble (2002, p.143) notes, 'score on immediacy, and are an unrivalled source of gossip. They convey how a particular politician thought and felt about events at the time, and the assumptions on which political calculations were made.' However, if the researcher begins with diaries s/he may well gain a superficial knowledge of personalities but is liable to 'take for new much that is not, and miss the real additions to knowledge' (Mowat, 1971, p.108).

Reliance on memoirs replicates many of the problems discussed above with the additional difficulty that the researcher must try to judge whether the writer has successfully battled with the ever present tendency to magnify his or her own importance in a given set of circumstances (Mowat, 1971, p.109; Catterall, 1994, p.34). The use of ghost-writers to help 'research' missing episodes, the desire to set the record straight or reinterpret one's actions and the 'natural' tendency to embroider and embellish, generally indicates that even the most interesting and well thumbed memoirs (Thatcher, 1993) are to be treated with extreme caution. Mowat (1971, p.109) once again pinpoints the great weakness of this source: 'no man is on oath in his memoirs. He is pleading at the bar of posterity, but will not hear the verdict.'

Secondary sources such as government official publications and debates (in Britain parliamentary papers and parliamentary debates) offer the political researcher a much more reliable starting point than biographies, published diaries and memoirs. Parliamentary papers (given a Command number) include parliamentary bills, treaties, reports of government departments (such as annual economic surveys), committees and commissions. They form the essential outer framework for political research and of course are often the result of the policy-making process. In this category we also find the publications of international organizations and institutions such as the European Commission or the UN. Whilst official papers and documents may seem rather dry and sanitized they are indispensable to the serious researcher who all too often will fail to study the actual Treaty or wording of the Bill, resting content with a summary (possibly defective and certainly selective) offered in tertiary accounts. However, official publications are both unwieldy and offer little to the researcher looking to generate an original contribution to the discipline. This is also true of the documents published in Britain under the heading of *Parliamentary Debates*. Although new researchers may feel that *Hansard* is a potentially rich source of information, the debates, by and large, record political talk and do not reveal the mechanics of administrative action. The lengthy mock battles in the Chambers are often dominated by individuals far removed from the policy-making process. For this reason, the *Debates* are well characterized by Mowat (1971, p.54) as 'low-grade ore for the historian . . . better to read the main arguments, and the votes, in a newspaper'.

However the analysis of newspapers themselves is not problem free. As Wilkinson (1994, p.50) outlines, newspapers offer a unique approach to the study of the past inasmuch as they are time-specific and do not have an eye on posterity. They are datable, published at set intervals and are linked in a unique way to a contemporary audience. A 'content-analysis' of newspaper material can therefore reveal much about the period under study: lifestyles, preoccupations, consumption and worldviews (in this respect *Keesings Archive* remains a valuable and under-used resource in political science). Unfortunately, the reliability and accuracy of newspaper material cannot be presumed and a full analysis of this source requires study of the role of editors and journalists, patterns of ownership and processes of production.

This brief review of the most commonly used secondary and tertiary sources in political science has tended to confirm the view that they are most effectively employed in combination with elite interviewing and/or with the analysis of primary documents. The analysis of primary documents however is in itself no easy task and, as Vickers (1995) shows, requires careful preparation to achieve success.

The analysis of primary sources

To the uninitiated the study of primary documents held in a record repository is often thought to be akin to research in a library. A short visit to even the most well organized record centre will quickly show this is a false analogy. In preparation for a visit to an archive new researchers should recognize three basic points. First, although record centres often share a common code of conduct, each repository is a unique institution with its own system of cataloguing and organization of material. Second, many record centres may have very rudimentary storage facilities and cataloguing may be primitive or even non-existent. Third, it is a rule of thumb amongst experienced researchers that you must be prepared to spend days, even weeks, wading through documents before you find material relevant to your research. By way of introduction to archival analysis this section will focus on how to track down the appropriate repository and then discuss in detail how best to analyse documents held in the repositories most useful to political scientists, the Public Record Office (now also called the National Archives) in London and the National Archives in Washington, DC. The first thorny question to consider is what constitutes a public record and why is it that some private records can escape the 30-year rule?

In the UK, the Public Records Act of 1958 defines public records as

> administrative and departmental records belonging to Her Majesty, whether in the United Kingdom or elsewhere, in right of Her Majesty's Government in the United Kingdom and, in partic-ular, – a/ records of, or held in, any department of Her Majesty's Government in the United Kingdom, or b/ records of any office, commission or other body or establishment whatsoever under Her Majesty's Government in the United Kingdom, shall be public records'. (The Public Records Acts of 1958 and 1967: http://www.pro.gov.uk/about/act/preact.htm, p.7).

In other words, public records are not simply the records of central government but cover a very wide remit to include records of bodies and establishments under government departments and other establishments and organizations as diverse as the Environment Agency, the Further Education Funding Council, the Imperial War Museum, the Post Office, the Royal Botanic Gardens at Kew and the University Grants Committee.

In addition, records of courts and tribunals (Supreme Courts; county courts, magistrates' courts, coroners' courts, courts-martial, naval courts, and Industrial Courts) are also considered public records. In the 1958 Act 'public records' include not only written records but records conveying information by any other means whatsoever (such as film, photographs and sound recordings).

The significance of whether a document is, or is not, a public record lies in the rules governing access to documents. On 1 January 1968 the Public Records Act of 1967 took effect, reducing the closure period on public records from 50 to 30 years. This granted the public a right of access to public records after the expiration of a period of 30 years 'beginning with the first day of January in the year next after that in which they were created' (http://www.pro.gov.uk/about/act/preact.htm,7). In essence, although some records may be retained by government departments (either because they contain private material relating to living individuals or the material is retained on the grounds of national security) most records will become available to the general public after the passing of 31 years. This, of course, covers all public records whether they are deposited in the National Archives, County Records Offices or elsewhere.

However, there are numerous records which fall outside the definition of a 'public record' that are of interest to political researchers. These include records of business associations and organizations (see Armstrong and Jones, 1987; Green, 1994; Crookham, 1997), trade unions (Crookham, 1998), political parties, groups and associations (Cook and Waller, 1994) and international organizations (see Box 7.2 for the joint UNESCO/International Council of Archives guide to the archives of intergovernmental organizations). Although some of the record repositories containing these records may voluntarily have adopted the strictures of the 30-year rule, others may have rather more liberal conditions of access depending on the wishes of the depositors of those records. For instance, the Modern Records Centre at Warwick University operates a 10-year closure period for its Trades Union Congress files, and many others are not subject to a closure period at all (although other restrictions may apply, such as vetting by an academic or advisory board). Similarly, at the National Museum of Labour History in Manchester, the archives of the Labour Party are subject to a 10-year rule, whilst the archives of the Communist Party of Great Britain are open for the most part except for a few embargoed files.

Box 7.2   UNESCO/International Council of Archives guide to the archives of intergovernmental organizations (select list)

European Commission
European Parliament
Economic and Social Committee of the European Communities
UN Economic and Social Commission for Asia and the Pacific
The Food and Agriculture Organization of the United Nations
Historical Archives of the European Communities
International Court of Justice
International Federation of Red Cross and Red Crescent Societies
International Labour Organization
International Monetary Fund
North Atlantic Treaty Organization
Organisation for Economic Co-operation and Development
Pan American Health Organization
United Nations Educational, Scientific and Cultural Organization
(UNESCO)
Western European Union
World Health Organization
World Intellectual Property Organization
World Bank Group
World Trade Organization

Source: http://www.unesco.org/archives/guide/uk/index.html.
Reproduced with kind permission of UNESCO and the International Council
on Archives.

Once it is clear that not all primary documents are 'public records' (and therefore not necessarily subject to the 30-year rule), researchers can begin the task of tracking down archives which may contain material relevant to their work. There are three strategies commonly used to select which archives will be of most use. First, there is no substitute for meticulously checking references in published books and articles pertaining to a research field. Through a careful process of cross-checking it should become clear which authors are seen as the authoritative figures in a particular area and the type of documentary material they have consulted. This can provide the basis not only for tracking down archives but also for beginning a search of the material in those archives. Second, the new researcher will find invaluable a number of published guides to archives. Of particular significance in the UK are the Longman

Guides to Sources in Contemporary British History (Cook and Waller, 1994; Cook, Leonard and Leese, 1994) whilst in the USA there are a number of general archive guides (Carson, 2001). Finally, there are some excellent web-based guides to archival holdings. In the UK the principal information gateway for archivists and researchers of British history is Archives on-line (known as ARCHON). This is hosted and maintained by the Historical Manuscripts Commission and provides information on all repositories in the UK and all those repositories throughout the world whose collections are noted in the indexes to the UK National Register of Archives (NRA). The National Register itself is perhaps the best place for new researchers to start searching for relevant archives. It contains references to papers of over 150,000 corporate bodies, persons and families relating to British history with a further 100,000 connected records (http://www.hmc.gov.uk/nra/abtnra2.htm). Searches can be conducted on-line in a variety of ways including corporate name search, personal and family name search and place name search.

In the USA, Columbia University Libraries Archive and Manuscript Collection provides excellent coverage of the main US sites. It includes national libraries, state archives and libraries, college and university collections, and historical society archives. It also discusses the merits of the finding aids available, which may be searched by name or topic (http://www.columbia.edu/cu/lweb/eguides/speccol.html).

Despite the burgeoning number of new collections constantly added to archives, there are two main repositories whose collections cannot be overlooked by students of politics and international relations in Britain and the USA. These are respectively the National Archives at Kew, London, which brings together and preserves the records of central government, and the National Archives and Records Administration (NARA) in Washington, DC, which makes available US government records and manages the Presidential libraries system. It is to conducting archival research in these central institutions that our attention will now turn.

Research in the Public Record Office (the UK's National Archives) and the National Archives, Washington

Although some political scientists simply choose to ignore the holdings of national archives, most would now agree with Rodney Lowe that for those interested in policy-making, there is no more important single source of information (Lowe, 1997, p.240). The great advantage of government records is that they reveal, 'not only the complete range of influences to which government was subjected at any given time but also what did not change' (Lowe, 1997, pp.240–1). In other words, they provide what Lowe term greater contextualization and balance, enabling the researcher to gain greater empathy with the past and therefore make a decisive contribution to understanding change over time. More specifically, the sheer volume of government records and the diverse range of government departments from which they are collected allow careful researchers the opportunity to make good gaps in knowledge and information that will inevitably arise from the analysis of other sources. Lowe lists four main advantages of using public records (Lowe, 1997, pp.241–2). First, they contain the widest range of information upon which policy is based. Second, in the bulk of records created by the 'lower-levels' of government we can trace policy implementation and therefore see how decisions taken by the 'core executive' are acknowledged, discussed and refined. Third, by sifting through departmental records it is possible to find clearly stated views of ministers and officials; this information would not necessarily be made public or even be found in Cabinet minutes. Finally, the files allow researchers to identify an important variable in policy-making, 'a distinctive "departmental" view transcending individual ministers and officials' (Lowe, 1997, p.242). In this way the files provide an opportunity for researchers to contribute to wider discussions in social science such as the agency/structure and the 'principal actor' debates. In short, there is now overwhelming evidence that the contents of national archives, if used with skill and judgement, can make a significant contribution to understanding the workings of modern government and the conduct of international relations. This is not to say that the use of public records is problem free and we will return to discuss some of the pitfalls towards the end of this chapter. However, it is now necessary to discuss each institution in turn, beginning with the Public Record Office (PRO).

As the National Archives for England, Wales and the UK, the PRO houses records from across central government and from the central courts (http://www.pro.gov.uk/about/access/sustem.htm). The percentage of records transferred to the PRO is between 1 and 2 per cent of total government records created in any one year, but this still amounts to approximately one mile of records each year (and of course the major government departments such as the Treasury contribute much more than 1 per cent). The Public Records Act

1958 places responsibility for the management of public records on government departments. Each has a Departmental Record Officer whose work on records is guided by the staff of the PRO's Record Management Department. Together with PRO staff, Record Officers select documents for permanent preservation at the PRO, although it is important to bear in mind that government departments remain the formal owners of records and can ask for their return at any time. The selection of records takes place in two stages. First, a record is assessed when it has passed out of active use (approximately five years after it was created). It may then be destroyed, provisionally considered worth preserving or kept for review at a later date. The second review takes place when the record is 15–25 years old and at this point records are identified which are worthy of permanent preservation.

It is commonly assumed by those new to archival analysis that the most important and controversial records of government will have been destroyed or retained. In general terms this is not the case. Records made available for inspection cover confidential, secret and top (or most) secret files. The principal barrier to the researcher is not the character of the records but the sheer size of the PRO's holdings (at the time of writing in 2003, the PRO held over 9 million individual files). In addition the researcher should be aware that the Public Records Act allows public records to be deposited at places other than the PRO. In general this covers records which are of local interest, including films and sound recordings, and records of national museums and galleries. Separate national records offices exist for Scotland and Northern Ireland. Records of departments mainly concerned with Scottish affairs, courts and individuals are located at the National Archives of Scotland in Edinburgh. The Public Record Office of Northern Ireland (PRONI) in Belfast, established in 1923, hold records of the provinces, Northern Ireland courts, local government records and private and business records.

Access to public records, as noted earlier, is governed by the so-called '30-year rule' which means that records are normally open to the public on 1 January of the year after that in which they became 30 years old. Some records may be retained for extended closure periods of 50, 75 or 100 years (for example, census returns which are always closed for 100 years). Others may be open earlier than 30 years (accelerated opening), such as annual reports and some published material. In general however records of the main government departments are still bound by the 30-year rule, although this may change when the proposals associated with the

Freedom of Information Act 2000 come into force in January 2005 (http://www.pro.gov.uk/about/act/).

The first question to be answered by a political science researcher new to the PRO is 'How can I turn an interest in a substantive topic into a researchable area in which files are available?' The first step is to translate this interest into a government department. This may appear to be straightforward but can in many cases turn out to be rather complex if your knowledge of government departments is limited. For instance, an interest in the government's employment policies in the interwar period will involve not simply an analysis of Cabinet documents but also those of, amongst others, the National Assistance Board (AST), the Board of Trade (BT), the Colonial Office (CO), the Foreign Office (FO), the Department of Education and Science (ED), the Ministry of Labour (LAB), the Treasury (T), and various private collections. The most reliable starting point for a new researcher interested in tracking down government departments is the Public Record Office *Current Guide* (PRO, 1996). This is generally available in libraries on microfiche and in hardcopy form at the PRO. It is not a catalogue of individual files or records held at the PRO, but rather describes the classes in which records are arranged. The three-part *Guide* contains, first, administrative histories of government departments (very useful if you are unsure which departments existed at a particular time); second, descriptions of the nature and contents of all the classes of records; and third, an alphabetical index to the text in Parts 1 and 2 covering personal, corporate and place names as well as offering a subject index. Using the *Guide*, it is possible to begin with an interest in the 1926 General Strike and, by following the cross-referencing to Part 2, end up with a list of relevant government departments including the Cabinet, the Treasury, the Admiralty, the War Office, the Home Office and the Ministry of Labour. You would now be armed with a two-part reference such as CAB 21 or HO 144. If you were unsure of the role or scope of the government department, Part 1 of the *Guide* would provide you with the necessary information.

Most other published PRO finding aids (see, for instance, Swann and Turnbull, 1971 and 1978; Cantwell, 1993; Atherton, 1994; Fowler, 1995) will also enable the researcher to track down a two-part reference. However, to order documents at the PRO, researchers require a three-part reference consisting of:

(a)   Departmental initial, such as T (Treasury), HO (Home Office), CAB (Cabinet);

(b)   class number, such as 236; 144; 21;
(c)   piece number, such as /32; /35; /3.

There are three routes to this full three-part reference (such as T236/32 or CAB21/3). First, it is possible to consult the hardbound volumes at the PRO which are organized on the basis of departmental initial and class number, and which list chronologically file by file the entire contents of the respective government department. In our view, this is far and away the most secure and comprehensive way to conduct research at the PRO. Second, it is often useful to begin with existing references found in tertiary sources. Authors who have used PRO files can save the new researcher much time and effort in tracking down relevant government departments and file piece numbers. The most relevant journals to consult in this respect covering British politics and international relations are *Contemporary British History* (formerly *Contemporary Record*) and *Twentieth Century British History*. Finally, the researcher can make use of the PRO's on-line guide to its holdings, PROCAT. This enables searches to be conducted using subject, place or name and can be narrowed in terms of a range of years or government department. PROCAT is part of the PRO Service Delivery Agreement under which it aims not only to make catalogues available on-line but, by 2005, to provide electronic access to the records of the core executive in the twentieth century (Foreign Office, Cabinet and Prime Minister's Office papers). Further details of how to conduct a search of the PRO using PROCAT can be found in Chapter 8 below, on the use of Internet resources.

A final, and important, issue to discuss relating to PRO records concerns the relative merits of the documents which are available for political researchers. The decision of the PRO to make available on-line the records of the core executive (particularly Cabinet and Prime Minister's Office files) by 2005 would imply that these records are of most use to social science researchers. However, this is a conclusion that has been vigorously challenged by Charles Mowat (1971) and, more recently, Rodney Lowe (1997). Cabinet records are of three main types: Cabinet Conclusions or minutes, Cabinet memoranda or papers, and the work of Cabinet committees. Most academic attention is focused on Cabinet Conclusions which record meetings of the Cabinet, giving time, date, names of those in attendance, a brief account of business and the conclusions reached by the Cabinet. Since they document decision-making, Cabinet minutes are obviously a vital component in piecing together the work of the government. Alongside Cabinet memoranda –

reports prepared by officials and ministers and circulated to the Cabinet as the basis for discussion – Cabinet minutes represent the endpoint of the decision making process. However, it is crucial to bear in mind that they are written with a view to recording conclusions rather than the full debate in Cabinet, and of course they reveal nothing of the evolution of policy or its implementation. As a guide to positions taken and arguments advanced in Cabinet, the circulated minutes are often misleading and incomplete. As Lowe (1997, pp.252–3) demonstrates in an analysis of Conservative Cabinets held in 1963, minutes can be an unreliable source of evidence, tending to under-estimate the wider political debate within which policy is formulated.

Similar considerations apply to the files of the Prime Minister's Office (PREM). Unlike Cabinet papers, the PREM records show the remarkable range of information, much of it sensitive, that is passed to the prime minister from all quarters of government. However as a guide to evolution of policy PREM files are equally unreliable. Few briefing documents are found in the files and there is little indication of the important decisions that would have been settled at lower departmental levels. Above all, as Lowe (1997, p.253) again points out, the papers 'can give a misleading impression of the Prime Minister's role and influence'.

To correct the imbalance that a focus on core executive records can produce, political researchers are well advised to base the bulk of their studies on the records of less fashionable government departments (Treasury, Foreign Office, Home Office, Ministry of Labour, etc.). This admittedly more difficult task requires not only the skills of a historian but also knowledge of the distribution of power and responsibilities within government to achieve what Lowe (1997, p.255) calls 'research in depth', which the volume of PRO material permits.

Many of the above remarks also apply to researching the records held at the National Archives in Washington. The National Archives of the United States is administered by NARA, an independent federal agency responsible primarily for managing US government records. NARA's 33 facilities hold approximately 21.5 million cubic feet of original textual materials, amounting to almost four billion pieces of paper from the executive, legislative and judicial branches of federal government. In addition, the National Archives multi-media collection includes nearly 300,000 reels of motion picture film, more than 5 million maps, charts and architectural drawings, over 200,000 sound and video recordings, 9 million aerial photographs, nearly 14 million still pictures and posters, and approximately 7,600 computer data sets (http://www.nara.gov/nara/whatis/records.html).

As with the PRO, NARA's Record Management Team determines which documentation should be preserved and less than 3 per cent of the government's records each year are judged to be historically significant and therefore become part of the National Archives indefinitely. The holdings of most interest to political researchers are subject to a '30-year rule' and include the General Records of the Department of State (RG 59), the General Records of the Department of the Treasury (RG 56) and the records of the National Security Council (RG 273). In addition, NARA is responsible for the Presidential Library system which makes available the papers, records and other historical materials of US Presidents since Herbert Hoover. The ten Presidential Libraries (together with the Nixon Presidential Materials Staff, and the Clinton Presidential Materials Project) contain a vast array of personal files and oral history collections which are not available at the main National Archive sites in Washington (see Box 7.3). These collections can include, for example, diaries, pre-presidential papers, presidential papers, financial documents, cabinet documents and White House central files. The Presidential Libraries are therefore a valuable (if somewhat unpredictable) source of information for political researchers.

The process of beginning research in the National Archives is very similar to that followed in the Public Record Office. However, having translated a broad interest into a specific government department (or departments), the task of tracking down documents is somewhat different. Three routes are available. First, as with the PRO, it is possible to begin by collecting references found in other academic publications. This should provide the necessary reference to the specific 'Record Group' which comprises the records of a government department. For instance, the Department of the Treasury is identified by Record Group (RG) 56. Within each RG, documents are organized into 'series', or sets of documents arranged according to the creating office's filing system. So, to continue our example, within the Treasury Department, the records of the Office of the Assistant Secretary for International Affairs 1934–70 are filed as RG 56.12. Eventually you arrive at a box number which may contain the documents you wish to see but, as there is no detailed catalogue to match that found in the Public Record Office (and box numbers may change) researching at the National Archives is more of a gamble.

The second route, and one recommended frequently by NARA

> ## Box 7.3   The US Presidential Libraries
>
> GEORGE BUSH LIBRARY
> http://bushlibrary.tamu.edu
>
> JIMMY CARTER LIBRARY
> http://www.jimmycarterlibrary.org/
>
> WILLIAM J. CLINTON PRESIDENTIAL MATERIALS PROJECT
> http://www.clinton.nara.gov
>
> DWIGHT D. EISENHOWER LIBRARY
> http://www.eisenhower.utexas.edu
>
> GERALD R. FORD LIBRARY
> http://www.ford.utexas.edu
>
> HERBERT HOOVER LIBRARY
> http://hoover.nara.gov
>
> LYNDON B. JOHNSON LIBRARY
> http://www.lbjlib.utexas.edu/
>
> JOHN F. KENNEDY LIBRARY
> http://www.jfklibrary.org
>
> NIXON PRESIDENTIAL MATERIALS STAFF
> http://www.nara.gov/nixon/
>
> RONALD REAGAN LIBRARY
> http://www.reagan.utexas.edu
>
> *Source*: Reproduced with the kind permission of NARA.

staff, is to use the *Foreign Relations of the United States* (FRUS) publications to identify relevant Record Groups, series and subseries. The *Foreign Relations of the United States* series presents the official documentary record of major U.S. foreign policy decisionsand significant diplomatic activity (http://www.state.gov/www/about_state/history/fruswhat.html). It is produced by the State Department's Office of the Historian, and comprises more than 350 individual volumes, the most recent of which contain declassified records from all the foreign affairs agencies (including Presidential Libraries, Departments of State and Defense, National Security Council, Central Intelligence Agency, Agency for International Development, and other foreign affairs agencies as well as the private papers of individuals involved in formulating US foreign policy). Volumes published over the past few years have expanded the scope of the series in two important ways: first, by including documents from a wider range of government agencies, particularly those involved with intelligence activity and covert actions, and second by including transcripts prepared from Presidential tape recordings (http://www.state.gov/www/about_state/history/fruswhat.html). Most major libraries contain the FRUS series (particularly for the post-1945 period) and the Department of State has recently placed some volumes on-line (http://www.state.gov/www/about_state/history/frusonline.html).

In addition, it is often useful to consult the web version of the *Guide to Federal Records in the National Archives of the United States* based on a hardcopy version with the same title compiled by Robert B. Matchette *et al.* in 1995. This version incorporates descriptive information about federal records acquired by the National Archives after the 1995 hardcopy edition went to press, and it is regularly updated to reflect new acquisitions of federal records (http://www.nara.gov/guide/). Finally, NARA aims to provide an on-line catalogue to list the agency's entire archival holdings by 2007. A prototype version of this catalogue, the National Archives Information Locator (NAIL), is currently available on the NARA website. However, whilst NAIL's coverage of NARA's holdings is significant, it is not a comprehensive resource and cannot yet be judged a reliable research tool, particularly for searches of federal records (where the *Guide to Federal Records in the National Archives of the United States* is a more reliable guide).

The National Archives of the UK and the United States are the two most significant record repositories for students of politics and international relations. This is largely because of the global political and economic reach of both the UK and the USA in the last two centuries. However, there are numerous other record centres around the world, as indicated in Box 7.4, operating on principles similar to those pioneered by the Public Record Office.

Conclusion: the value and limits of documentary and archival analysis

Documentary and archival sources offer great opportunities for political scientists to develop novel accounts and interpretations of significant events. Politics may not be defined solely by a focus on the 'state', but as a concept it remains central to any definition. It follows therefore that the workings of the state, as revealed in public records and the private papers of key individuals, are a vital resource

Box 7.4   National archives: worldwide

Australia
Website: www.naa.gov.au

Canada
Website: www.archives.ca/

France
Website: www.archivesnationales.culture.gouv.fr/

Germany
Website: www.bundesarchiv.de/

India
Website: www.nationalarchives.nic.in

Italy
Website: archivi.beniculturali.it/

Japan
Website: www.archives.go.jp/index_e.html

Malaysia
Website: www.arkib.gov.my

Netherlands
Website: www.nationaalarchief.nl/

New Zealand
Website: www.archives.govt.nz

Russia
Website: www.rusarchives.ru

South Africa
Website: www.national.archives.gov.za

Sweden
Website: www.ra.se/

Source: Accessed January 2003 National Archives of Australia (Canberra)
http://www.naa.gov.au (Factsheet 193), reproduced with permission.

for political research. However, as with all sources and methods, it is prudent to ask what other types of information may usefully complement this approach and what are the limitations of documentary records? These issues are often discussed in terms of the quality control criteria: *authenticity, credibility, representativeness* and *meaning* (Platt, 1981, pp. 31–66; J. Scott, 1990, p.19; Harrison, 2001, p.131).

The authenticity of a document concerns its genuineness: 'whether it is actually what it purports to be' (Scott, 1990, p.19). This involves a consideration of the notion of 'soundness' (is the document an original or a copy and has it been corrupted in any way?), and 'authorship' (is it possible to authenticate the identity of those responsible for producing the document?). In general terms the authenticity of public records can be established without much difficulty. The form and content of such records are usually compatible with the procedures known to have been used by the government department responsible for its creation. However, many such records are undated and the precise author of the record may be difficult to identify (particularly given the frequent practice of officials producing papers presented by ministers). These obstacles can usually be circumvented by careful analysis of a wider range of public records.

Authenticity presents more of a problem when considering private papers and documentary sources such as diaries or memoirs. In the twentieth century, the Zinoviev Letter (allegedly signed by Zinoviev and other members of the Communist International, dated 15 September 1924 and addressed to the Communist Party of Britain), is perhaps the most famous example of a document whose authenticity has led to protracted debate amongst political scientists and historians (see Mowat, 1971, pp.199–212). More recently, questions have been raised over the authenticity of the 'Mitrokhin Archive' (smuggled out from the KGB foreign intelligence archive: see Andrew and Mitrokhin, 2000), and the claims made by Peter Wright in *Spycatcher*, particularly concerning the so-called 'Wilson Plot' which, according to Stella Rimington, Wright later admitted to be 'not true' (P. Wright, 1987; Rimington, 2001, p.189). Often there is no sure-fire test which can establish beyond doubt the authenticity of documentary material. However, in most cases, as Scott (1990, pp.21–2) indicates, it is possible to relate the document in question to what is known about the conditions surrounding its production and so to be wary about diaries and letters discovered in unusual circumstances rather than in known and trusted archives.

The criterion of credibility is closely related to that of authenticity. Once a document has been authenticated (beyond reasonable doubt), it is then necessary to ask 'how distorted its contents are likely to be (J. Scott, 1990, p.22). In other words, how sincere and accurate was the author of the document? This requires that the researcher pay particular attention to the conditions under which the document was produced and the material interests that may have driven the author to write the document. Once again this criterion presents fewer problems for public records than for other documentary sources. For instance, a Treasury official may have little choice or discretion in producing a document for a minister. This is not the case, however, for private diaries when, as illustrated above, the author may have written the diaries in order to present an over-dramatized account or may have omitted certain relevant details to secure wider public acceptance.

Perhaps the most serious challenge facing users of documentary sources concerns their response to questions of representativeness and meaning. Scott (1990, p.24) notes that researchers should be sure that the documents consulted are 'representative of the totality of relevant documents'. This requires that consideration be given to the survival and the availability of relevant documents. As noted above, the selection of public records is formalized and carried out according to established and accountable procedures, whereas other primary and secondary material may be collected, retained and archived on a much more *ad hoc* basis. This can all too easily result in the survival of an unrepresentative selection of documents. In addition, it often means that the number of public records available will significantly outweigh other documentary sources. This can give rise to specific problems, including the alleged 'top-down bias' introduced by a focus on public records. As a corrective, Lowe (1997, p.245) advises researchers to seek out other public and private archives as an essential counterweight to the PRO. For instance, in respect of British politics, the Institute of Contemporary British History sponsors a regular series of 'witness seminars' at which participants pool their memories of particular events. The transcripts of the seminars are published in the journal, *Contemporary British History*, and in this way they complement the oral history archive at the British Library of Political and Economic Science (Lowe, 1997, p.245: also see Plummer, 1983, on the diversity of collections of life-documents). This strategy, which should be extended to include personal interviews wherever possible, goes someway to help the researcher tackle the related problem of meaning in both its literal and interpretative guise.

For students of modern politics and international relations there should be little difficulty establishing the literal meaning of documents (unlike the situation facing the mediaeval historian). However, all users of documents face problems of interpretation, outlined succinctly by Scott (1990, p.31) as involving, 'interpretative understanding of individual concepts, appreciation of the social and cultural context through which the various concepts are related in a particular discourse, and a judgement of the meaning and significance of the text as a whole'. This requires that the researcher discover as much as possible about the conditions under which the text was produced and, on that basis, make sense of the author's situation and intentions. This will require extensive biographical investigation of key individuals and willingness on the part of the researcher to become immersed in the social, political and economic context under study. Through analysis of news, film, music and other media is it possible to gain greater awareness of the context and in that way conduct a type of participant observation (albeit at one remove).

Documents, of course, do not speak for themselves but only acquire significant meaning when situated within a context set by vigorous analytical and methodological assumptions. To enable other scholars to judge the worth of research produced from documentary sources it is therefore necessary to state the working assumptions which have guided the selection of material. This is particularly important given the range and diversity of documentary sources now available to the researcher. Disagreements between researchers in political science cannot, as Gamble (2002, p.142) points out, often be resolved into a simple matter of 'fact', because the problem 'is one of different perceptions of the same event, none of which are obviously false'. It is certainly true that since 'reality is constructed and experienced in so many different ways, determining what *actually* happened in any final sense is an aspiration impossible to achieve' (Gamble, 2002, p.142). However, careful use of a wide range of documentary material is one of the most reliable methods open to the political researcher and provides an opportunity for the production of authoritative studies, even if the 'definitive account' remains just out of reach.

Chapter 8

The Internet and Political Research

This chapter discusses how effective use may be made of the Internet in political research. Authenticity can be a problem and some of the precautions that need to be taken resemble those used in relation to archival sources. CD-ROMs and government documents on-line are also important sources for political research. On-line polling represents a new and innovative development in survey work. Elite interviewing may also be conducted on-line. The Internet is not so much transforming political research, as open up a range of new ways of undertaking it.

One example is the way in which the Internet has considerably reduced the transaction costs of obtaining some kinds of information. Government documents which might formerly only have been available by visiting a foreign country, xeroxing them and mailing them home can now in principle be accessed and downloaded within a matter of minutes. Later in the chapter we discuss how use can be made of documentary and data archives that can be accessed through the Internet. Other materials are available on CD-ROM.

A note of caution is, however, necessary. We have not yet reached a position where electronic resources can entirely replace paper-based ones. Internet enthusiasts claim that one can look up a fact more quickly and easily on the Internet than in a reference book, but that is not necessarily the case. Libraries are having to invest in electronic and paper-based resources in parallel. One cannot be connected to the Internet on aircraft and only with difficulty and some expense in trains. Paper-based resources are still highly portable and can comfortably be read outside on a day when the sun is shining.

Even more important, materials from the Internet should be approached with at least as much (perhaps even more) rigour as other types of research materials. The sheer volume of information on the Internet makes it particularly important that a systematic approach is deployed in its use. The origins of materials may not always be clear, particularly as it is possible to set up 'mirror' sites that are deliberately intended to mislead. Even government websites change constantly, making 'monitoring very difficult' (S. Wright, 2002, p.139). Authenticity can be a particular problem in research based on Internet sources. In many ways there are similarities between the Internet and documentary research and many of the same precautions need to be taken (see Chapter 7).

In conducting a web search, the questions that one asks in relation to sampling about representativeness are also relevant. Indeed, the way in which a search for material on the web is approached represents a form of 'snowball' sampling. This is a very useful technique in elite interviewing, but no one would claim that it is a probability sampling method. Much depends on the starting point that one selects. The web perhaps has better signposts than a maze, but one could still arrive at one's destination while having missed a lot on the way. The activity of 'surfing' the web can be intriguing and revealing, but it lacks the systematization one would expect to find in research. However, it may help less hierarchical, more lateral and hence more innovative forms of thinking.

Nevertheless, even if the web-like character of the Internet allows us to think in new and different ways, the basic organizing concepts that are deployed in social science research still have to be applied. Problems of reliability arise. Websites change very quickly and the old material is not always archived. That is why it is always important to date references to websites, but it would be possible for an unscrupulous researcher to attempt to make false claims. Questions of validity arise in terms of whether material from websites measures what it is supposed to measure. For example, how can one verify claims by non-governmental organizations about the influence they have exerted on policy?

Websites are designed for a variety of reasons, some commercial, others to recruit support for a political campaign, yet others to indulge a personal whim. The needs of a researcher are not generally in the forefront of the mind of the site designer. Immediacy is an important criterion: one needs to address issues that are going to capture the attention of surfers before they move on to another site. Websites can represent a form of electronic journalism. As such, they perform a useful function, but most researchers would not be very impressed by a study that relied primarily on the synthesis of stories from different newspapers. Such stories might be a useful (if not unbiased and undistorted) source of information on particular events, but they would provide a starting point for research, rather than its main source. For example, they could be used to inform questions asked in interviews. The same considerations apply to websites, but they may be even more inclined to editoralize than newspapers. If one buys a 'quality' newspaper, one expects some semblance of objectivity, albeit from a particular slant or political perspective. A free access website may feel entitled to put across a particular point of view, but the extent to which this is being done may not always be made clear.

Searching the Internet

There is a vast amount of information available on the Internet. An advertisement on American television for a service provider showed the customer encountering a message, 'You have reached the end of the Internet. Please click to go back.' Of course, unlike the *Hitch Hiker's Guide to the Galaxy*, one will never reach 'the restaurant at the end of the universe'. What is more likely is that the user will go round in circles without finding the information s/he actually needs. This is where search engines become important. Their use is analogous to the way in which one might type in keywords in an electronic catalogue in a library to locate books or articles on the subject that you are interested in.

Yahoo! was for a long time regarded as the best way of locating information on the Internet. It sorts information into categories and also allows the user to make a search country-specific. The categories and the information placed into them are, however, constructed through a process of human decision-making. Yahoo! emphasizes the importance of the distinction between 'a directory that happens to be searchable, [and] a search engine . . . Searchable directories and search engines treat information differently. They approach it differently, store it differently, and present it to the world differently' (Yahoo!, 2002b).

Yahoo! maintains that 'one important differences between search engines and directories is that directories have structure. You can navigate the structure and peruse the information contained within it, making choices as you go along' (Yahoo!, 2002c). It is thus possible to browse through a rich hierarchy of information, a collection of categories and subcategories. The information is organized into 25,000 categories that range from the very general to the very specific. Yahoo! starts with fourteen very general categories, including, Business and the Economy, Government, Recreation and Sports. The White House site is in the category Government: US Government: Executive Branch: the White House.

Set up in 1998, Google has become an increasingly popular alternative to Yahoo!. Google is a search engine, which means that it generates a lot of raw data by indexing all the web pages it finds by crawling over the web. Yahoo!'s perspective on search engines is that they 'provide good results for very specific requests, and often poor results with general requests' (2002a). If all the material that Google generated was not ordered in any way, it would not be very helpful. Google overcomes this problem by using the link structure of the web to determine what is important and what is not. A link from one page to another is interpreted as a 'vote'. The more votes a page has, the higher it appears on the list of search results. Users are therefore likely to find very quickly the material that is most relevant to their enquiry. For an example of a search using Yahoo! and Google, see Box 8.1.

Electronic resources for political research

These come in a variety of forms, but a key shared property is that they involve a considerable saving of time and effort for the researcher. They also usually incorporate sophisticated search facilities which enable researchers to download what they need or to receive it in a variety of forms. Visits to distant libraries are replaced by resources readily accessible from the researcher's own computer. The resources dealt with here are CD-ROMs; government documents on-line; and access to both documentary and data archives.

CD-ROMs

The key advantage of the CD-ROM is that it involves a vast amount of information to be stored on a small disc placed in the computer (sometimes the information is accessible on-line from the researcher's library). For example, the complete edition of Margaret Thatcher's public statements on CD-ROM is made up of a total word count of around 14 million (see Box 8.2). This would have required 50 large volumes to be reproduced in a print format. 'One of the appealing features of CD-ROMs is that bulk creates no problem whatsoever and the structure of costs is

Box 8.1 Occam's Razor

A search was conducted for information on William of Ockham or Occam, the mediaeval monk and philosopher who made an important contribution to social science methodology by developing the concept of parsimony. This was popularly known as 'Occam's Razor' and these two words were typed into the search box on Yahoo and Google.

Yahoo! provided two direct references to 'Occam's Razor', sites which outlined the essential features of the concept. It was possible to ignore a site in the 'clubs and organisations' category that referred to an 'independent improvisation comedy theatre troupe' at the University of Chicago.

By clicking on to William of Ockham at the top of the Yahoo listing, a further series of sites was generated, including a brief biography. Two of these referred to his famous razor, but others provided context, including 'Ockham and Nominalism', 'Ockham and Infallibility', 'William of Ockham Archives'. One-line descriptions of the content were helpful. For example, 'Ockham and Nominalism' stated: 'he probably never anticipated his dream coming true: the death of universals', identifying him as a premature post-modernist.

Google generated 21,900 references, but the first ten would provide the basic information that a student would need to understand the concept. For example, the first reference was to 'Occam's razor . . . a logical principle attributed to the mediaeval philosopher William of Ockham.' A social scientist could use the descriptions to eliminate those that referred to theology or topics in natural science. One could also eliminate 'a fantasy sci-fi story set in an on-line virtual reality fantasy role-playing game in the near . . .', while another referred to crop circles as an illustration of the principle. The statement of the number of categories associated with each reference was also helpful as it gave some idea of the extent of the material on the relevant site.

In this case, the more structured information on Yahoo! would probably be more helpful to someone approaching the topic for the first time, but Google gives a better idea of the rich variety of applications of the concept.

Search conducted: 12 June 2002.

entirely different. A single disc provides more than sufficient capacity for a complete edition in written form and extra units of data have a very low marginal cost' (Oxford University Press, 1999, p.5).

The discs cost relatively little to produce and distribute, and hence editors do not face the kind of selection problems that face editors of printed collections. Often the only limitation is the

---

Box 8.2   Example of a CD-ROM: Margaret Thatcher's complete public statements 1945–1990

Benefits to researcher: offers as comprehensive as possible a coverage of her public statements, including materials that are not readily accessible, e.g., transcripts of television and radio programmes, speeches to the 1922 Committee.

Organization of material: the material is grouped around a list of themes which are themselves grouped in families for ease of presentation on the screen. For example, the family 'housing and local government' includes a theme 'local government – community charge'.

Statements are graded in four levels of importance. The software allows the researcher to concentrate on the most important or range progressively more widely across the whole range of statements.

1. Seminal statements, 3 per cent of the total, e.g., the Bruges speech on Britain and the EU.
2. Major statements, including all the bigger set-piece speeches and lengthier interviews, about 50 per cent of all material.
3. Minor statements, including many impromptu comments, about 37 per cent of all material. Of use to anyone studying a particular episode in depth, e.g., Falklands War.
4. Trivial statements, included on the disc for sake of completeness, about 9 per cent of all material. Includes material relating to her constituency (Finchley). May be of value for some in-depth studies or biographical work.

Example of a search
The search facility was used to locate Mrs Thatcher's famous 'no such thing as society' statement. 'Society' as a search term generated too many responses, but the addition of 'such' and 'thing' as search terms produced a shorter list with the article in *Woman's Own* having 'no such thing as society' in brackets in the index. The full transcript shows that Mrs Thatcher makes the statement in two different forms during the interview. An appendix gives an elucidation statement issued by 10 Downing Street in response to a request from *The Sunday Times*.

---

availability of the original record. The compilers of Margaret Thatcher's public statements found over 7,100 statements that they could list and a record of some kind was found for 95 per cent of them. Eighteen statements had to be excluded from the disc for copyright reasons, principally interviews with ABC television in New York.

The record of her statements also becomes better over time. The greatest difficulty was experienced in the period before 1970 when she was not sufficiently prominent to be newsworthy. For example, one of the authors attended a speech by her at his university in 1966 that did not even attract local press attention. The Press Association, a major source of political material for the British press, kept no archive of its output, otherwise it might have been a principal source for the disc. 'Thousands of hours of Prime Ministerial audio tapes appear to have been lost or destroyed by the Central Office of Information' (Oxford University Press, 1999, p.6). However, over time more 'impromptu' material came to be recorded, 'matching pace with the use of handheld tape recorders by journalists and the development of even lighter and more manoeuvrable television cameras' (Oxford University Press, 1999, p.14).

The experience of compiling this disc of Thatcher's public statements showed the importance of completing such a task relatively quickly. Finding transcripts for statements made on party business, particularly during elections, was especially difficult as no government records were kept and the editors sometimes had to rely on privately made recordings:

> Full records of all but one of the Conservative Party's press conferences during the 1979 General Election have vanished and even the 1987 election launch no longer survives in full form . . . Left another ten or twenty years a disc of this kind would have been much more expensive to produce and significantly less complete. (Oxford University Press, 1999, p.6)

Despite the fact that a CD-ROM can hold several thousand pages of text, editors are not free of all selection decisions. There are costs associated with obtaining and transcribing entries. In the case of the Thatcher disc, the editors made a distinction between 'public' statements, the defining characteristic of the collection, and those that have an essentially private character. Although logically coherent, this selection criterion does pose some problems for the researcher. Most researchers would not object to the exclusion of hundreds of goodwill messages sent to local Conservative Associations that are present in the Thatcher manuscript archive. However, messages to business and interest group conferences are placed in a similar category, but might be of considerable interest to some researchers, for example those working on business–government relations or pressure groups. Nevertheless, the CD-ROM contains material of considerable value in one location, much of it not readily available elsewhere.

More generally, CD-ROMs 'offer students access to quantities and qualities of material previously reserved for academic élites' (Ludlam, 1995, p.350). Browsing the material is usually relatively easy, thus replicating one of the advantages of traditional libraries. 'The immeasurable advantage of electronic documents is that the "retrieval" software supplied with them enables vast volumes to be scoured for key terms (words, dates etc.) or patterns of words, and results obtained in seconds' (Ludlam, 1995, p.349).

Government documents on-line

The increasing availability of official government documents on-line is one of the main benefits of the Internet for the political researcher. In the past it might have been necessary to visit other countries to obtain documents. For example, when undertaking research on air pollution in California in the early 1990s, Grant (1995) had to search for documents in the state library or obtain them from state or legislative officials. They then had to be shipped back to England. Most of these documents could now be downloaded from the web in a matter of minutes.

The UK Government has set itself a target of providing 100 per cent of services on-line by 2005. The Office of the e-Envoy has been set up with a staff of 244 and £52 million annual expenditure to give a clear lead on this initiative. The Government on the Web project noted in its April 2002 report that all the major Cabinet departments had well-developed websites. Only 66 out of 376 central government organizations still did not have a site, but these were mainly small government bodies providing a specialist service within government itself.

There has been a considerable improvement in the availability of documents to download on-line. Dunleavy, Margetts, Bastow, Callaghan and Yared found (2002, p.15):

> Perhaps the biggest changes in the features provided on central government Websites in the two years from 1999 to 2001 has been the expansion of electronic publishing facilities ... The proportion of agencies providing downloads of their documents on-line has more than doubled from two fifths to nine tenths in two years. The proportion of agencies providing their press

releases and annual reports on-line has tripled in the same period, although at least a quarter of agencies do not provide these seemingly essential materials on-line.

The particular document that a researcher needs may not be immediately evident and the quality of search facilities is therefore an important issue. Dunleavy *et al.* found (2002, p.16) 'that the proportion of sites with a search engine grew by almost half of its 1999 levels in the period up to 2001. But there are still poor facilities on central agencies' sites for finding publications.' Of course, the principal purpose of government sites is to serve citizens and enterprises not researchers. However, the research conducted in the e-government project exposed more fundamental problems in the government's use of the web which are not necessarily confined to the UK.

The research found that public agencies often lag behind private sector organizations in monitoring how their websites are being used: by whom, and which parts of the site are being well used and which are not. In part, there is a practical issue about making the transition to new modes of operating in organizations which developed routines based on manual and paper-based processes and then adjusted these to conventional information and communication technology systems. There is still a lack of a clear idea of what constitutes 'good practice' for a public agency website. Margetts and Dunleavy argue (2002) that the fundamental problem is a cultural one. The most important determinant of effective change is the transformation of organizational cultures and personal mind-sets which allow an agency to move towards more digital modes of operating. The more effectively this is achieved, the greater the benefits for researchers.

There are also broader political problems with government websites. Wright sets out a powerful critique of the way in which the Downing Street website has developed. It was originally supposed to offer a two-way link between government and people, but by 2002 there were only negligible opportunities for feedback from citizens. 'The website can thus be said to have failed to achieve part of its founding rationale. The informative capabilities of the website have been favoured ahead of generating "two-way" communication' (S. Wright, 2002, p.140). He admits, however, that 'The problem for Downing Street is drawing the line between "abuse" and legitimate criticism of the government' (Wright, 2002, p.139). New technologies do not resolve old problems; they just make them reappear in new ways.

Using the Internet to access archives

The Internet may be used to access both traditional documentary archives and electronic data sets. Most Western European countries have an official data archive containing data of interest to political scientists. The Internet enables potential users to search the contents of such data archives, and to order the data sets that they find interesting. Documentary archives are placing their search facilities online and are also making some key documents downloadable over the Internet. There are, however, severe limitations to this process. Bromund (2002, p.109) notes that: 'For the foreseeable future, scholars who wish to do original research in contemporary British history will not be able to rely exclusively on on-line sources.' There is simply so much paper awaiting conversion to electronic form that contemporary historians are 'never likely to be as well served on-line as, for example, the early modern era' (Bromund, 2002, p.121). See Box 8.3 for a discussion of how to access the PRO on-line and Box 8.4 for a discussion of how to access data archives on the Internet.

On-line polling

The Internet presents a number of opportunities for the adaptation of traditional research techniques. One of these is on-line polling. Its advocates claim that it has a number of advantages over more traditional polling techniques. It is increasingly being used in politically related work. For example, from the spring of 2002 *The Daily Telegraph* has been obtaining most of its public opinion surveys from the Internet, using the company YouGov which has built up expertise in this area. The company claims that the general election survey it undertook for the Economic and Social Research Council produced a much better prediction of the actual result (accurate to 0.7 per cent) than any other pollster (YouGov, 2002a).

The advocates of Internet polling claim that it is more able to reach groups that other forms of polling have difficulty in contacting. In particular, well-educated people with high incomes are frequently away from home and therefore cannot be contacted easily in door-to-door surveys. They are particularly likely to avoid street interviewers. Telephone interviewing often does not work particularly well with this group either as they often use telephone answering machines. However, they are likely to be connected to the Internet and to be frequent users of it.

Box 8.3 Using the web to conduct a basic search for primary documents at the PRO

One of the most useful websites to students of politics and international relations is that of the Public Record Office (www.pro.gov.uk). In particular its on-line catalogue, PROCAT, contains details of over nine million files, organized by creating department (www.pro.gov.uk/catalogues/procat.htm). Once you have tracked down your files it is possible to order them on-line, request that they be copied and even, with those on the PRO-ONLINE system, download digital images of documents as Adobe Portable Document Format (PDF) files (see www.pro-online.pro.gov.uk). However, the first task is to locate files relevant to your research. There are three simple rules for conducting a successful search using PROCAT:

1. *Begin by using the Guided Search.* This enables those new to the PRO to enter a term related to their research area – a subject, place or name – or opt for a broad pre-defined search such as Government or Foreign Affairs. This will produce a list of *information leaflets* providing useful advice on records for readers carrying out research in a particular area (from Admiralty Charts to Women's Service in the First World War). The leaflets will indicate relevant government departments and class numbers (for instance, T/236: Treasury files, Class 236).

2. *Next, conduct an Index Search.* This useful function enables researchers to quickly search for a name or term and will direct readers to the richest sources in the catalogue (again revealing departments and class numbers). However, an index search will not pick up every occurrence of a name or term and so to conduct an exhaustive search it is necessary to choose the Search the Catalogue option.

3. *Finally search the catalogue.* Here it is possible to look for words or phrases and narrow down a search by entering dates and government department initials (e.g., FO). Only by searching the catalogue is it possible to arrive at the three-part reference needed to order individual files (eg. T/236/371). However, care needs to be taken to maximize PROCAT's searching function as shown in the following example. A search for the Korean War (entering the dates 1950 to 1953, and no government department) will produce in excess of 271 'hits' covering thirteen government departments. To narrow down the search it is best to click on one of these government departments, such as the Foreign Office. This reveals over 96 Foreign Office files relating to the Korean conflict and gives the full reference and title for each file (e.g., FO 371/99594, 'Allegations against HMG's part in the Korean War', 1952). Armed with the full reference it is now possible to order a file prior to visiting the PRO in person. Finally, by using the 'Go to reference' facility, researchers can type in FO 371/99594 and scan the catalogue either side of this reference to track down related files.

> ## Box 8.4   Using the Internet to access data archives
>
> A useful starting point is CESSDA (the Council for European Social Science Data Archives). Its website http://www.nsd.uib.no/cessda/index.html, has links to the data archives across Europe that are CESSDA members as well as North American and other archives.
>
> Each data archive tends to have a number of ways that users can search the archive on-line. Some users may know the exact title of the study (e.g., the data set) they are looking for, and can search for it using its title. Other users may be interested in exploring an archive more widely. This is typically possible with a key word search (e.g., 'racism', 'national identity', 'environment', 'trust'), which will identify all studies that in some way use the key word in question. For example, using the key word 'racism' would bring up all opinion polls that had a question referring to racism, and so on.
>
> Once the search for interesting data is complete, it is also possible to order studies over the Internet by filling in an on-line form. Here it is customary to specify in what form one would like to receive the data: either on a CD-ROM (which is sent in the post) or on guest File Transfer Protocol (FTP) file storage (which means that a registered data archive user receives a username and password for accessing the selected data on-line). Either way, it is also usually possible to request the data in a specific format, e.g., to be formatted for a specific computer software such as ASCII, SPSS or SAS.
>
> There may be a charge for data that is intended for funded research, but there is typically no fee for data that is intended to be used for unfunded research and private study.

It is also claimed that Internet polling produces more honest and thoughtful answers. Because they are working to time budgets, street and telephone interviewers are inclined to put questions in a rapid-fire manner, which can lead to answers that are often rapid or ill thought through. It is argued that on-line polling gives more time for a reflective answer, although that is not to say that respondents actually complete polls in such a way.

A further claim is that Internet polling eliminates the problem of interviewer bias and, in particular, the problem of respondents giving the answer that they think the interviewer wants to hear. Respondents are more likely to be honest, particularly when it comes to politically sensitive topics. They are less likely to give 'politically correct' answers which can be a problem in surveys on, for example, attitudes to ethnic minorities or migrants. It can also be difficult to get accurate responses to surveys on the environment because of respondents thinking that they should prioritize the environment as an issue and support stringent environmental policies. There also tends to be a discrepancy between reported and actual behaviour (e.g., in the use of recycling facilities).

The biggest potential drawback with on-line surveys is that of sampling bias. Telephone interviewing only really took over when almost everyone had access to a telephone. A large proportion of the population is still not on-line and those that are do not constitute a representative cross-section of the population. The young, the better-educated and the well-off are heavily over-represented. YouGov use a number of techniques to try to overcome this problem.

Their sampling methods can be divided into three distinct types. *Passive sampling* involves a survey sitting on a site and all visitors (or every Nth visitor) being invited to take part. Visitors to the site are greeted with the banner 'Get paid to vote. Click here to earn ££s.' There is usually some specific incentive for participation, such as the chance to win a cash prize. For example, visitors to the site in June 2002 were offered cash prizes worth £8,000 in total to record their experiences of the National Health Service. *Active sampling* occurs when YouGov contacts the respondents and only they are able to take part in the survey. Lists of respondents can either be provided by the client or by YouGov itself. YouGov's experience is that there is a greater need for incentivization with this type of sampling. *Combination sampling* takes elements from both approaches. The precise degree to which the two are mixed depends on the specific requirements of the survey. The two methods could be used side-by-side, one after another. For example, visitors to a website may be invited to register for a survey and record certain demographic information. A certain proportion of respondents (e.g., a nationally representative sample) could then be targeted separately (YouGov, 2002b).

YouGov had recruited by the spring of 2002 a total of 60,000 registered potential respondents. Thus, even though the elderly, for example, are proportionately under-represented, they are still present in large numbers. It is possible to ensure that those respondents invited to participate in a survey do constitute a representative national cross-section in terms of age, gender, occupation, previous voting behaviour or other relevant requirements. As an additional precaution, YouGov usually interviews on-line between 2,000 and 3,000 respondents, far more than in most conventional polls. It also weights its raw data to ensure that the social and demographic profile of its respondents fits that of the population as a whole. YouGov is also alert to the danger of members of minority pressure groups 'piling in' to affect the results of a particular survey. There is no evidence that this has occurred, but YouGov considers that it has mechanisms to alert it to unusual and unexpected changes in its recruitment patterns.

Just as Internet banks can offer better rates than conventional ones because customers act as their own cashier, so in Internet polling all one has to do is set up the site and the poll and the respondent does the rest. There is no need to hire and train teams of interviewers to be deployed in shopping centres or to staff telephones. The risks of using 'clustering' to reduce costs in door-to-door interviews are also reduced, as are the biases that are introduced by interviewer selection of respondents in quota sampling.

When telephone polling was first introduced, there was considerable scepticism about it and resistance to its use. W. Miller felt able to describe (1983, pp.223–4) telephone interviews as 'part of what I call the *new technology norm*, which differs from the traditional survey norm of the 1930s in a variety of interconnected ways. It is the *combination* of several interlocking changes that makes the new technology norm excitingly differently from the old.' It is possible to extend this argument to the Internet and to argue that on-line polling offers a cost-effective technique which has some advantages over more traditional methods.

Elite interviewing on-line

Researchers at the Department of Political Science at the Australian National University have developed a method for realtime interviewing on-line using standard World Wide Web browsing software. This approach was developed 'for the study of closed, finite groups of policy makers and political participants (policy "elites" and advocacy coalition members)' (Chen and Hinton, 1999, p.1). Given the nature of the target group, access to a computer is not likely to be a problem. The principal motivation for developing the method was to meet the requirements for inexpensive interviewing, an imperative in a country the size of Australia where respondents may be dispersed around the various state capitals, or even further afield. The approach also saves on transcription costs and is clearly applicable in a variety of research settings.

On one level, the technique could be seen as an extension of e-mail interviewing where a series of e-mails are exchanged between researcher and research subject. Respondents who might not otherwise be accessible, or face serious time constraints, can be contacted in this way. 'While the methods are similar, the on-line interview and the email interview differ in the realtime aspect of the interview which can limit the *immediacy* of e-mail communication' (Chen and Hinton, 1999, p.8). E-mail exchanges can be protracted, particularly if time has to be spent clarifying questions.

The technique involves using a web page as an interviewing 'screen' so that the subject is questioned in realtime. The interview is conducted in a series of 'rounds' and is therefore more ordered than a traditional interview which in elite interviewing can often take a conversational form. One participant enters a message and the other responds, so that the discussion is broken up into a series of time lagged 'chunks' in the form of sentences or paragraphs. 'As neither is able to directly see the other person, all non-verbal communication is lost and the method lacks the ability of the researcher to conduct observation based research during the course of the interview' (Chen and Hinton, 1999, p.4). Presumably the technique could be combined with video conferencing, but this would greatly increase the cost and one would not be able to observe the respondent's normal working surroundings. One of the practical advantages is that the complete text of the interview can be placed on a file accessible to interviewer, eliminating transcription costs.

One of the drawbacks of this technique is that 'the on-line interview tends to be shorter and may need to be restricted to the gathering of low-cost supporting evidence' (Chen and Hinton, 1999, p.9). In some respects it is like a telephone interview, except that costs are normally lower and a transcript is automatically generated. Chen and Hinton admit (1999, pp.15–16) that the potential of their technique is limited to 'the possibility of becoming a useful low-cost adjunct to existing interview and survey methods in the social sciences'. It may be of particular value to cost-constrained graduate students. In general, however, the interaction between interviewer and respondent is more important in elite than in mass interviewing. Interviews are often semi-structured and the face-to-face method allows respondents to make long and detailed responses to questions. There is probably less scope for on-line methods to displace more traditional techniques in the area of elite interviewing than in relation to polls of the general population.

Conclusions

The Internet is making a whole range of different forms of data easier for the researcher to locate, acquire and search. It has considerable cost-saving potential for social science research. It is also makes it easier for students to undertake relatively advanced forms of research as part of their learning experience, giving them 'hands-on' experience of the identification and analysis of relevant data. It is also opening up new ways of applying old research techniques, particularly in the area of mass surveys. However, it could not be said that it is revolutionizing political science research; rather, it is opening up new and more cost effective ways of undertaking research.

Chapter 9

Elite Interviewing

This chapter is concerned with a technique particularly used by political scientists, elite interviewing. It explains what is distinctive about this technique and examines the problems associated with its use. Researchers using this technique need to decide who they are going to see, how they are going to access their interview targets, the best way to conduct the interview and how they should analyse the results. When it is carried out effectively, this technique can make a considerable contribution to the understanding of political phenomena.

The majority of work by political scientists is concerned with the study of decision-makers and hence a key research technique for political scientists is what is known as elite interviewing. This may be defined both in terms of the *target group* being studied, an 'elite' of some kind, and the *research technique* used, most characteristically what is known as semi-structured interviewing. It is often the most effective way to obtain information about decision-makers and decision-making processes. More generally, 'elite interviewing can be used whenever it is appropriate to treat a respondent as an expert about the topic in hand' (Leech, 2002a, p.663).

Unlike, for example, electoral studies where the balance of knowledge and expertise is usually in favour of the interviewer, elite interviewing is characterized by a situation in which the balance is usually in favour of the respondent. This is because of their high levels of knowledge of the subject matter under discussion and their general intellectual and expressive abilities. Techniques that work very well with surveys of the electorate where each voter has one vote may not be appropriate. Indeed, one of the defining characteristics of elite interviewing is that some respondents may count more than others in terms of their influence on the decision-making process.

In survey interviewing, the emphasis is on standardization. The respondent is presented with a structured questionnaire and interviewers are trained so that the questionnaire is administered in a standardized way. Any variation should arise from the respondent's views rather than the research instrument or its administration. In practice, this may not be easy to achieve, but the techniques and expertise developed and accumulated through many decades of survey research are intended to maximize standardization. In elite interviewing, standardization may hinder the successful completion of the research. Not only may the approach used differ from one project to another, but interviews within a single project may have to be handled differently. There is no standard set of techniques that can be applied, although this chapter will attempt to offer some guidelines.

Despite its centrality in the study of politics, there is not a very large literature on elite interviewing. Three of the most useful studies are Dexter (1970); Moyser and Wagstaffe (1987); and Rubin and Rubin (1995). Burnham (1997) contains a number of studies in which PhD students reflect on their own experience of elite interviewing. In part the lack of a literature may be because it is difficult to generalize from a series of 'how it was for me' studies. The paucity of the literature requires that this chapter should give more specific guidance to intending researchers about the practical use of the technique. It is possible to derive some guidelines based on the work that has been undertaken. The broader methodological issues raised by the technique are returned to at the end of the chapter.

The key guideline must be not to base any piece of work entirely on elite interviewing. This is consistent with the principle of triangulation which 'entails using more than one method or source of data in the study of social phenomena' (Bryman, 2001, p.274). 'The best research on elites has utilized a combination of methodological approaches to deepen the research findings' (Hertz and Imber, 1995, p.ix). One should also use other sources and techniques such as archives, materials on the Internet and observation at meetings of, for example, legislative bodies. In some cases, of course, elite interviewing may serve as a supplementary technique. For example, a student may be undertaking an archive-based project, but may also interview key individuals who are still alive.

Researchers using elite interviewing as a technique must cover four key points:

(a)   decide who you want to see;
(b)   get access and arrange the interview;
(c)   conduct the interview;
(d)   analyse the results.

Decide who you want to see

It is self-evident that who you want to see will be determined by the purposes of your study. Let us suppose that, as is popular in contemporary political science, you are seeking to study a particular policy community or policy network. One of your concerns will be to establish which actors are included in the community or network and what its boundaries are. Reading secondary sources and visiting websites may give you some ideas about who is included and who is excluded.

Conventional sampling techniques will not usually help you in elite interviewing unless you are going to use a standardized questionnaire and a mass sample. This is not appropriate, however, in most elite studies as respondents are not of equal weight. A more usual technique is what is referred to as 'snowball' or 'referral' sampling. In practice, this means that you start out with a few key informants that you have identified from your literature and Internet search. You then ask them to name other key individuals you should see who are relevant to your study. Your 'snowball' thus grows larger and larger as you gain access to a network of individuals in a particular policy arena. There may be national variations in the effectiveness of this technique depending on the density of elite interconnections. 'German elites are strongly characterised by dense sectoral and territorial networks, so that if you are able to secure access at one point, you will be more than likely to be recommended to others within the network' (Paterson and Grix, 2000, p.18).

The problem then becomes when to stop. The most frequently asked question posed by students who intend to use elite interviewing in their research is 'How many respondents should I interview?' There is no simple answer to this question, as in large part it should be determined by the objectives and purposes of your study. Sometimes it is possible to interview the whole universe of respondents when the total number is relatively small. For example, as part of a study of the relationship between bankers and farmers, it was possible to interview all nine heads of agricultural departments in the main English and Irish banks, plus their equivalents in three specialist agricultural lending institutions (Grant and MacNamara, 1996, pp.427–37).

What one has to bear in mind is that elite interviewing is a very time-intensive technique. If one adds together the time involved in setting up the interview; travelling to and from it; the interview itself; preparing the transcript; and analysing the transcript, then a figure of at least twelve hours per interview is not unrealistic. Berry (2002, p.680) estimates that transcription takes two hours for every half-hour of interview. Ten interviews will consume 120 hours of research time, or three 'standard' working weeks. It is important for a researcher to consider how much time to allow for interviewing in terms of the overall time budget for the thesis or project.

In practice, it is relatively unusual for a researcher to undertake insufficient interviews or to neglect to interview key actors. Rather, the contrary is the case: researchers tend to undertake too many interviews, thus extending the completion time for the project. A point is reached where each additional interview yields diminishing returns. One needs to be able to recognize when the 'saturation point' is reached in a series of interviews where each interview is adding relatively little to the stock of information or understanding. Bearing in mind all these caveats, 20–30 interviews might be a reasonable target for a project in which elite interviewing was the principal method. For example, the well-regarded study of the Treasury by Deakin and Parry (2000) was based on 30 interviews with senior officials.

Get access and arrange the interview

The biggest problem in getting an access to a member of an elite group is that such individuals are usually very busy and they have to be provided with some convincing motivation for seeing a researcher. Goldstein (2002, p.669) comments, 'Frankly, "getting the interview" is more art than science and, with few exceptions, political scientists are not particularly well known for [their] skill at the art of "cold calling" '. In a study carried out in Russia it took 15–20 calls to arrange a single interview (Rivera, Kozyreva and Sarovskii, 2002, p, 683). One PhD student found that a government department had decided not to give interviews to research students. As Stedward writes (1997, pp.153–4), 'it's worth pointing out to interviewees some benefit of their participation (if you can't think of one, then ask yourself why anyone would agree to be interviewed by you!)' Most usually, this will be because they are interested in the topic you are researching.

There are probably certain advantages in this respect in being a researcher in a foreign country, or at least in a stable democracy. Drawing on their experience of elite interviewing in Russia, Rivera, Kozyreva and Sarovskii note (2002, p.684), 'respondents in more politically unstable environments may be a good deal more suspicious about the goals and purposes of the research project'. Nevertheless, respondents outside your home country may consider that they will learn something from you about policy design and implementation in your own country that may be of use to them. As Paterson and Grix caution UK researchers (2000, p.18), 'make sure that you are not only well informed of your German research topic, but also the UK equivalent, be it a company, policy or attitude, as interviewees will often ask about them'.

Some elites are more difficult to access than others. Members of legislatures tend to be saturated by requests for research interviews. It is characteristic of business elites that they 'are quite good at insulating themselves from unwanted disturbance' (Thomas, 1995, p.4). Non-governmental organizations, on the other hand, are usually quite keen to have opportunities to put their case across. Before research is started, one of the design questions that should be confronted is whether the target group is likely to be accessible.

Stedward (1997) offers some good practical advice on what she calls *negotiating* access, including a sample letter sent to a potential respondent. As Stedward points out (p.153), particularly in large organizations, it is important 'to target appropriate individuals to interview'. In order to do this, one has to gather as much information about the organization as possible. In the case of public sector bodies, websites or directories may include lists of officials and short descriptions of their duties (e.g., the Civil Service List in the UK).

Having identified your target, you need to contact them by letter (or, if you have the address, preferably by e-mail). Researchers should provide a concise and honest account of what the research is about, what they are seeking to achieve, and why they wish to interview the particular person approached. It may be necessary to follow up the initial contact with a telephone call and this may require getting round the 'gatekeepers' the targeted individual has surrounded herself or himself with. As Stedward comments (1997, p.154), 'The way you handle the phone call is as important as the letter. The best advice I can give is based on my own experience, and it is very simple: be prepared, polite and persistent.'

One risk when dealing with a large organization is of being fobbed off. In some large organizations, you may find yourself being shunted to someone with a title such as 'Director of Lateral Planning', a not particularly well-regarded official who can be kept occupied talking to inquisitive researchers. This is probably less of a problem than it was in the past, as personnel policies have become more ruthless. One way of dealing with such a situation is to appeal to the vanity of the person concerned and ask them to set up interviews with more powerful or relevant members of the organization.

A more common problem is to find yourself placed in a public relations programme designed as a 'one size fits all' option for anyone from a foreign dignitary to a researcher. In such situations the researcher should try to negotiate to see the key interview targets either then or on a subsequent occasion. Again, appealing to the professional skills of the public relations person may work as they may want to show that they can meet any reasonable request.

Sometimes you will be invited to lunch. This is to be avoided if at all possible (lunch after the interview is a different matter as it may lead to valuable revelations in a more informal setting). It is difficult to know whether to concentrate on eating or talking (it would be discourteous to eat little). It is difficult to take notes and eat, and the tape recorder may pick up a lot of background noise.

Researchers need to be realistic about the number of interviews they can undertake in one day. If you manage to fit two into a day, given the scheduling constraints of most elite group members, you are doing well. There is a need to allow flexibility in the timetable as the interview may be rearranged once or twice. This can be infuriating, but the researcher needs to be patient: the interview is more important to the researcher than it is to the respondent. In a busy city, sufficient time has to be allowed to travel from one location to another. Researchers need to budget some 'buffer time' anyway for a first review of their notes or recordings. Elite interviewing is very demanding for the researcher in terms of the level of concentration required and some recovery time is needed. Harrison recalls (2001, p.101) 'three interviews of forty-five to sixty minutes was my personal best; after this, I began to suffer from writer's cramp and my brain was struggling to function'.

As in all types of interviewing, the initial impression the respondent forms is important. Knowing how to dress for interviews poses some difficult problems. The cardinal rule is that researchers should avoid drawing attention to themselves by their dress; it is the questions to be asked that the researcher requires the respondent to focus on. Very conservative dress is not always appropriate. Thomas recalls (1995, p.15):

> I routinely don a (conservative) navy suit; however, in a computer company I found that I stood out like a sore thumb by comparison to the pullover sweater and slacks that were the norm . . .

people chided me for dressing too much like a consultant – a comment that was tantamount to an insult.

It is important to arrive on time for your interview. Arriving late creates an unprofessional impression and may cut down the time available. The interviewee may, of course, arrive late, something that reflects the balance of power in the interview. That cannot be avoided, but researchers need to sort out the logistics of the interview beforehand. They should make sure that they know the location of the interview site beforehand (this is particularly important in long streets where they could find themselves half a mile or more from their destination). Plan to arrive in the vicinity ten to fifteen minutes beforehand: one can always browse in a shop or have a cup of coffee. Remember that in some buildings security checks may take some time. Allow time to get from the reception desk to the actual location of the interview. These may seem trivial points, but there is nothing worse than arriving for an interview that has taken much planning and effort to secure late and flustered.

Conduct the interview

The cardinal rule for conducting the interview is: be prepared. It is waste of time asking questions which can be answered from the Internet or published sources. The respondent will respect the researcher more if s/he can show that s/he is familiar with the subject matter and can ask well informed and penetrating questions. Instead of providing generalities or platitudes as answers, the respondent will then engage in a fruitful dialogue with the researcher.

Most interviews are conducted by a single individual, but sometimes research partners will conduct the interview together. In that case, it is important to have agreed in advance who will cover which topics and what the general approach to the interview will be. Sometimes researchers are faced with more than one respondent. This is not an easy situation to handle, as it is difficult to know who to look at or respond to, particularly if the different roles of those present are not made clear. This can always be probed by asking, 'So your main responsibility is . . .?'

One of the most vexed practical questions in elite interviewing is whether to use a tape recorder or take notes (if a researcher does use a recorder, they should take back-up notes anyway). A tape recorder gives a complete record of the meeting, but it may inhibit respondents from being as frank as they would be in its absence. Cultural differences can be important here. Experience suggests that North American respondents are usually comfortable with a tape recorder, British respondents less so (although not Irish respondents). With the exception of a few interviews at a senior level, Deakin and Parry (2000, p.12) were able to tape their interviews at the British Treasury. Unlike earlier researchers on the Treasury, their experience 'was that the inhibiting effect was minimal and the advantage of generating a text agreed between subject and interviewers was very substantial'. 'German elites in general are likely to agree to use of tape recorders in interviews . . . but the higher the interviewee up the hierarchical scale, the less likely you are to get a frank answer' (Paterson and Grix, 2000, p.18). Researchers using a tape recorder should ask permission to do so at the beginning of the meeting. Good miniature models with attached microphones are available on the market. Ensure beforehand that the batteries are fully charged and that the machine is working properly! It should also be noted that the transcription time for a typical taped interview will be much longer than for an interview at which notes have been taken.

Elite studies, particularly of legislators, have been successfully carried out using standardized questionnaires (see, for example, Presthus, 1973 and 1974). Equally, there may be occasions in the early stages of a research project when a few unstructured interviews would help the development of the research design. Such an interview would take the form of an exploratory conversation around a structured theme. Thus, with this format 'the researcher suggests the subject for discussion but has few specific suggestions in mind' (Rubin and Rubin, 1995, p.5). This form of interview may be useful when the researcher still has a limited understanding of a topic. Their very lack of structure, however, means 'that the interviews will not be a very consistent source of reliable data across interviews' (Leech, 2002a, p.665).

The semi-structured interview does not follow one common format. 'Many qualitative interviews have both more structured and less structured parts but vary in the balance between them' (Rubin and Rubin, 1995, p.5). Despite their variability, three general propositions may be made about such interviews.

First, the respondent will have a list of topics or questions s/he wants to cover. These may take the form of precisely formulated questions, as in the example provided by Stedward (1997, pp.164–5). More experienced interviewers may consider that standardization of the form in which most questions is put is of secondary importance as the answers are not usually quantified. They are more comfortable working from a list of topics. 'In contrast to a predefined questionnaire, the interview guide is used as a check-list of topics to be covered, although the order in which they are not discussed is not pre-ordained' (Devine, 1995, p.138). In any case, the questions asked will vary depending on the particular expertise of the respondent.

Second, there is a need to prioritize the topics to be covered. The length of interviews can vary considerably. Charles Raab (1987, p.120) probably holds the UK all comers' record for an interview lasting fifteen hours. More typically, a busy individual may set aside 45 minutes or one hour for an interview, a time which cannot usually be extended. Everything has to be covered in the time made available. As Stedward says (1997, p.155) there is no point in asking a question if one can get the information elsewhere. In broad terms, questions or topics may be classified as 'essential', 'necessary' and 'desirable'. Essential questions are those which, if they are not answered, would mean that the interview is a failure. Necessary questions are those which are important to the project and should be covered if at all possible. Desirable questions are those that can be inserted if time permits.

Third, the interviewer must not seek to impose too rigid a frame-work on the interview. 'Qualitative interviewing requires listening carefully enough to hear the meanings, interpretations, and under-standings that give shape to the worlds of the interviewes.' (Rubin and Rubin, 1995, p.7). The interviewer must allow the respondent to open up new topics that may lead to areas of inquiry that had not been previously considered. 'The advantage of the informal inter-view is that it leaves the investigation open to new and unexpected information' (Daugbjerg, 1998, p.15). There needs to be a willing-ness to redefine the objectives and the scope of the project in terms of the material obtained from the interviews. 'Interviewees can confirm or reject one's initial interpretations and, consequently, make the subsequent analysis more precise' (Daugbjerg, 1998, p.16).

Within the interview, a delicate balance has to be maintained between, on the one hand, covering the ground the researcher thinks is important and, on the other hand, allowing the respondent to open up new areas without going off on irrelevant tangents. It is questionable whether one should follow Bryman's (2001, p.312) advice that 'In qualitative interviewing, "rambling" or going off at tangents is often encouraged – it gives insight into what the intervie-wee sees as relevant and important.' One wants to understand the respondent's definition of the situation, but one is also trying to place that definition in the context of a theoretically informed research project. One cannot let the respondent entirely control the interaction. Striking the right balance is one of the most difficult tasks in elite interviewing, given the balance of authority between the interviewer and the respondent, and the fact that respondents tend to do most of the talking. Harrison notes (2001, p.102), 'a careful balance needs to be struck here between the methodological need to remain "neutral" and the practicalities of getting a respondent talk or cutting them short if they are going off on a tangent'. It requires a combination of firmness and tact. Harrison advises (2001, p.102), 'if you want to "steer" the discussion into a certain direction, you must *never* show your approval or disapproval of a voiced opinion, but signal your understanding or interest in a particular topic in more "neutral" terms'.

The interview experience may, of course, differ considerably in terms of the effects of the cultural context within which it is conducted. Reflecting on her interviewing experience in Japan, Koen notes (1997, p.32) 'In Western countries, people want precise questions and will give you as precise an answer as possible. In Japan this did not seem to work.' One strategy suggested by local experts was to ask very broad and general questions. Another was to keeping asking the same question in a slightly different form.

Proceeding from a basic model suggested by Rubin and Rubin (1995), the interview may be seen as going through a series of stages. These can be seen as a means of developing rapport between the interviewer and the respondent. 'Rapport means more than just putting people at ease. It means convincing people that you are listening, that you are understand and are interested in what they are talking about, and that they should continue talking' (Leech, 2002b, p.665).

The opening stage begins with some informal conversation structured by the exchange of business cards (having one is essential as this is a key ritual, especially in East Asian countries, as well as giving you information about how you can contact the respondent again). One needs to establish an atmosphere of mutual trust without being grovelling or sycophantic. Cultural factors will be important in this stage of the interview. For example, informal directness characterizes the USA, especially the west coast.

There should then be some discussion of the purposes of the research. Respondents vary in terms of how much they want to know (they will normally have been sent a short description in advance). On the whole, it is better to offer too much than too little, but without consuming too much interview time.

Early questions should deal with matters that the interviewee certainly knows about and feels good about. In this respect unstandardized approaches are similar to more standardized forms of interviewing by starting with questions that do not challenge the respondent too much and building rapport. Opening questions also provide an opportunity to steer the interview by indicating what the interviewer knows about already and what s/he wants to explore. For example, Grant's opening question in an interview with a Californian legislative aide was: 'I'm fairly familiar, I hope, with the structure of Californian politics, I know in general how things work, what I'm not sure about is how things work in relation to air quality management, as far as the Senate is concerned. There seem to be a number of committees involved.'

As the interview progresses, one moves into the more central questions. For example, in the interview cited above, a key question was 'How much are people concerned in this about the whole issue of global climate change?' As the interview progresses and rapport develops, one can move into more difficult or sensitive questions. In the cited interview, the legislative aide was asked about a prominent state senator, 'Is he a bit politically isolated?' The initial response was, 'He tends to be very independent within the Democratic Party, I guess that's a gracious way to say it', before proceeding to a very full analysis of the strengths and limitations of his position.

Probing can play an important role in successful interviewing. 'Insufficient probing indicates boredom or inattention: too much probing and the researcher turns into an inquisitor' (Rubin and Rubin, 1995, p.150). The Rubins distinguish usefully between three types of probe. Continuation probes signal for more detail. They may even be executed non-verbally, but typically would be questions like 'So what happened next?' Clarification probes are used when it is unclear what is being said. An example would be 'Could you say a little more about that?' Completion probes return to something that was said earlier such as 'You said earlier that . . .'

At the end of the interview, respondents should be given an opportunity to say whether there any aspects of the topic being discussed which have not been covered which they think are important. There should be a quick summary of any documents, names and addresses or other information to be exchanged subsequently. Casual conversation may resume. This may lead to more valuable information being made available.

Bizarre incidents can sometimes disrupt an interview. Stedward comments (1997, p.158) 'It's an obvious point, but no less important for that, to caution against interviews conducted under the influence of alcohol.' In practice, following this counsel may be difficult if the respondent arrives at the interview already drunk. There is no easy way to deal with incidents such as these, but they emphasize that successful interviewing requires good interpersonal skills. These include a certain level of self-confidence balanced by a willingness to listen and learn from others.

Respondents may ask to see a transcript of the interview or chapter drafts. Such requests can yield additional information or helpful comments. They do not usually lead to an attempt to censor the results or exercise undue influence on them. In ethical terms, such requests would seem to be reasonable and help to ensure access for future interviewers.

Although the interview needs to have some structure if the results are going to meet research objectives, it is important to avoid dominating the interview and to let the respondent's voice come through. It is their perception of the situation that researchers can obtain from this type of interviewing.

The contribution of interviews to the research may well change as it proceeds. In the early stages, there may be many themes that interest the researcher who will be defining, refining and exploring them. In the central part of the research process, the researcher will have become more selective and will be focusing on a more limited range of themes. In the final interviews, the interviewer may wish to check emerging interpretations with respondents.

Follow-up interviews with respondents do not generally yield good results. Particular points may be pursued by e-mail or on the telephone. If one does go back to people on repeated occasions, a professional relationship may become personal, reducing the research utility of the transaction. There is also a danger of becoming over-reliant on 'key informants' who, although they may be 'inside dopesters', are offering their own particular interpretation of events which may 'capture' the researcher. Indeed, this would be a key distinction between the use of interviewing by journalists and researchers.

Once a standardized questionnaire has been designed and implemented (an expensive exercise), the researcher is stuck with the results it has yielded. With semi-structured interviewing, the researcher can redesign the questions as the research proceeds to take account of new themes. This does not mean that the researcher should lose sight of the original goals of the research or its central theme, but it is possible to take account of new topics revealed by the research.

Ultimately, elite interviewing is a technique in which, even if practice does not make perfect, experience is invaluable. One way of trying to give students some prior experience is through role-playing exercises. Some people are, however, more temperamentally suited to being good interviewers than others. As Stedward observes (1997, p.152), 'given the nature of the research method, you should also give some consideration as to whether it is right for you. Techniques can be learned and skills developed, but it is an unalterable fact that some people will never make good interviewers because they are uncomfortable with the process.' Harrison warns (2001, p.102), 'close face-to-face involvement with your subjects means that this way of exploring controversial issues is not for the sensitive or faint-hearted'. Researchers should confront issues of this kind before embarking on their research.

Analyse the results

After the interview the researcher should read through the notes taken or listen to the tape as soon as possible. If any parts of the notes are difficult to read, they should be clarified while the interview is still fresh in the researcher's mind. From the notes or tape, the researcher should highlight any new points that need to be followed up in subsequent interviews. Harrison notes (2001, p.102), 'the transcription process for me proved crucial in that it allowed me to become "familiar" with my data by milling over them time and again'.

Researchers should try and build in routines of self-evaluation. After each interview, they should reflect carefully on what is going right or wrong. Are the interviews covering the topics the researcher wants to cover? If not, is the researcher allowing the balance of the interview to swing too much in favour of the respondent? Alternatively, is the researcher adhering to too rigid an interview structure or leading the respondent towards particular kinds of answers? Is the understanding of the topic too broad or narrow? Is there anything that could be excluded? Are there new angles that have to be followed up?

The researcher should then code the data to pick out themes. The point of this task is to make a judgement about the data in the light of the theoretical framework. One can use a very simple coding frame, numbering topics or themes from one to N and then putting a note in the margin of a copy of the interview whenever they occur. There are computer programmes (the best known are Nudist and Qualidata) which allow the researcher to analyse qualitative data, and these may be particularly useful if the researcher is engaged in some kind of content analysis. If the research is concerned with the interpretation of meaning as it is constructed by respondents, such an approach may be too mechanistic.

Particular care needs to be taken in writing up data of this kind. It is essential that early on in the analysis, as part of the general discussion of methodological issues, the researcher provides a short account of the way elite interviewing techniques were used in the research. This should include a discussion of their importance relative to other techniques. Publications should include a table categorizing the respondents interviewed (e.g., Commission officials 8, UK government officials 6, German government officials 7, EU level lobbyists 6, and so on).

Quotation from the elite interviews can do a great deal to enliven a publication. However, there is a risk of making excessive use of quotations. One does not want sections of a book, article or thesis to be nothing more than a series of quotations with linking sentences. In particular, researchers should not place too much reliance on any one respondent, however eloquent they may be or however much their views may support the argument being made. A journalist may be happy with selective quotations that happen to support the particular line taken in the story, but researchers have a duty to consider conflicting explanations and contradictory points of view.

Conclusions

Elite interviewing may lead to good (topical, interesting, incisive) writing about political themes and that is no bad thing given the turgid character of much contemporary political science literature. However, is it good social science? This in part depends on what one defines as good social science. Critics portray qualitative research 'as being unrepresentative and atypical. Its findings are impressionistic, piecemeal, and even idiosyncratic' (Devine, 1995, p.141). Quantitative data sets can be re-examined by other researchers. Records of qualitative interviews can also be opened for scrutiny by other researchers, although problems of respondent confidentiality may arise. Even if they are available, they may not reveal how the nature of the interaction between the interviewer and the respondent has affected the data. Two researchers might interpret the same data in very different ways.

However, if one is interested in actors' perceptions of the world in which they live, the way in which they construct their world and the shared assumptions which shape it, there is much to be said for the model of the elite interview as an extended conversation. The advantages of qualitative research are clear 'where the goal of a piece of research is to explore people's experiences, practices, values and attitudes in depth and to establish their meaning for those concerned' (Devine, 2002, p.207). The way in which is this exploration is conducted is, however indirectly, informed by the theoretical concerns of social scientists and is undertaken by a researcher seeking to gather data systematically to pursue defined questions in a reflective fashion. 'While quantitative research is usually reliable, qualitative research tends to be valid' (Devine, 1995, p.146). It is certainly not difficult to identify classic political science texts which have been based on elite interviewing (e.g., Heclo and Wildavsky, 1974).

The reality of modern democracy is that many political decisions are taken by small groups of highly qualified and knowledgeable individuals. The term 'policy community' may have fallen out of fashion, but many 'under-ventilated' (Heclo and Wildavsky, 1974, p.xx) policy communities remain in existence. The shared assumptions and meanings which inform these private worlds still require exploration, and elite interviewing remains the most appropriate technique. It is a technique whose exercise benefits from the accumulation of experience, but it is also accessible to students starting out on their research careers. Elite interviewing brings the world of the practitioner and the academic together in a hopefully fruitful mutual dialogue.

This chapter has tried to explore some of the issues and problems that arise in elite interviewing and to offer some practical guidance. Elite interviewers must be prepared to explore the world of the respondent sympathetically without being captured by it. They must have a research design that is flexible and open to new ideas and interpretations, while still being informed by an over-arching theoretical framework and a central research question. There is a limit to the utility of the advice that can be offered, as much depends on the ability of the researcher in managing a series of pressures (of time, of interpretation and of judgement). Nevertheless, skilfully executed elite interviewing can add significantly to our stock of political knowledge and understanding.

The further methodological development of elite interviewing must be related to the current emphasis on seeing qualitative and quantitative approaches to research as complementary rather than competitive. Devine notes (2002, p.207) that 'To date . . . there have been few genuine attempts in political science to bring quantitative and qualitative data together to address consistencies as well as inconsistencies.' This theme is one that is returned to in Chapter 12.

Chapter 10

Participant Observation and the Analysis of Communications

Introduction

This chapter introduces three contrasting methods of research. First, it looks at participant observation, which is a qualitative research strategy which is popular in anthropology and sociology but has been relatively little used in political science. Second, it examines two methods of analysing communications: content analysis, which attempts to be precise, scientific and quantitative; and discourse analysis, which, like participant observation, is a qualitative technique but is becoming quite fashionable as a research strategy in social science.

Participant observation, or ethnographic research as it is now widely called, has rarely been used by political scientists. This is surprising as it seems a very appropriate research strategy in certain political situations, for example in studying small political groups and movements, especially those on the fringes of the political system which may adopt a culture of secrecy. Researchers who have used this method argue that it is able to provide accurate and useful insights into these small political movements and to explain why people join them and remain as members in spite of existing in a hostile political environment (D. Scott, 1975, p.214). To understand why people join revolutionary movements or far-right groups and to appreciate their motivations and rationalizations, it would seem that participant observation is a better strategy than, for example, semi-structured interviewing or a social survey.

Content analysis refers to any technique used for drawing inferences by objectively and systematically identifying specified characteristics of messages (Holsti, 1969, p.14). It was stimulated by the explosion in communications produced by governments and the media after the Second World War. Content analysis is a quantitative technique for analysing communications and was particularly popular during the

Cold War when it was used to analyse the content of Soviet communications, especially in the newspapers and television.

Discourse analysis is a more qualitative technique for analysing communications. It has become extremely popular as a method of analysis and has spread from linguistics and semiotics to the social sciences, including politics and international relations.

Participant observation

Participant observation (Box 10.1) has been defined as 'a process in which an investigator establishes a many-sided and relatively long-term relationship with a human association in its natural setting for the purpose of developing a scientific understanding of that association' (Loftland and Loftland 1984). More concisely, it is 'a research strategy in which the observer's presence in a social situation is maintained for the purpose of scientific investigation' (Schwartz and Schwartz, 1955).

Box 10.1   Definition of participant observation

Participant observation is a research strategy whereby the researcher becomes involved in a social situation for the purpose of understanding the behaviour of those engaged in the setting. The involvement can be intense or slight, open or covert, but extends over a significant period of time. The researcher observes and records the behaviour of the people in the social setting and may collect additional evidence through formal or informal interviews and the collection of documentary materials. The outcome of the research is a detailed account of the activities and behaviour of those involved in the social situation.

Source: adapted from Loftland and Loftland (1984), p.12.

As a research methodology, participant observation was first developed by social and cultural anthropologists to study groups and communities belonging to cultures different from that of the investigator. The aim was to describe accurately, and in detail, the customs, rituals, institutions and belief systems of those communities and therefore provide accurate information about groups which were relatively unknown to western scholarship. Classic works were published on such groups as the Trobriand islanders (Malinowski 1922), Andaman Islanders (Radcliffe-Brown, 1964) and the

Samoans (Mead, 1954). These studies showed the diversity of human institutions and behaviour that had developed in different societies across the world.

These early studies were criticized for making unrealistic assumptions about these communities, for neglecting the research context, and for failing to live up to their aspirations. Thus researchers often wrongly assumed that the communities they studied were isolated and had distinct boundaries. They neglected to research the colonial context within which they were embedded, and sometimes their research was not as accurate as they claimed it to be (Freeman, 1984). The researchers often wrongly assumed that the groups studied would not be significantly disturbed or influenced by the presence and activities of the researcher and that accurate and complete observations and records could be made of the cultural, social, religious and political lives of the community, despite the constraints of gender, culture and language that inevitably handicapped the researcher.

Participant observation established itself as the core field methodology in anthropology and quickly spread to sociology, where it has been successfully used for studying groups and communities in modern societies which otherwise would be difficult to access and research. Groups defined as marginal, criminal or excluded have been widely researched by sociologists using participant observation. Classic studies in sociology include Whyte's study of an Italian community in Boston (Whyte, 1993), Becker's study of drug users (Becker, 1963) and Humphreys' study of gay men (Humphreys, 1970). In Britain, groups as diverse as gypsies (Okely, 1983), the civil rights movement (Purdie, 1990), women drug users (Taylor, 1993) and football hooligans (Giulianotti, 1995) have been studied in this way (see Box 10.2).

In political science, the use of participant observation as a research strategy has been relatively rare. Major examples were the studies by Richard Crossman of the roles of cabinet minister and backbencher (Crossman, 1975; Morgan, 1981). Crossman was involved in politics as both an enthusiastic participant and also as a social scientist. He wrote, 'Unlike most of my colleagues in the Council chamber [a reference to local politics] and in Parliament, I was an observer as well as a doer, a political scientist as well as a journalist MP' (Crossman, 1975, p.11). Crossman wanted to make a major academic contribution to the study of Cabinet government and British politics. He wrote: 'My ambition was to write a book which fulfilled for one generation the functions of Bagehot's *English Constitution* a hundred years ago, by disclosing the secret

Box 10.2   Participant observation case study

The problems of finding an appropriate methodology to research particular communities are well illustrated in Okely's research on Traveller-Gypsies. Her sponsors wanted her to carry out 'scientific' research involving questionnaires, large samples and quantitative analysis that would be representative of Traveller-Gypsies as a whole. This, the sponsors felt, would make the research more authoritative and would therefore influence administrators and policy-makers. However, attempts to administer a lengthy questionnaire by a local council official proved hopeless. The Gypsies' answers were 'brilliantly inconsistent' and impossible to code. A scientific sample could not be obtained. Gradually it was accepted by the sponsors that participant observation provided more reliable, accurate and detailed evidence of Gypsy attitudes, opinions and behaviour (Okely, 1983, pp.38–9).

operations of government, which are concealed by the thick masses of foliage which we call the myth of democracy' (Crossman, 1975, p.11). Crossman thus used his position as a political insider to be not only a backbencher and a cabinet minister but also a participant observer. In particular, he wished to test his hypothesis about the power of the prime minister.

Crossman kept a detailed diary, dictating the events of each day on to a tape. His observations lack the rigour and systematic collection of data associated with positivist research methods and he makes no attempt at impartial and objective analysis. In fact, he records his own forthright views as part of his data. Nevertheless, his diaries provide a detailed and fascinating account of his work and activities as a backbencher and cabinet minister. At the time of their publication, they were a breakthrough, as previously such accounts had had to be carefully vetted and rendered anodyne. It is noteworthy that the government attempted to prevent publication of the Crossman Diaries on the grounds that they needed official approval to be published; however, the courts allowed publication to go ahead.

Participant observation in action

The participant observer shares in the life of the community being studied, being involved consciously and systematically, as far as circumstances allow, in the activities of the group and even in their interests and affections. If this aim is achieved, there will be two consequences: first, the subjects of the study will learn to take the research for granted and will thus behave almost as though he or she were not there; and second, the researcher will get 'under the skin' of his/her subjects and learn to think almost as they think. Whyte argues that 'if people accept you – you can just hang around and you can learn the answers in the long run without even having to ask the questions' (Whyte, 1993, p. 303).

Much deeper knowledge about the motivations, beliefs and behaviour of individuals and groups is thus obtained by participant observation. The views of individuals can be compared with their behaviour and, as time progresses, greater knowledge and understanding of the individuals and community is acquired. Because the observer, as a researcher, is at least to some extent detached from the groups and the situation, comparisons can be made with other groups in similar situations.

To be successful, participant observation requires a high degree of commitment by the researcher. The social scientist must study the group or community over a long period, normally for several months or even years. This long-term involvement allows researchers considerable opportunities to modify and change their original hypotheses and theories during the course of the research process. As new data and evidence are collected, the original hypotheses may be rejected and new ones developed which can then also be tested. Participant observation thus allows for constant modifications in the research design as the project evolves. As Gans argues, 'one of the major pleasures of participant observation is to come across unexpected new topics of study' (Gans, 1967, p.xxi). This is in sharp contrast to more quantitative and deductive approaches to research where hypotheses are either confirmed or rejected as a result of specific testing procedures.

The traditional role of the scientist is that of a neutral observer who remains unchanged and uninfluenced by the objects of his or her research. However, the role of the participant observer is quite different. He or she must share in the activities and sentiments of those who are being studied. Thus the observer will be changed in the course of the investigation and the community or groups will also be changed to some extent by the presence of the researcher. However, researchers have found that although the observers becomes involved and changed by their role as participant observer, it is important to maintain a degree of detachment so as to maintain the role of observers and researcher, otherwise there is the risk of complete integration into the group. The observer must therefore negotiate a role which is acceptable to the group and where s/he can function as both participant and observer (Bruyn, 1962).

This problem of remaining detached and as objective as possible is one of the greatest challenges for the participant observer. The longer a researcher shares in the activities and experiences of the group being studied, and the more the researcher is accepted by the group, the greater the temptation to empathize with them. The researcher may thus gradually become integrated into the group or community and may lose the ability to criticize them. At that point the chance of giving a full account of the group, warts and all, may be lost, since it could become too painful to publish the negative side of the group's activities.

Community studies

There have been some well-known studies of urban communities using participant observation, and interestingly they show the limitations of this method for studying politics. Gans and his wife bought a house in a new suburb – Levittown, New Jersey – in order to study the dynamics of the creation of a new community and to challenge the denigration of suburban life that was common in academic circles. Gans used a combination of methods to collect his data, namely a questionnaire, semi-structured interviews and participant observation. He was most enthusiastic about the latter, which he felt was the only method 'that enables the researcher to get close to the realities of social life' (Gans, 1967, pp.449–50). Not surprisingly, Gans found it easier to study the associational life and community culture of Levittown than politics. He made an important distinction between the public performance of local government and the workings of actual (substantive) government as, in the latter case, key policy decisions were taken secretly in caucus meetings. Gans writes, 'The workings of actual government are hard to fathom for the caucus meets in total privacy, no minutes are kept, and no outsiders are permitted. The press cannot attend and I was refused admission even though I promised not to publish anything on what took place' (Gans, 1967, p.317). Thus while Gans felt he could access the realities of social life, he was unable to access fully the realities of political life.

In Britain, the Banbury Restudy highlighted some of the problems of using participant observation to study a sizeable community (Stacey *et al.*, 1975). The Banbury restudy was a second community study of the Oxfordshire town of Banbury, following an earlier study by Magaret Stacey (Stacey, 1960). The research team for the restudy was located in the same building as the local Labour Party and quickly became identified as part of the Labour Party network. While this opened some doors for the research, other doors were firmly closed. Thus the researchers quickly accumulated much more information and knowledge about Labour Party activities in the town than they learnt about the Conservatives, who were the dominant party in the community (Bell, 1977, p.52). The researchers found that it was more difficult than they expected working with the different political parties, even though the three researchers specialized in covering the major parties. The researchers also found that they became partisan about the parties they were researching and thus found it hard to agree on a common analysis. In fact, this specialization seems to have contributed to conflict within the research team (Bell, 1977, p.60). The personal strains of intensive field work, the problems of over-identification with particular groups and the difficulty of obtaining comprehensive coverage are all well illustrated in this study.

Types of participant observation

The literature on ethnographic fieldwork and participant observation in particular, makes distinctions between active and passive forms of investigation, the degree of involvement of the social scientist in the research process, and whether the observer's role is known to the subjects of the research or is concealed from them (Burgess, 1984). These distinctions have been used to develop ideal types of field research roles. The classic typology has been developed by Gold, who described four categories or ideal types of role. These were (1) 'the complete participant', (2) 'the participant as observer', (3) 'the observer as participant', and (4) 'the complete observer'. These ideal types describe roles the researcher can adopt in their research. The first two roles are those normally adopted by participant observers in the field. The last two categories seem rather peripheral to the idea of participant observation, although the third category, 'the observer as participant', can be modified to create a useful category of non-participating observer. The final category, 'the complete observer', does not involve participation at all and can therefore be ignored as a form of participant observation.

The complete participant
The complete participant involves the researcher in joining the group without revealing his identity as an observer. This strategy involves

ethical and methodological issues and is a source of considerable controversy. The researcher may decide that covert research is the best strategy because of fear that he or she would otherwise be denied access to the group. Even when less important and more accessible groups are the focus of research, social scientists may be nervous about being refused access. In these circumstances covert research may appear to be an attractive strategy.

Covert methods are also often justified on the grounds that the observer will have less impact on the groups observed and that the data will therefore be more valid and authentic: if you tell the subjects about your research this will influence their attitude towards you and hence their behaviour. If you do not tell them you may have a better chance of access (though possibly less if you are socially and culturally distanced from the group). The subjects will also have no reason to modify their attitudes and behaviour in your presence. But if you conceal your research role, then are you, as a researcher, being dishonest, unethical and acting as a social science spy?

The social science disciplines have strong codes of ethics which condemn covert methods of social research. The code of practice of the British Sociological Association (BSA) states:

As far as possible, sociological research should be based on the freely-given informed consent of those studied. This implies a responsibility on the sociologist to explain as fully as possible, and in terms meaningful to participants, what the research is about, who is undertaking and financing it, why it is being undertaken, and how it is to be promoted. (BSA, 1994)

Many social scientists take the view that

it is wrong for an inquirer ostensibly to take up membership in a community with the intention of conducting a sociological inquiry without making it plain that is what he is doing. His self-disclosure might occasionally hamper the research he is conducting but the degree of injury suffered does not justify the deviation from straightforwardness implied by withholding his true intentions. (Shils, 1979)

The most remarkable and controversial example of covert participant observation was carried out by Laud Humphreys in a study of gay men. He adopted the role of lookout voyeur to observe homosexual encounters in men's toilets. He took the registration numbers of his subjects' cars and, via contacts in the police, was able to obtain their addresses. A year later he interviewed a sample of the subjects under the pretext of carrying out a social health survey. In this way he was able to collect more information about them. Their names were kept confidential and the data were later destroyed (Kimmel, 1988, p.23). Not surprisingly, Humphreys' methods caused considerable controversy. He was accused of gross deceit, failure to observe the ethical standards of his profession and violating the privacy of a marginal and vilified group. On the other hand, his research was praised by some members of the gay community for shedding light on a little-known group and for helping to contradict commonly held stereotypes and myths.

Do groups who might refuse permission to researchers have a right to privacy, freedom from disturbance to their reputations and respect which might be undermined by research? The strong response of professional bodies is 'yes', and this is often reinforced by legislation (for example, in Canada and some American states, where researchers have to obtain informed consent from the subjects of their research).

However, there may be cases where the public interest is served by covert participant observation. The public has a right to know, for example, about organizations which put up candidates for public office or are thought to exercise influence on public policy; examples of such groups might be the National Front or the British National Party, the Freemasons and the Ku Klux Klan. However, many social scientists would argue strongly that covert research is not only unethical but also unnecessary. Groups and institutions are surprisingly willing to co-operate with bona fide researchers and to allow them access to their personnel and files. Heclo and Wildavsky, for example, obtained permission to do a study of the higher Civil Service in Britain and produced a fascinating study based on observation and informal interviewing. This study described the informal culture that existed in the executive branch of government, particularly in the Treasury (Heclo and Wildavsky, 1981). Even studying criminal groups is not impossible using open methods. Klockars' study of the professional fence encountered few problems, despite the fact that the author was open about his research intentions (Klockars, 1975). In Scotland, Giulianotti was able to study two rival groups of football hooligans (see Box 10.3) despite the problems of gaining access, and their culture of violence (Giulianotti, 1995).

Box 10.3   The research bargain

Giulianotti had been engaged in research on the Aberdeen Casuals, a group of football hooligans associated with this Premier League Scottish club. He wished to extend his research to an even more notorious group, the Hibs Casuals, a group associated with the Hibernian Football Club of Edinburgh. Giulianotti was concerned about the difficulties of gaining access to the group, first, as he was an Aberdonian, and second, as the Hibs Casuals had recently been targeted in the media as both criminals and violent, which might make them suspicious of approaches which they might suspect as being part of a police undercover operation. In the event he found that he had something to trade which made his presence tolerable to the Hibs Casuals: they were keen to know about the Casual scene in Aberdeen and to compare it with the situation in Edinburgh. Giulianotti was thus able to gain access to the Hibs Casuals but to retain his status as a researcher somewhat detached from the group and its activities. In exchange, he provided information about the Aberdeen Casuals (Giulianotti, 1995, pp.3–6).

The participant as observer

The participant as observer role involves situations where the researcher is open about his research and negotiates the agreement of the group to allow him or her to participate in their activities, but not to be fully integrated into the group because of his or her research role. The main distinction therefore between the complete participant and the participant as observer is that the latter does not conceal his or her research role.

The role of participant as observer is the strategy most often adopted by researchers engaged in such studies. It avoids the ethical problems associated with covert participant observation and enables researchers to prioritize their research. Thus Roy argues:

> The participant as observer not only makes no secret of his investigation; he makes it known that research is his overriding interest. He is there to observe . . . the participant observer is not tied down, he is free to run around as research interests beckon; he may move as the spirit listeth. (Roy, 1970, pp.216–44)

A critical issue for researchers undertaking the role of participant as observer is how access is negotiated to the community or group which they wish to study. These problems are well illustrated in Whyte's *Street Corner Society*, referred to earlier as one of the classic participant observation studies. Whyte came from an upper-middle-class family and knew little or nothing about working-class life in deprived areas. Imbued with ideas of social reform and intellectual curiosity, he decided to embark on a study of a slum district in Boston. Once he had chosen a district to research, Whyte was confronted with the problems of how and where to start. Initially he made various attempt to make contact with the people in Cornerville, which was the name he gave to the locality. Initial attempts through a housing survey and 'chatting up' young women proved unsuccessful, and finally a social worker introduced him to Doc, the leader of a street gang in the district. He calls the gang 'the Nortons'. Whyte explained his project in detail to Doc, who agreed to help Whyte to get as complete a picture of the community as possible (Whyte, 1993, p.291).

One danger of participant observation research is that of over-rapport, or the researcher being 'captured' by part of the organization or group being studied. In a study of a trade union branch the researcher, Miller, became very close to the trade union leaders. They provided him with lots of information, some of which was very confidential and delicate, in relation to the internal workings of the branch. The leaders co-opted him into friendship to such an extent that he was unable to question closely their attitudes and running of the branch. Challenges to their opinions and policies would have opened up severe conflict. Miller therefore felt he had to drop areas of investigation disapproved of by the leadership. Thus he not only learnt the views of the branch leaders but came to see the situation from their point of view. In other words, he was so attuned to the sentiments of the leaders that he became ill-attuned to the less clearly articulated feelings of the rank and file. He was captured by the branch leaders and became their agent (A. J. S. Miller, 1952, pp.97–9).

The observer as participant, or 'non-participant observer'
The 'observer as participant role' as described by Gold, covers situations in which contact with informants is brief, formal and openly classified as observation. He defines this role very narrowly, stating: 'The observer as participant role is used in studies involving one-visit interviews. It calls for relatively more formal observation than either informal observation or participation of any kind' (Gold, 1958). This definition of the third category of participant observation research is so narrow that in practice it fails to include any form of

participant observation. It can be replaced with a category which describes situations where the researcher has failed to negotiate the access he or she would have liked, and so conducts the research at some distance from the community or group under investigation. To distinguish it from Gold's definition, it can be redefined as that of *the non-participant observer*. The researcher's role is known and s/he is able to conduct the research but not with the level of intimacy and involvement that is characteristic of either the complete participant or the participant as observer roles. The role of non-participant observer is thus often imposed on social science researchers, either because they have failed to convince groups to allow them access, or because of the nature of the situation in which the research is being conducted. For example, a male researcher carrying out research in many situations would find it difficult or impossible to observe many activities of female groups and individuals. Similarly, a female researcher might find it difficult to access male domains. It would be hard, for example, for a female researcher to carry out research on an exclusively male group such as the Freemasons. In these kinds of situations, the researcher would occupy the observer as participant role or, more accurately, the non-participant observer role.

A good example of research using the non-participant observer role, as defined more broadly than by Gold, is the study of a Catholic community in Belfast described by Frank Burton in his book *The Politics of Legitimacy* (Burton, 1978). Burton lived in a working-class Catholic community in Belfast for eight months, staying in a house with two other English students. The house was used as a drop-in centre for young adolescents and some adults in the area, whom Burton used as informants about the local situation. Burton states that:

> most of the information I received came through general discussions between conversationalists in the house' . . . 'because of the relationships that were established in the house, we were introduced into the community through the clubs and through people's homes. This enabled me to see which groups in the community I had little contact with and those with whom I was well acquainted. (Burton, 1978, pp.166–7)

Burton argues that gradually, over time, his role as a student researcher was accepted in the local community but, because of the conflict situation in Belfast, this acceptance was only partial. Again he states:

That I was only a partial insider was never an entirely open topic of conversation. But enough had been shown to me to enable me to assess the significance of Fianna membership and to be seriously impressed by the militancy of these adolescents. I came to realise that the length of the war in Ireland has created potential cadres of youth who are able to assume IRA status when their age allows it (Burton, 1978, p.175)

The research that Burton undertook to describe how the political, ideological and military struggles in Belfast in the early 1970s are expressed within a local community was extremely ambitious and dangerous. He could not expect to gain insider status in a war situation and there is no evidence in his book that he ever met or interviewed members of the Irish Republican Army (IRA) group whom he argues ran the local community. His role as a partially accepted outsider is illustrated by the remark of one of his informants: 'I don't care if you are an army spy, I like you' (Burton, 1978, p.176).

Another example of the non-participant observer role is provided by Beynon's study, *Working for Ford* (Beynon, 1973). Beynon writes very little about his research methods, though it is clear that he never worked for Ford and was refused co-operation by the Ford management at the Halewood plant. This seems to have included being banned from entering the plant. Beynon's information about workers' experiences of working for Ford thus comes largely from interviewing workers in local pubs close to the plant and unstructured interviews with workers on picket lines. Shop stewards form a significant proportion of his interviewees (Beynon, 1973).

The studies by Burton and Beynon draw attention to the unsystematic and incomplete nature of participant observation research. Participant observation can be done by a single researcher, as in Whyte's study, *Street Corner Society*, or a team, as in the Banbury Restudy (Stacey *et al.*, 1975). But although the studies provide very rich data and can be full of insights, they are rarely systematic, quantifiable and representative. In Burton's study of a local community in Belfast, the informants are largely those young people and adults willing to drop in for recreation to the student house where he was living. These young people understood very well that there were certain issues they were not supposed to discuss as this might provide information to outsiders about the IRA or IRA activities. Burton also has little to say about the role of the Catholic Church in this community, which seems to be another limitation of his study.

Beynon's informants are similarly obtained in a haphazard

manner and it is impossible to know how representative they are. Many commentators draw attention to the danger of researchers seeking out like-minded people and in Beynon's account, *Working for Ford,* it seems very clear that he has sought out and interviewed people with similar political views to his own, thus giving his own hypotheses and views every chance of being confirmed and reinforced (Beynon, 1973).

One dimension of the non-participant observer role that is often emphasized is the brevity of the researchers' contacts with the subjects of the research and the research situation. Whyte lived in Cornerville for three-and-a-half years and developed a very rich and detailed knowledge of the members, the structure and the activities of the Norton Street gang. He also learnt a lot about the groups and institutions with which they came into contact. Although Burton stayed in Belfast for eight months, his knowledge and contacts with key institutions in the local community seem much more limited and partial. This is largely explained by the fact that he was studying a community at war. Thus although he argues that the local community was run by the IRA he was obviously unable to study this organization or interview any of its officials.

The attractions and problems of participant observation

The attractiveness of participant observation as a strategy for research is very great. It provides an opportunity for inductive methods of research, enabling researchers to spend lengthy periods of time in close contact with the people, groups, institutions or community that they are researching. The observer is able to collect a great deal of information in an informal and relaxed way, then use these observations to analyse and explain the situation under investigation. The longer s/he is in the research situation, the more the observer comes to understand and empathize with the subjects of his or her research. If researchers stumble across new information that they had not previously come across or anticipated, they can incorporate it in the analysis. In this way, participant observation is more flexible than a survey, where it would be harder to develop and test new hypotheses half-way through the project.

The results of participant observation studies tend to be highly readable and detailed accounts of small groups and communities. They are rich in details about the activities, beliefs and rationales of the groups. They are all the more interesting because they are generally about groups and communities that are little known to the reader (for example, gangs, sects, criminals or fringe political parties). Participant observation is often praised for its flexibility, because a wide variety of groups, tribes, communities and institutions have been studied using this approach. Indeed, it may be the only method of researching particular groups.

However, the problems of participant observation are formidable. Researchers need a regular routine and a systematic procedure for recording conversation, impressions and the activities of the group. They cannot rely on their memory and ability to recall conversations and events accurately. Many researchers are thus suspicious of evidence from participant observation, regarding it as unsystematic and unquantifiable, too impressionistic and subjective. Whyte sometimes wondered if just hanging about on street corners was an active enough process to be dignified by the term 'research'. Perhaps he should be playing a more positive role in asking questions and interviewing people more formally; one of the skills he had to learn was when it was appropriate to ask questions as well as what questions to ask (Whyte, 1993, pp.303–4).

A single researcher or even a team of researchers can only observe a certain amount. The group, village, trade union branch or constituency party may be totally unrepresentative. The informants may be unrepresentative even of the group being observed. There is the danger of serious conflict between the roles of participant and observer. The researcher is always in danger of 'going native' or being captured by part of the organization. The role of researcher is hard to sustain in a small group situation. The researcher is bound to make friends with some of the members of the group being studied. S/he develops obligations and reciprocal relations and feels the necessity to return the help and assistance s/he receives.

For the researcher, participant observation is also a costly research strategy in that it demands a high level of commitment in terms of time, energy and concentration. It takes time to gain access, to be accepted, to learn the languages, nuances and rites of the group. It tests the ability of the researcher to overcome differences of language, class, articulation, gender, culture and behaviour.

Perhaps the major issues to confront the researcher are the ethical ones. Participant observation is replete with ethical problems such as whether to adopt an overt or a covert strategy. How far should one participate in the group's activities? How far should one condone or turn a blind eye to anti-social or illegal activities carried out by the group? How far should one participate in such activities?

How should one publish material that has been obtained without the knowledge and agreement of the subject? How should one publish materials that may upset or harm the individuals involved in the study, especially as they may not have given their informed consent?

To summarize, participant observation is an open-ended and spontaneous method which gives the researcher tremendous responsibility in negotiating access, deciding on the relevance of information and the importance of events. The challenge for participant observation research is to convince other scholars that the descriptions and analysis presented by means of this case-study approach are accurate and valid, and are not merely impressionistic accounts of alternative lifestyles. If the obstacles are successfully negotiated, the researcher gains access to a situation rich in new information, data and opportunities for analysis and publication.

Content analysis

Content analysis is a technique for analysing the content of communications. Whenever somebody reads, or listens to, the content of a body of communication and then summarizes and interprets what is there, then content analysis can be said to have taken place. There are two main methods by which this can be done: first by qualitative methods of analysis, whereby the importance of the content is determined by the researcher's judgement. The researcher decides on the intrinsic value, interest and originality of the material. S/he decides on a topic or hypothesis to investigate, determines which documents or other communications are appropriate sources of evidence, and then selects a sample of texts to investigate and analyse. This process results in a subjective assessment of the content and value of the material. It relies heavily on the judgement and expertise of the researcher.

Second, content analysis can be done quantitatively. Quantitative content analysis was stimulated by the need to develop a more objective and systematic method for analysing the rapidly increasing volume of communications produced by governments, companies and other organizations, but in particular by newspapers and television companies. Berelson, one of the pioneers of content analysis research, defined quantitative content analysis as 'a research technique for the objective, systematic and quantitative description of the manifest content of communication' (Berelson, 1952, p.18). The analysis thus proceeds under clearly specified conditions which make it systematic and objective. As the procedures are clearly determined, content analysis can be replicated by other researchers.

In their study of agenda setting in the USA, Baumgartner and Jones use content analysis to show how issues are taken up by the media in a positive or negative way and how this influences how policy issues rise and fall on the national agenda. They also examine how this impacts on policy outcomes. (Baumgartner and Jones, 1993). They analysed the titles of over 22,000 articles from *The Reader's Guide to Periodical Literature* and the *New York Times Index* from 1900 to 1990. They analysed a wide range of issues including nuclear power, pesticides, smoking, child abuse, drugs, urban affairs and automobile safety. They used keywords to indicate the issue area covered by the articles and to classify them as including positive or negative coverage. They used this data to indicate the salience of the issues and the intensity of support and opposition to the activity. A variety of data is used to show the response of government and other elites, and the policy impact. They argue that policy-making in the USA is punctuated by bursts of intense activity which change the understanding of issues and lead to major policy changes. Those who dominate a policy area at one time may be marginalized in the future as the issues are redefined and new players come to dominate the area. (Baumgartner and Jones, 1993).

There are a number of steps under which a content analysis project normally proceeds (Box 10.4). First, a research topic is selected and hypotheses developed. The topic might be, for example, the attitude of the British press towards entry into the Euro system. One possible hypothesis is that 'The broadsheet press are more supportive of joining the Euro than the tabloids.' A sample of broadsheet and tabloid newspapers could then be selected over a particular time period (or example, since the latest British general election).

Box 10.4   A content analysis project

1. Select a topic and develop research hypotheses.
2. Choose the appropriate communications sources (e.g., newspapers, television programmes, party manifestos, etc.).
3. Decide on the basis of sampling the material.
4. Define the categories for analysis.
5. Develop the procedure for coding the material.
6. Choose the quantitative measure for analysing the data.

The next step in the analysis would be to choose appropriate documentary sources to analyse. In this case an obvious choice would be to choose editorials or leading articles to represent the policy stance of the paper. A procedure would then be devised to classify whether the leading articles were for or against entry to the Euro. This could consist of the number of positive or negative statements in each leading article. Formal instructions would be developed specifying how statements should be selected and classified and a quantitative system developed to classify whether the article was for or against entry. For example, the number of positive statements minus the number of negative statements would lead to a positive or negative score, and would also indicate how strongly the article supported a particular position. Finally, it would then be possible to classify the positions of the newspapers and to decide whether the hypothesis is correct or should be rejected.

This may seem a rather cumbersome procedure for analysing the contents of a newspaper, but it is a more precise and systematic way of analysing the content of leading articles than, say, reading a selection and gaining an impression of the policy position. Content analysis enables researchers to produce concrete evidence to back their analysis (see Box 10.5 for an example).

Box 10.5   Content analysis example

In Britain an interesting content analysis has been done on the publications of the far right-wing, anti-immigrant party, the National Front. Billig analysed a number of National Front publications and distinguished between those produced for wide dissemination among the general public and those produced for limited circulation among the membership. He used content analysis to distinguish between the surface values of National Front ideology and the underlying and more concealed ideology of the movement. He showed how the publications produced for wide public consumption emphasized racist anti-immigrant themes while those produced for internal consumption were extremely anti-Semitic. He concluded that the National Front was not merely an anti-immigrant party emphasizing racist and extremely nationalistic themes, but was in reality also a fascist party which was continuing to perpetuate an anti-Semitic Nazi ideology. These fascist themes were concealed from new members and the general public but were appreciated by long-standing members (Billig, 1978).

Content analysis has been used in a wide variety of contexts. For example, Berelson and Salter (1946) used it to investigate the treatment of majority and minority Americans in popular magazine fiction. They formulated a series of hypotheses about the roles they expected different ethnic groups to play in magazine stories: for example, they hypothesized that 'The overwhelming majority of heroes or approved characters will be from the majority group, that is, white American Protestants.' In contrast, they hypothesized that members of minority groups were most likely to be cast as villains or minor characters. These hypotheses yielded three main categories for analysis: first, the ethnic identification of the characters and whether they belonged to the majority group or to a minority; second, their role in the story; and third, the degree of approval of disapproval associated with the role. Berelson and Salter were able to confirm their hypothesis convincingly.

Content analysis has been widely used to analyse the policies of political parties and how these change over time. A major study of ideological and policy change using content analysis was carried out by Budge, who co-ordinated a study based on party manifestos (Budge, 1999). The aim of the study was to compare the stance of British political parties in the General Election of 1997 with their policies in previous elections. Party manifestos were chosen for analysis as these are key statements of party policy representing their promises and commitments to the electorate; parties often argue that the electorate should measure their success and hold them to account by their promises in their manifestos. Also, given that manifestos are updated and issued at each general election, they provide an ideal means of plotting changes in party policy over time.

Categories for analysing manifestos had already been developed by the Manifesto Research Group of the European Consortium for Political Research. These categories covered 56 policy areas and included the stance of parties on particular issue areas such as whether they supported the expansion or contraction of social services, and whether they supported or opposed issues such as multi-culturalism or traditional morality. Each sentence in each manifesto was counted under one, and only one, of these 56 policy area. The resulting numerical distribution was then percentaged out of the total number of sentences to standardize for the different lengths of the manifestos. This enabled comparisons to be made between the manifestos of different parties and between the 1997 manifestos and earlier ones. (A full account of the development of the percentage measurement can be found in Budge, Robertson and Hearl, 1987, 15–38, 417–71.) Budge then used the percentages of sentences on left- and right-wing policies to develop a left/right

coding scale so that he could plot the leftward or rightward movement of the parties between elections, based on the statements in
their manifestos. He did this for the period since the Second World
War.

Budge's content analysis confirmed well-known historical
trends such as the leftward movement of the Conservative Party
between 1945 and 1951, the rightward movement of the Labour
Party in the 1960s, and the rightward movement of the
Conservatives after 1959, which become most pronounced in the
1980s. Most recently his analysis emphasized the strong rightward
movement of New Labour after 1992 and the emergence of the
Liberal Democrats as the most left-wing major party in Britain,
especially as far as social and environmental issues are concerned
(Budge, 1999). He argued that this research helps to provide a
more complete analysis of elections by providing concrete
evidence of how the parties have presented their polices to the
electorate in their attempts to win votes. It complements research
on how voters react to policy initiatives by the parties. (See Box
10.6.)

Box 10.6   Extracting policy positions from political texts using words as data

Traditional content analysis treats texts as narratives to be read, understood and interpreted for meaning. Political texts can be analysed and
coded by trained experts who may classify them as, for example,
conservative, liberal or socialist. This method is highly labour-intensive,
expensive and subject to coding errors as some texts may be wrongly
categorized. The approach developed by Laver and his colleagues
replaces the hand-coding of texts by experts with computerized coding
schemes. Specified words in known political texts are linked to prede-
termined policy positions and given a word score. Computer coding of
word scores in new political texts is used to estimate the policy positions of these new texts. The known (reference) texts act as a benchmark for estimating the policy positions of the similar new (virgin) texts
about which nothing is known. The texts are treated as collections of
word data which can be quickly and accurately coded by computer. The
assumption underlying the analysis is that key words such as 'privati-
zation', 'choice' and 'nationalization' can be linked to specific policy
positions and these meanings are stable over time. Laver and his
colleagues used the method to analyse party manifestos and parliamentary speeches in Britain, Ireland and Germany (Laver, Benoit and Garry,
2003).

One area where content analysis is regularly used is in the measurement of bias in newspapers or television programmes. In the British General Election of 1997, Norris and her colleagues carried out research into the bias in television news programmes. They analysed how much news was devoted to each of the major parties, what issues were prioritized, and what was the balance between positive and negative messages. The research also included the news coverage of a range of newspapers and assessed the balance between newspapers and television news programmes. Each news story was measured on a seven-point scale ranging from +7 for a highly positive story to 1 for a highly negative story. They concluded that the large majority of stories were well balanced, including both positive and negative elements (Norris *et al.*, 1999).

The advantages and limitations of content analysis

The great advantage of content analysis is that a large quantity of documentary or other communication material can be analysed in a precise and systematic way. Convincing evidence can thus be produced to test hypotheses about, for example, the policies of political parties, the stereotyping of minorities in television programmes or the bias in editorial comment. As the categories, coding system and the sampling of materials are open to scrutiny, the analysis can be replicated and the results confirmed. The method can be used to measure changes over time, as shown in Budge's research on party manifestos. Content analysis can be used to analyse a wide range of material from newspaper reports, television programmes, government documents and also politicians' speeches and radio broadcasts. As the material is public, there are no problems of access and informed consent, although these would arise if the researcher wished to access material in private collections.

Content analysis is a laborious and time-consuming technique. Care must be taken to check the authenticity of the material, ensure a representative sample of documents is selected, and to construct good categories and develop appropriate measures. A major limitation is that the importance of a theme is usually measured by the number of times it appears in the material. This limits the scope of the analysis. Themes which occur infrequently may be neglected or ignored altogether, even though they may be important. This is a limitation of a quantitative approach to content analysis. Also, if the categories are very broad, then interesting material may be neglected.

It goes without saying that the coding of the material is critically important and must be carefully checked.

Quantitative content analysis is most valuable when a high degree of precision and objectivity are needed to produce clear evidence to test hypotheses, perhaps about controversial and sensitive issues.

Discourse analysis

The growth of interest in qualitative approaches to social research can be seen in the growing interest that has been developing in discourse analysis. This has occurred as scholars have realized the importance of language (and in particular political language), and how political concepts, ideas, language, behaviour and institutional arrangements are loaded with assumptions about the nature of the social and political world and our understanding of it. A recurrent theme in the literature on discourse analysis is that discourses reproduce the everyday assumptions of society and that those common perceptions and understandings are encouraged and reinforced by those with access to the media, such as politicians, journalists and academic experts. Language and discourses therefore frame and constrain given courses of action, some of which are promoted as sensible, moral and commanding wide levels of support, while others are discouraged as stupid, immoral and illegitimate. The general public are thus guided as to how they should respond to particular crises or events. It is the function of discourse analysis to reveal the bases of these common assumptions and to show how they relate to different interests in society.

Howarth argues that discourse theory begins with the assumption that all objects and actions are meaningful and that their objectives are a product of historically specific conditions. Discourse theory therefore needs to research into the origins of social practices and institutions and must critically analyse the discourses that are linked to them and continue to give them legitimacy and meaning (Howarth, 2000).

A strong theme in discourse analysis is that it should contribute to human emancipation (Fairclough 2000). Discourse analysis should be critical because language can be used to deceive and to manipulate those to whom it is addressed. Language and discourse are dominated by the powerful in society who can impose meanings and explanations of social reality which protect their interests and undermine those of the rest of society, by spreading confusion and deceit in discourses that allow oppression and exploitation of the weak to continue.

As is the case with complex and controversial concepts, discourse analysis is hard to define. Howarth argues that there are five major approaches or ways of defining discourses (Howarth, 2000, 2–5). He argues that positivists and empiricists define discourses as 'frames' or 'cognitive schemata', which are defined by McAdam and his colleagues as 'the conscious strategic efforts by groups of people to fashion shared understandings of the world and of themselves that legitimate and motivate collective action' (McAdam, McCarthy and Zald, 1996, p.6).

This definition complements a critical approach to discourse analysis as it encourages research into the motivations behind the construction of these shared understandings and on the success of these groups in achieving their goals. It is also essentially a political definition, focusing on attempts by groups to impose their assumptions and values on others in order to promote their own interests.

Second, Howarth contrasts this positivist approach with a realistic approach which assumes that discourse is a structured system in its own right. The social world is assumed to consist of independently existing sets of objects with inherent properties and causal powers. The interaction of these objects causes events and processes in the real world. Discourses are particular objects in their own right and as such contribute to the creation of events and social processes. The aim of discourse analysis is to expose and explain the role of discourses and to show how they contribute to the causation of events and social processes, and in particular to show how powerful they are (Howarth, 1998).

A Marxist approach to discourse analysis emphasizes the relationship of discourse to the contradictory processes of economic production and reproduction in capitalist societies. Discourses are ideological systems of meaning which legitimate capitalist exploitation. They are supported and reinforced by capitalist elites and by their supporters in politics, the media and education, to legitimate their control over the system and the unfair share of economic resources and political power that they hold. The role of discourse analysis is thus emancipatory, to expose the role of the dominant discourses in legitimating a grossly unfair economic and political system and proposing an equalitarian alternative.

Critical discourse analysis is similar to the Marxist approach, but emphasizes a sociological rather than an economic framework within which to carry out discourse analysis. In this approach, human meanings and understandings are seen as crucial in explaining the social world. Social action always involves interaction and therefore communication, so language and discourse are an integral part of social activity. Social practices always involve language in a combination of action and reflection, as people develop constructions of the world to justify their actions.

Fairclough argues that critical discourse analysis sees language as one element of social practice and aims to see how it is articulated along with other elements. Critical discourse analysis is particularly concerned with social change and with how it relates to social relations of power and domination. The role of critical discourse analysis is to expose the way in which language and discourses are used by the powerful to confuse and exploit the mass of the population (Fairclough, 2000).

Finally, Howarth argues that post-structuralists and post-Marxists regard social structures as inherently ambiguous, incomplete and contingent. In these perspectives discourses constitute symbolic social systems, and the task of discourse analysis is to examine their historical and political construction and functioning (Howarth, 2000).

It is easy to see why discourse analysis should be attracting the attention of political scientists. Politics can easily be described as a struggle to control the dominant political language. The political party that is able to control the political agenda, to impose its ideas and concepts on the media and the electorate, is in a strong position to win elections. Hall demonstrates how Margaret Thatcher and her advisers were able to construct a dominant political discourse based partly on traditional Conservative values such as patriotism or law and order, but also on economic ideas based on classical economic liberalism (S. Hall, 1983). The Thatcherites made a virtue of private enterprise and individual worth which was supported by massive privatizations and sales of council houses to sitting tenants. Thatcherism as a political discourse dominated British politics for 20 years and was only seriously challenged when the modernizers captured control of the Labour Party and transformed it into New Labour.

Fairclough argues that the 'creation' of New Labour involved the reinvention of the Labour Party and the creation of a new political discourse which has successfully incorporated elements of Thatcherism and has thus undermined the ability of the Conservatives to present a coherent and consistent programme to the electorate (Fairclough, 2000, p.21). The ideology of New Labour which Fairclough presents is one of a party which accepts capitalism, national self-interest and economic competition between states. It claims to be patriotic, economically competent and in favour of enterprise and economic success. At the same time there is an attempt to marry capitalism with elements of Labour's traditional concerns so that New Labour's rhetoric includes an emphasis on fairness, social inclusion and greater social justice. But the assumption is that the positive values of Old Labour cannot be achieved without the success of British capitalism. Economic success in the global world economy is necessary for a thriving welfare state, including good healthcare provision, pensions, and support for poor families.

New Labour has thus worked hard to create a new dominant political discourse which includes some Thatcherite themes such as those of national renewal, individual responsibility, maximizing competition and limiting government. This is balanced by the more caring rhetoric of fairness and social cohesion. But the two discourses are linked together by New Labour spokesmen. The state is seen as having a duty to ensure that everybody and all groups are included in society and guaranteed a reasonable standard of life and are given a stake in its present and in its future, while citizens have a responsibility to contribute to society by working and being financially independent (Fairclough, 2000, p.92).

Fairclough emphasizes that the political discourse of New Labour is a process rather than a finished product. New Labour does not control the political agenda. It has to respond to events at home and abroad over which it has no control. The discourse of New Labour is thus constantly changing in response to new challenges and developments, some of which it can exploit and some of which it has to contest.

As befits an analysis from the perspective of critical discourse analysis, a key goal of Fairclough's study is to expose the contradictions in New Labour's discourse. There are lots of contradictions between New Labour's political rhetoric and its political achievements. An example widely cited is the promise of a Freedom of Information Bill and the resulting legislation which failed to deliver the 'open government' that was promised. In opposition Tony Blair promised:

Our commitment to a Freedom of Information Act is clear, and I affirm it here tonight. We want to end the obsessive and unnecessary secrecy that surrounds government activity and make government information available to the public, unless there are good reasons not to do so. So the presumption is that information should be, rather than should not be, released. (Fairclough, 2000, p.146)

In the event, the Bill was widely regarded as a victory for those who wanted to preserve secrecy in government, with numerous exemptions from the Bill and blanket exemptions from disclosure if an authority or department could show that disclosure would prejudice the working of government. Thus the presumption of release could easily be circumvented by an unwilling department. The dichotomy between rhetoric and reality is always likely to be large in politics, but with the great emphasis New Labour places on presentation and spin, the gap is particularly great in its case. This dashing of people's expectations is likely to lead to growing disillusion with politicians and politics and a growth in alienation and apathy.

Using discourse analysis

The growth of interest in discourse analysis has not led to agreement on how studies using this approach should be carried out; rather, there are a number of assumptions and guidelines that underlie discourse analysis. There is widespread agreement that scholars using this approach do not wish to be limited by the straitjacket of the traditional scientific approach to research, with its emphasis on testable hypotheses, research design and empirical analysis leading to generalizations; they prefer to be free to carry out in-depth and considered qualitative research. On the other hand, they do wish to conduct rigorous analysis that is accepted as such by other scholars.

Schmidt defines discourse as 'whatever policy actors say to each other and to the public in their efforts to generate and legitimise a policy programme. As such discourse encompasses both a set of policy ideas and values and an interactive process of policy construction and communication' (Schmidt, 2002, p.210). She defines discourse analysis as a descriptive language or an analytic framework that allows the researcher to identify, describe and analyse important phenomena when they occur, that applies only under certain conditions, and for which theories can be developed and tested. She describes this approach as 'discursive institutionalism' (Schmidt, 2002, p.8). She uses discourse as a framework for analysing the policy adjustments of Britain, France and Germany to the challenges of globalization and Europeanization, in particular to show what these changes were and how they were legitimized by the political elites in those three countries. The result is a major study of the leading states of the EU (Schmidt, 2002; see also Box 10.7).

Box 10.7   The role of discourse in the political dynamics of adjustment in Britain, France and Germany

Schmidt argues that in terms of both policies and practices Britain, France and Germany have followed very different paths in their adjustment to globalization and Europeanization. She believes that this has been partly due to their success or failure in generating political discourses that have legitimizsed neo-liberal reforms. Britain under Mrs Thatcher generated a political discourse which legitimized neo-liberal reforms and this was so successful that the policies were continued by her successors, John Major and Tony Blair. In France, a coherent discourse to legitimize neo-liberal reforms was not generated as successfully as in Britain, with the result that there has been considerable resistance to social welfare reforms and a more open, market-oriented economy. In Germany institutional fragmentation has made it harder for the government to persuade the opposition, its social partners and the *Länder* governments of the need for neo-liberal reforms, although the economic crisis may force their acceptance (Schmidt, 2002).

There is widespread agreement that discourses are systems of signification: that is, that reality is socially constructed by people who give meaning and significance to objects in the material world. These discourses may often be organized in terms of binary opposites contrasting, for example, the First and Third Worlds; good and evil; development and under-development; and democracy and authoritarianism (Milliken, 1999).

Discourse analysis illuminates the dominant ideas and identifies those who legitimate these ideas. In policy arenas the most influential spokesman are likely to be politicians, leaders of pressure groups and expert journalists and academics. It is thus relatively straightforward for researchers to obtain a representative selection of texts on a particular policy area for investigation and analysis. They can then describe the main features of the dominant discourse in this arena, and show who are accepted as the legitimate representatives, the knowledgeable and authoritative spokespersons. They can then determine who is allowed to contribute to the debates and whose views are excluded and suppressed. This latter analysis may be very challenging as those who are silent or who are silenced may be difficult to discover. However, this is an important point of discourse analysis because of its commitment to a critical understanding of the construction of social reality. It is much easier to analyse the dominating and hegemonic discourses and to explain how they are organized, their content, their internal contradictions, why they are successful, how they are legitimized and what the consequences of the dominance are likely to be, than it is to analyse the passive alternative discourses of those excluded from the policy area. An analysis of the different discourses that supported or opposed the war on Iraq would reveal the importance and power of different groups in gaining access to the media and the strategies they use to gain legitimacy for their proposed courses of action.

There are, of course, a great many discourses taking place at any one time. Discourses compete with each other, challenge each other and overlap with each other. Dominant discourses which are so widely accepted that they are considered to be common sense may still be challenged and even undermined over time, so that they are replaced by new discourses articulated by new elites. Thus a major role of discourse analysis is to explain how this happens and to show, for example, how the hegemony of Thatcherism in 1980s Britain was replaced by the dominance of New Labour's double-barrelled rhetoric linking elements of Thatcherism to elements of social democracy.

Discourse analysis is thus a relatively new research methodology in political science. It is attractive as it focuses on the origins, content and transformation of the dominant political discourses in society. These discourses frame the political agenda and limit possible opposition among groups which may be adversely affected by their political consequences. Discourses provide legitimacy to political institutions, including the state, and to the policies and actions of politicians and other political actors. They provide a rich area for research.

Conclusion

This chapter has introduced and discussed three very different research strategies. The first of these, participant observation, has been largely neglected by researchers in political science but is one which has been usefully employed in sociology to study small groups and communities. It has the advantage of providing rich material and insights, especially into individuals and groups on the fringes of society who are often overlooked by more conventional means of research (such as social surveys and elite interviewing). A major challenge in participant observation is maintaining objectivity and detachment from the group and finding a means of recording observations and collecting material in a systematic and accurate way.

In contrast, content analysis is a quantitative research strategy. This is a more rigorous and systematic technique for analysing the content of communications, whether these are written or spoken. Recently content analysis has been much used to test the objectivity of newspaper and television reporting and to analyse the policy positions of parties as declared in their manifestos. Content analysis research can be easily replicated by other researchers, which makes it attractive as a source of evidence to test hypotheses. However, quantitative data may miss subtleties and nuances in the material which a sensitive and experienced researcher would wish to include in his/her analysis.

Discourse analysis is a qualitative research strategy comprising a number of approaches under in this general term. It is very similar to qualitative content analysis and involves the analysis of the dominant discourses or political languages that frame our social and political world and our understanding of it. It is the function of discourse analysis to describe these discourses, to reveal the assumptions on which they are based and to show how different groups and interests in society benefit from or are oppressed by these discourses. Language and discourses are politically constructed and are used by the powerful to legitimate their actions.

Chapter 11

Ethics and Political Research

This chapter explores what ethical problems are and how political scientists should respond to them. Our understanding of ethical problems is affected by different cultural and intellectual traditions. The dilemmas that arise from these different approaches cannot necessarily be resolved by reference to standard principles of ethical conduct. It is, however, possible to categorize ethical problems by looking at them in terms of relationships with sponsors and gate-keepers. Fraud and plagiarism is a serious problem in social research. Professional codes of conduct are often too generally worded to provide much help, but the increasing resort to ethics committees in universities may constrain research as well as guide it.

Political research cannot be properly conducted in a moral vacuum. It has consequences for those who participate in the research and those who are influenced by it. Researchers and those who read their research needed to be aware of the functions performed by social research in an economy that is increasingly knowledge-based. Social science research should not be viewed simply as an objective search for truth. It can show the way to greater profits: for example, by providing a better understanding of consumer behaviour that allows market niches to be exploited. It can provide greater understanding of voter preferences in a way that allows politicians to package their messages more effectively. Although social science research is often critical of existing policies and practices, a call for further research can be used to delay change or deflect criticism. Given this background, it is not surprising that the ways in which research is funded can pose difficult moral choices, as can the compromises that have to be made with 'gate-keepers' to gain access to research sites in organizations.

The nature of ethical problems

Barnes (1979, p.16) defines ethical problems as 'those that arise when we try to decide between one course of action and another not in terms of expediency or efficiency but by reference to standards of what is morally right or wrong'. It is very easy as a researcher to become caught up in the excitement of the research itself, to be driven by the internal dynamic of a process which is making new discoveries in terms of theoretical perspectives, methodologies or empirical findings. The impact the research may have can easily be ignored, particularly when the achievement of the individual researcher's career goals are significantly dependent on whether the research is successful or not. There is a need for researchers to remind themselves to show 'principled sensitivity to the rights of others' (Bulmer, 2001, p.46).

The stance an individual takes on particular ethical dilemmas is often influenced by major belief systems that are religious in origin (e.g., Judaeo-Christian or Islamic). Even in relatively secular societies, these beliefs may be deeply embedded in the culture. Thus, in a society influenced by a Christian tradition, the maxim 'Do unto others as you would have done unto you' may have a subconscious influence on the moral choices that people make. However, as society becomes more fragmented and heterogeneous, these ethical codes become more contentious. In post-modernist conditions, individuals can feel comfortable about 'picking and mixing' from a variety of traditions to construct their own individual combination of beliefs. Ethical standards derived from religious traditions can no longer readily be appealed to as a means of resolving disputes. For example, two students want a snack. The first student suggests going to a fast food outlet to buy a burger. For this student, the choice is a simple one of expediency and efficiency: a standardized product is available at an affordable price. The second student is a vegetarian. For her, the decision to purchase a burger raises important moral issues.

Decisions about what is right and what is wrong may thus be influenced by cultural traditions, but also by individual choices. It is often suggested that researchers should be guided in their professional lives by codes of conduct drawn up by associations representing their disciplines. Such codes have proliferated in recent years but, as we shall see later in the chapter, they often take lowest common denominator positions which place few restrictions on researchers' behaviour. The difficulty of drawing up codes is in part a reflection of the diverse and even contradictory viewpoints that people hold. However, 'this indeterminacy does not mean that ethical issues can be ignored' (Bulmer, 2001, p.56).

Two broad approaches to ethical problems

There are two broad intellectual approaches to ethical problems in social research. Deontological theory 'derives from the Greek "deon", meaning duty. The most famous advocate of this approach was Immanuel Kant, who argued that morals ought to be based on obligations to others' (Kent, 2000, p.62). In this approach ethical judgements would be guided by a set of principles that base moral choices on obligations and duties to others. 'Research ethics take on a universal form and are intended to be followed regardless of the place and circumstances in which the researcher finds themselves' (May, 1997, p.55).

Not surprisingly, such an approach is not generally popular with researchers who find it rather restrictive. However, there are objections other than the question of the convenience of researchers. It is not necessarily evident what the good is that researchers are meant to maximize. In terms of an injunction to avoid deception, it is rather utopian. Should researchers be held to higher standards of behaviour than the population at large?

Not surprisingly, researchers are more comfortable with the consequentialist approach that arises from the utilitarianism of John Stuart Mill. Mill 'argued that people should seek to act in accordance with the consequences of their behaviour and minimize suffering and maximize well-being' (Kent, 2000, p.62). The problem with this approach is that it is rather elastic and could be used to justify a very wide range of research practices. Mill himself referred to the criticism 'that a utilitarian will be apt to make his own particular case an exception to moral rules and, when under temptation, will see a utility in the breach of a rule, greater than he will see in its observance' (Mill, 1910, p.23). For example, the frequently cited Milgram experiments discussed in Chapter 2 induced volunteers to give electric shocks to actors who exhibited signs of pain. They have been justified both on the grounds that they provided interesting insights about passive acceptance of apparently immoral commands from authority figures and that the volunteers were not harmed but often gained insights about themselves.

In practice, it is often difficult to predict what the long run outcomes of research might be. Indeed, this risk might be increased if we believe that the proponents of chaos theory who have argued that very rare events will occur more often than a Gaussian or bell-shaped normal distribution would suggest. In more practical terms, the benefit and harm resulting from research is sometimes difficult to estimate (see Box 11.1).

> ## Box 11.1   Did this research stigmatize the socially excluded?
>
> Grant (2001) undertook research into the relationship between social exclusion and environmental policy, particularly policies related to climate change. The research investigated the attitudes and knowledge on environmental questions of socially excluded groups (e.g., lone parents, the unemployed); their environmentally relevant consumption patterns; and whether their consumption patterns were more inefficient (related to their circumstances rather than choices they made). The research revealed that differences between countries were sometimes more powerful than those between the socially excluded and the rest of the population, and that there were considerable differences between the different socially excluded groups. Policy measures would need to be sensitive to these differences and seek to empower the socially excluded. The research was open to the ethical objection of 'ecological stigmatization'. It was suggested that it was blaming the socially excluded, who had many other problems in their lives, for environmental imbalances that were in fact largely caused by the more prosperous.

Five basic ethical principles

Modern approaches have tried to reconcile the conflict between the approaches based on moral duty and on utilitarianism by specifying a set of basic ethical principles that should guide research and then using these to advise researchers against certain forms of conduct. The form in which these are stated varies in the literature, but five basic principles may be discerned:

1. Beneficence or the avoidance of harm: researchers ought to seek to do good rather than cause harm.
2. Veracity or the avoidance of deception: they ought to tell the truth and keep promises.
3. Privacy or autonomy: individuals have a right to limit access to information about themselves.
4. Confidentiality: closely related to the notion of privacy, the right to control the use of information about oneself.
5. Consent: the notion of informed consent, often recommended as an operational principle for the conduct of research.

Not surprisingly, each of these principles gives rise to difficulties. The implementation of the beneficience principle necessarily involves making difficult judgements about likely consequences with the researcher always tempted to construct a justification that will permit research to proceed. Particular difficulties may arise when researchers in a team fall out with each other, as happened in the second study of the community of Banbury in Oxfordshire. In a note on Bell's account of what happened, Newby comments (1977, p.65):

> When invited to do so [the other members of the research team] understandably declined to waive the rights they have under the law and which might have enabled a more personally authentic, but also more vituperative and offensive, account to be published. It seems necessary to state, then, that the published account is both less frank – but, some might agree, less inaccurate – than the original draft.

The principle of veracity is perhaps more straightforward in its application. Researchers should be honest about what they are doing and should report their results fully and truthfully. Even if they are not motivated by a concern about the subjects of the research, they should be aware of their duty to future researchers. This arises both in terms of not making it more difficult for research to be carried out on the subject in future and also in providing a full and accurate basis for future work (subject to conditions about the release of data which protect confidentiality). This is assisted by such practices as depositing data in archives which allows it to be re-analysed by future researchers. The principle of veracity perhaps encounters its greatest difficulty in cases where covert participant observation may appear to be justified (e.g., in studies of extremist political movements).

There is increasing concern about violations of privacy and it is certainly important that individuals should have the right not to participate in research. It is possible that 'people can feel wronged without being harmed: they may feel they have been treated as objects of measurement without respect for their individual values and sense of privacy' (Social Research Association, or SRA, 2002, p.14). There is a difficult balance to be drawn between 'society's desire, on the one hand, to expose the hidden processes at work in modern society and, on the other, to protect the privacy of individuals and to recognise that there are private spheres into which the social scientist may not, and perhaps even should not, penetrate'

(Bulmer, 2001, p 49) For example, do investigations into freema sonry reflect a kind of social voyeurism about a secret society, or are they justified because of fears that freemasons have penetrated particular social institutions such as the police and may grant favours to their fellow masons?

Individuals may be particularly concerned about how the data collected is used, a concern expressed in the notion of confidential- ity. These concerns have been reflected in increasingly stringent data protection legislation. There is a concern about balance here and whether data protection legislation might make some forms of valid and useful research increasingly difficult.

The doctrine of informed consent is sometimes used to resolve some of these issues. Informed consent has been particularly impor- tant in medical research and was restated at the Nuremberg trials of Nazi war criminals after some particularly cruel experiments. The monitoring of its use is spreading to social research with universi- ties increasingly introducing ethics committees to vet research before it proceeds. 'Informed consent is generally taken to mean that those who are researched should have the right to know they are being researched, and that in some sense they should give their consent. (Bulmer, 2001, p.49). As a principle, this is straightforward and attractive, but its application may be more problematic: 'Medical models can be inappropriate in social settings' (SRA, 2002, p.24). In medical research persuading someone to take place in a clinical trial is common practice, but in social research it may be seen as coercion. In a sample survey in which interview length has to be restricted to encourage respondent participation, a full explanation of the purposes of the project might depress response rates. Thus, 'there are many situations where it is not possible to be completely open to all participants, and sometimes a full explana- tion of one's purposes would overwhelm the listener' (Bulmer, 2001, p.52).

It is evident that these various principles pose questions as much as they provide answers, although that can be useful as a checklist. As Mill reminds us (1910, p.23), 'It is not the fault of any creed, but of the complicated nature of human affairs, that rules of conduct cannot be so framed as to require no exceptions, and that hardly any kinds of action can safely be laid down as always obligatory or always condemnable.' This suggests that we might need a rather different kind of approach which understands the interactive, dynamic character of social research. Such a framework is provided by Barnes (1979, p.15) who sees social inquiry 'as a process of inter- action and negotiation between scientist, sponsor, gatekeeper and citizen'. The next part of the chapter considers each of these relationships in turn.

The relationship with sponsors

Social science research is expensive. Success in obtaining funds is one of the key indicators used to measure the progress of a researcher's career. It might therefore seem that the researcher is at the mercy of powerful sponsors who might wish to bias the research in a particular direction in order to pursue their own particular ends. The example usually produced in support of this argument is Project Camelot, a research project sponsored by the US Army in the 1960s. It set out to measure and forecast the causes of revolution in developing countries with the objective of yielding information that would reduce the incidence of insurgencies. It was exposed in Chile and was eventually cancelled by a Presidential directive. The alternative possibility, that researchers may be able to manipulate and mislead sponsors, is less often considered. After all, the money being disbursed does belong to the sponsors.

Who are the funders? It is difficult to make generalizations about them. As Barnes points out (1979, p.78):

> [sponsors] have in common with one another nothing more than the possession of resources and an interest in using them to promote social research. There is little that can be said about ethical dilemmas that can apply equally to a government department, a charitable foundation and a commercial enterprise.

For the political scientist, the two most important categories are government (including international bodies) and private foundations. Government funds for social science research in the UK are provided through the Economic and Social Research Council (ESRC). The ESRC has a responsibility to the academic community to maintain standards and foster high quality research which it seeks to do through extensive processes of consultation and peer review of research proposals. However, it is also answerable to the community of practitioners and in particular to government departments. The ESRC has decided to place a greater emphasis on quantitative skills training, arguing that these were in demand from government departments. There is no doubt that policy-makers in both the public and private sectors have a preference for what is seen as 'hard' data. Researchers in the social sciences were concerned that quantiative methods were being privileged. This was of particular concern to political scientists and sociologists who considered that qualitative data could yield in-depth insights which were often not generated through the use of quantitative techniques. Sponsors may not seek to influence just the substantive content of research programmes, but also the research techniques used.

The European Commission has become an important funder of social science research. Its 'COST' (the French acronym for 'European Co-operation in the Field of Scientific and Technical Research') programmes have facilitated networking across Europe between researchers who may then make an application for one of its 'framework' programmes. The successive 'frameworks' set out research priorities and themes which, understandably enough, reflect the current policy concerns of the European Union. It has been suggested that applications have a greater chance of success if they include a partner from a Southern European country. Although some partnerships have been highly successful, in other cases the search for a partner to secure funding has produced collaborators who seem to have priorities other than the pursuit of research.

Despite the policy emphasis of European Commission research, the mechanisms for integrating research findings into the policy process do not always seem to be well developed. It has been suggested that the principal agenda of the Commission is to develop a cohort of researchers with a European orientation and to engage in an activity (research) which is seen to add legitimacy to a set of polit-ical institutions often seen as lacking in that quality. This reminds us of the point made at the beginning of the chapter that research may have broader political purposes that go beyond the development of theories, the collection of data or problem solution. Because the researchers are getting funding, and the sponsoring institution is seeing its particular agenda pursued, an implicit collusion can be developed between sponsor and researcher which permits a neglect of any consideration of whether there is value for money beyond the achievement of the contracted research deliverables. This suggests that there is a third model beyond those of 'sponsor as exploiter' and 'researcher as exploiter', which is one of joint collusion between elites (a consideration that will be returned to at the end of this section).

Whereas the UK has a specialized research organization for the social sciences, the publicly funded research body in the USA, the National Science Foundation (NSF), covers everything from biology to polar research. The NSF was established by legislation in 1950 with the mission 'To promote the progress of science; to advance the national health, prosperity, and welfare; and to secure the national defense.' Its statement of activities includes the word 'scientific' twelve times and 'engineering' ten times (National Science Foundation, 2002). A political science programme was set up in 1965, but concerns about the standing of political science at the NSF led the APSA to set up a special committee of investigation.

APSA had three chief concerns about the relationship:

[a] perceived failure of the NSF to support political scientists whose NSF grant was criticized in the Congress, the token budgetary increase ($10,000) awarded to the political science program at NSF for budget year 1998 and, in justification of that budgetary decision, the statements of an NSF administrator that research in political science lacked innovation and excitement. (Report of a Committee, 2000, p.895)

The committee found that 'the discipline of economics appears to enjoy a favored position within the Division of Economic and Social Sciences'. In contrast, political science was 'perceived at NSF as not very exciting, not on the cutting edge of the research enterprise, and in certain quarters as journalistic and reformist' (p.895). It is curious that being seen as 'reformist' should be seen as a criticism, given that one outcome of research could be suggestions about how institutions could function more effectively. Congress appears to have been particularly upset by a research project to study the recruitment of congressional candidates. There is certainly a potential tension in criticizing the body that is the ultimate source of a project's funding.

One of the most interesting observations in the APSA report is that, although it refers more than once to a perceived shrinkage in funding for political science research, 'it seems clear to us that we know too little about the full range of funding sources for research in political science' (Report of a Committee, 2000, p.897). What this does draw attention to is the pluralism and diversity of funding sources in the United States which means that a researcher who is denied by one sponsor may have success elsewhere.

Private foundations are a particularly important source of research funding in the US. The most important from the viewpoint of social science research include Carnegie (founded in 1911), Rockefeller (1913) and Ford (1936). Foundations in Europe are generally on a smaller scale with one of the most important being

Germany's Volkswagen Foundation which was established when the shares of the state-owned car company were sold to private shareholders. Two of the most important foundations providing funds in Britain are the Leverhulme Foundation and the Nuffield Foundation.

The Ford Foundation has been particularly important in foreign affairs research and has been criticized for trying to build international knowledge networks that foster American intellectual hegemony. In general, however, the private foundations are relatively benign funders. They intrude less into research than public funders. They are more open to projects that are critical of government policy (Barnes, 1979, p.79). The outlook of their staff is often pragmatic and utilitarian, driven by a need to dispose of the available funds in accordance with the trust deed. A broader concern is that 'philanthropy has totally changed its character. From being charity to the poor, it has become an élite subsidising élites' (Whitaker, 1979, p.235).

The conventional picture of the relationship between sponsors and researchers has been that sponsors enter into negotiations with researchers 'from a position of strength' (Barnes, 1979, p.78). The researcher is seen as a supplicant for funds without which the research cannot proceed. Hence, the sponsor may push research in directions that are ethically undesirable. Examples can be found that would fit such an account, but which may not encapsulate the broader picture. Information asymmetries do not necessarily favour the sponsor. A successful researcher is one who knows how to fit her own particular interests into the current agenda of the sponsor. Thus the question that needs to be asked 'is not whether a sponsor should impose conditions but rather what these conditions ought to be' (Barnes, 1977, pp.6–7). It should also be noted that the agenda of the sponsor and the researcher may be markedly different from that of the citizen.

Gatekeepers

One of the characteristics of political science research is that it is often undertaken in organizational settings: pressure groups, political parties, government departments and so on. In order to gain access to such institutions, it is often necessary to negotiate with gatekeepers who may deny access to the institution, ration it, or impose conditions on the way in which the research is carried out. The extent of the difficulty that they can present is encapsulated by the almost despairing comment by Barnes on the final page of his book, 'And gatekeepers? Maybe there would not be any in an ideal world' (Barnes, 1979, p.188).

If access is denied, then the research cannot proceed, but the onus of responsibility for denying access rests with the gatekeeper. If access is rationed to, say, one visit (as does happen), then the effectiveness of the research may be severely undermined. However, the problem is a practical rather than an ethical one. Indeed, some institutions and organizations are besieged by researchers and there is perhaps some responsibility on researchers to engage in self-regulation. On a research visit to the House of Commons, a Canadian researcher encountered five academics he knew (Docherty, 2002, p.7). 'Members of parliament are, justifiably, getting tired of talking to us and organising our mail' (Docherty, 2002, p.8). His suggested solution was that academics should collaborate with each other in the data-gathering phase of their projects.

Research subjects may ask to see drafts of the research output. This is not usually deployed as a means of exercising censorship and can lead to useful comments that enhance the quality of the research. Indeed, some researchers consciously build seeking feedback in this way into their research planning. In their work on public expenditure Thain and Wright circulated 25 drafts of working papers in the Treasury and spending departments. 'Interviewees were then invited to comment on revised drafts of working papers and later chapters of the book based upon them' (Thain and Wright, 1995, p.9).

Publications may, of course, give rise to offence. Cowell-Myers carried out a second wave of interviews with members of the Northern Ireland Assembly. One woman 'who had participated in the first round of interviews insisted that she "was sick of doing favors for Americans" and would not allow me time with her unless I was willing to pay!' Her reaction was perhaps less surprising when one considers that it was probably a reaction to an article Cowell-Myers 'had written for *Women and Politics* based on the first interviews in which her comments on gender and the other women in the Assembly were portrayed as the anomalies they are among politicians in the rest of the advanced industrialized world' (Cowell-Myers, 2002, p.9). Cowell-Myers understandably wished to adhere to her interpretation of her research results, but the consequence was that her second wave of interviews were biased towards nationalist members of the Assembly.

Usually researchers encounter more subtle techniques than denial of access. These may be defined as *co-option, restriction* and *diversion.* An established organization with strong institutional defences is likely to resort to co-option as a technique to deal with potential critics. In their research on the Treasury, Deakin and Parry encountered the technique of 'what could be crudely called co-option'. They noted: '[the] Treasury does indeed contain a remarkable number of exceptionally able people. This makes the task of conducting interviews there challenging . . . It is easy, in such company, to be flattered into believing that what you hear presented with such beguiling fluency is the whole story' (Deakin and Parry, 2000, p.3).

Hennessy encountered the problem of restriction in his study of Britain's preparation for nuclear war during the Cold War period. The study only became possible when restrictions to access to documents at the PRO were relaxed. However, certain documents were still closed. To some extent it was possible to piece together their contents from other documents in the files or, in one case, from a scribbled note that had been inadvertently left in the file. Hennessy asked for permission to visit the government's secret (but by then stood down) headquarters for nuclear war in a quarry near Bath known by the code name 'Turnstile'. The careful wording of the note from the civil servant who gave permission for the visit led him to believe that he might be shown only some of what was there. 'It could be . . . that we were . . . not taken through the final "turnstile" to the last arena of British Central Government. I have no means of knowing for sure, but I think it very likely. Indeed I am virtually sure of it' (Hennessy, 2002, p.176).

Well-established organizations may have routines for processing visitors. When Grant was undertaking research on environmental policy in the USA, he arrived at a research site in California where a large notice welcomed 'our distinguished visitor from England'. The organization's public relations function had taken charge of the visit and he was led off on a visit to the laboratories that were not the main focus of his research.

In negotiations with gatekeepers, the balance of power generally lies with the organization being investigated rather than with the researcher. No one, of course, is obliged to open their organization to research, although concerns about transparency and accountability might motivate them to do so. Researchers need to be on their guard in their dealings with gatekeepers because of the subtle control techniques which they may deploy. It is an area where experienced researchers have something of an advantage. However, to treat gatekeepers simply an as obstacle to be overcome would overlook the fact that there may be ethical considerations which influence the stance that they are taking. Unhindered access is not an inviolable right of the researcher.

Citizens

In the relationship with citizens, the advantage is generally with the researcher and there is therefore a greater potential for harm. Barnes argues (1979, p.23) that at one time social science research tended to follow a natural science paradigm in which

> [citizens] and scientists were not only socially but also analytically and epistemologically unequal; the new knowledge that was expected to emerge was perceived as a source of enlightenment for the elite. With the passage of years, citizens have come much closer to scientists not only socially but, with the decline of positive theories of knowledge, epistemologically as well.

Data protection legislation (see Box 11.2) provides an important means of protecting the citizen in relation to the collection of survey data. It should be noted that: 'In many of the social

---

Box 11.2   Principles of data protection in the UK

Anyone processing personal data must comply with the eight enforceable principles of good practice. They say that data must be:

- fairly and lawfully processed
- processed for limited purposes
- adequate, relevant and not excessive
- accurate
- not kept longer than necessary
- processed in accordance with the data subject's rights
- secure
- not transferred to countries without adequate protection.

In particular, political opinions are defined as 'sensitive personal data'. The data subject must give explicit consent to the processing of this data. Explicit consent is further defined as a 'freely given, specific and informed indication of his wishes'.

Source: http://www.dataprotection.gov.uk/principl.htm, 27 March 2002.

inquiries that have caused controversy, the issue has had more to do with intrusion into subjects' private and personal domains or by overburdening subjects with "too much" information, rather than with whether or not subjects have been harmed' (SRA, 2002, p.14). The collection of survey data generally involves a brief interview to which the citizen can withhold consent. Similarly, participation in focus group work is subject to consent by the citizen. In this type of work it is more practical to apply the doctrine of informed consent as the timescale permits fuller information to be given to participants.

Some qualitative forms of research such as observation or more intensive forms of interviewing make greater demands of subjects. They may be seen as intrusive by socially excluded groups in society, such as the homeless or women who are victims of violence. They may question why they should advance the careers of researchers when the chances of meaningful social or policy change resulting from the research are actually quite small. Such a perception is not misplaced given that, as has been argued earlier, the role of research may be more conservative than researchers often claim. However, groups that are 'researched out' by repeated inquiries may develop their own protection systems, setting up their own gatekeeping mechanisms (Barnes, 1979, p.164).

Social scientists have to pay some attention to the preferences of citizens as unco-operative members of the public can obstruct research in practice and in principle (Barnes, 1977, p.5). Citizens may therefore not be as weak in relation to researchers as some conventional accounts allow. The question of the relationship with research 'subjects' is usually one of the areas addressed in professional codes of ethics (see below). Failure to manage this relationship in a satisfactory way may increase pressures for the establishment of ethics committees in universities, increasing the transaction costs of research and perhaps discouraging innovation.

The problem of fraud in research

The pressures to succeed in modern academic life can lead students at undergraduate and postgraduate levels but also researchers to present fraudulent results. Krull notes (1999, p.145) that there is an increasing assumption that the big scandals which emerge are simply the tip of the iceberg. 'We have to pay more attention to the wide range of opportunities for committing scientific fraud' (Krull, 1999, p.146). In political science research this may involve tampering with

data to make results look more convincing, or even creating ficti-
tious interview results. A more common form of fraud is plagiarism.
This has come to mean 'the act of stealing or *presenting as one's
own,* the ideas or work of someone else' (Grix, 2001, p.120).

Rosamond (2002, p.166) notes that: 'Plagiarism is widely thought
of as perhaps the most grievous academic crime.' It has become an
increasing problem for universities as web technology has allowed
access to a wide range of papers without charge, leaving aside the
'essay mills' that sell 'off the peg' research or undertake customized
work. Rosamond makes a distinction between four approaches to
plagiarism. It can be seen as a spill-over from sloppy scholarship or
in legal terms as a breach of intellectual property rights. From an
ethical perspective it can be seen as a breach of another person's
human rights. Perhaps its most corrosive effect, however, is 'as an
infringement of those informal practices – as opposed to formal rules
– that allow academic life to proceed'. Above all, *'trust* is the cultural
glue that enables academia to function successfully' (Rosamond,
2002, p.168).

Krull (1999) conceptualizes fraud as a moral slippery slope. He
quotes Park as stating 'that few scientists ever set out to commit
fraud. "They simply reach a fork in the road and they take a wrong
turn" ' (Krull, 1999, p.144). Simple error is possible in any
research process. This may then be compounded by negligence, a
failure to observe proper procedures and processes. Researchers
may then succumb to fudging or fabricating data and finally to
plagiarism.

Researchers may justify such conduct to themselves as a means of
arriving at results that would have been obtained anyway under
conditions of extreme time pressure. Campbell observes (P.
Campbell, 1999, p.159): 'it seems inevitable the more pressure
people are under to deliver results in a fixed and constraining time,
the more likely it is that misconduct will ensue unless adequate
measures are in place to prevent it'. The increasing use of electronic
citation scores, and the ranking of journals in terms of prestige,
places researchers under increasing pressure to deliver results.

Professional codes of conduct

Professional associations of social and political scientists now generally provide 'codes of conduct' or 'ethical guidelines' for their
members. Indeed, it has been necessary to revise existing codes
'partly [as] a consequence of legislative changes in human rights and

data protection, but also [as] a result of increased public concern about the limits of inquiry' (SRA, 2002, p.1). Drawing up such codes of conduct is not an easy task. It is difficult to write them without enunciating conflicting principles. Social researchers face 'conflicting obligations not all of which can be fulfilled simultaneously.' Above all: 'Even within the same setting and branch of social research, individuals may have different moral precepts that guide their work. Thus no declaration could successfully impose a rigid set of rules to which social researchers everywhere should be expected to adhere' (SRA, 2002, p.2).

Another problem is the extent to which codes of conduct can be enforced. Political science is not a profession like law or medicine where a failure to follow the professional code of conduct can lead to withdrawal of a legal sanction to work. Given that researchers are generally concerned about their reputations, censure by a professional body might be regarded as sufficient punishment. However, those who breach ethical codes of conduct may be unlikely to be concerned about such judgements. In any case, perhaps the main function of such codes should be seen as 'educational' (SRA, 2002, p.2) enabling researchers to deal with ethical dilemmas they encounter in the course of their work. On a collective basis, they should be moved towards 'the establishment of systems for "research governance" – ways of discovering and sharing information that are open to public scrutiny and can be seen as subject to the highest ethical standards' (SRA, 2002, p.1).

This section compares and contrasts three codes of conduct: the Social Research Association, the American Political Science Association and the Political Studies Association (PSA) of the UK. They will be examined first in general terms; then in terms of the advice they offer about relationships with sponsors, gatekeepers and citizens; and finally in relation to the specific issue of the conflict between professional and political roles.

Although not specifically written for political scientists, the Social Research Association code is seen as offering a 'gold standard' in terms of its detailed but also very balanced advice. It was originally produced in the 1980s, drawing on the code of the International Statistical Ethics Committee, and was thoroughly revised in 2002. It is constructed on the basis that, while social research should be properly conducted, due recognition should be given to its social value. The code is organized under the following main headings: obligations to society; obligations to funders and employer; obligations to colleagues; obligations to subjects; ethics committees; and a standard protocol for checking ethical considerations (which is particularly helpful). It provides exten-sive references for further reading and also a contact e-mail address where researchers can obtain further advice.

The APSA code is very detailed (23 pages) and sometimes seems to be written in a rather legalistic language, perhaps reflecting the society in which it was drawn up. Indeed, paragraph 6.1 of the code reminds political scientists of their obligation as citizens to co-operate with grand juries, other law enforcement agencies and institutional officials. A report on professional ethics produced in 1968 led to the establishment of a Standing Committee on Professional Ethics. The statement of ethical principles was thor-oughly revised in 1968 and further changes in relation to ethics in tenure and promotion were approved in 1998. The code opens by emphasizing that political scientists 'frequently encounter ethical problems unique to their professional concerns' (APSA, 2002). However, many of the matters that the code deals with seem to be ones that would be matters for general codes for all academics or university procedures (e.g., recruitment and hiring, tenure and promotion, sexual harassment). Indeed, the code incorporates the statement on professional ethics of the American Association of University Professors.

The PSA statement is a rather minimalist one, occupying two pages in the members' handbook. This may reflect a lack of enthusi-asm among some members of the Association for having a code at all. Many of the statements are of a rather general and common sense character, such as, 'members should conduct themselves in a manner that does not bring into disrepute the discipline and their profession'; 'Members should perform the work they undertake for their institutions in a timely, competent and efficient manner'; 'The development of knowledge depends on high personal standards of scholarly conduct' (PSA, 2002, p.83). Despite its brevity, the code does address in a way that the other two did not the question of rela-tionships between colleagues. PSA members are advised that 'They should not prejudice individuals, communities, agencies or institu-tions against a colleague for reasons of personal advantage. (PSA, 2002, p.83). More surprisingly, 'Members should not allow intellec-tual difficulties or personal animosities among colleagues to impinge on students' relationships with those colleagues' (PSA, 2002, p.84). Perhaps the inclusion of these statements says something about rela-tionships between colleagues in British political science departments or about British political scientists!

Each of the codes has something to say on the subject of relations with sponsors. The SRA sets out what funders can expect from researchers and what researchers can expect from funders. The code emphasizes that 'Research cannot be exempt from quality assurance procedures. High quality research demands high qualities in ethical standards and a concern to ensure that procedures agreed to at the design stage are maintained throughout a project' (SRA, 2002, p.9). The APSA code sets out principles for funding agencies, universities and researchers. Particular American concerns are reflected in the inclusion of a statement that research should not be sponsored as a cover for intelligence activities (a practice that is nevertheless not unknown). The PSA provides one line of advice, 'Members should not allow the undertaking of sponsored research to damage or otherwise impair the academic integrity of their professional conduct' (PSA, 2002, p.84).

Relationships with gatekeepers are a particularly difficult area for political scientists. The problems they face are rather different from those encountered in other areas of social research. The SRA implicitly views gatekeepers as protecting relatively vulnerable research subjects, hence the recommendation that the responsibility of protection should not be devolved on the gatekeeper but that informed consent should be obtained directly from the research subjects. Researchers are also cautioned about inadvertently disturbing the relationship between subject and gatekeeper. Political scientists really need advice on how to deal with powerful gatekeepers who impose unacceptable conditions on access or seek to manipulate research findings. Unfortunately, the two political science codes are silent on this important subject.

All the codes have something to say about responsibilities to citizens. The SRA sets out the useful general principle that 'in planning all phases of an inquiry, from design to presentation of findings, social researchers should consider the likely consequences for society at large, groups and categories of persons within it, respondents or other subjects, and possible future research' (SRA, 2002, p.5). It is also pointed out that 'One way of avoiding inconvenience to potential subjects is to make more use of available data instead of embarking on a new inquiry' (SRA, 2002, p.13). The APSA has only two paragraphs on 'principles governing research on human subjects'. Its recommendation on the subject is rather flabby: 'Possible risk to human subjects is something that political scientists should take into account' (APSA, 2002, p.21). Perhaps this is because since 1991 there has been a regulation setting out a Federal Policy for the Protection of Human Subjects. The PSA advises its members to treat their research subjects 'fairly', elaborating this statement in terms of informed consent and not promising 'greater confidentially than can be realistically guaranteed' (PSA, 2002, p.84).

There is a potential conflict of interest between the roles of political scientists as academics and in public life. Fenno argues (1990, p.24) on the basis of his research experiences in the USA that the key value of professional credibility depends on 'some separation between the world of political science and the world of politics . . . some kind of boundary between them'. In Fenno's view (1990, pp.24–5), 'There is a big need in our business for more people to study politicians, not to become politicians.' His stance is similar to that of a founding member of the profession in the UK who scrupulously refused to place an election poster in his window in a marginal constituency.

In practice, this separation can be difficult to maintain. Universities like their academics to appear on radio and television and to secure column inches in the press. Universities may operate their own studios to facilitate this process. However, if one is on a late-night phone-in show, academic detachment will hardly meet the needs of the presenter or the audience. They want crisp and preferably controversial statements that will maintain a healthy queue of calls on the monitor.

This issue is one that the PSA addresses in the first paragraph of its guidelines. 'Members are entitled to hold political opinions and to act politically. However they have a general duty not to present their own political convictions as though they carry the authority of professional knowledge' (PSA, 2002, p.83). In practice, this difference may be difficult to maintain. For example, supposing a political scientist is on a radio phone-in show on British membership of the Euro which he or she supports; what constitutes an expert opinion and what is a political value judgement? The APSA advises its members that 'Academic political scientists must be very careful not to impose their partisan views, conventional or otherwise, upon students or colleagues' (APSA, 2002, p.8). Leaving aside the question of whether one could 'impose' anything on as quirky and individualistic a character as the average political scientist, where does one draw the line between explaining to students one's own stance in relation to an issue and imposing views on them? Ethical codes of conduct can help us to think about difficult issues of conduct, but they cannot always resolve them.

Conclusions

As the SRA points out (2002, p.1) 'In recent years ethical considerations across the research community have come to the forefront'; yet this trend is not reflected in most books or articles by political scientists. Researchers may discuss the research procedures they have used in their study (although often that discussion is rather cursory), but there is rarely any reference to ethical dilemmas. This chapter has shown that many ethical problems do arise in the course of research. 'Researchers may have high moral aspirations, but their expectations concerning their colleagues' ethical behavior seem to be quite low' (Krull, 1999, p.144). A study at the well known Center for Disease Control and Prevention in Atlanta 'found that more than half of 400 medical researchers knew of cases where their colleagues had cheated in clinical trials' (Krull, 1999, p.145). Can we be satisfied that political scientists have higher standards than medical researchers?

A failure to respond to these issues may lead to a greater reliance on ethics committees in universities. These were originally used in relation to medical research where there are particular problems in relation to patient confidentiality and harm to individuals. There are risks in this approach that may have the effect of strengthening the position of gatekeepers who object to research simply because it is inconvenient or involves risks:

> [researchers] in the USA have had problems with [such committees] being more concerned about legal threats to the employing organisation than with the 'benefits to society' of the proposed research. These ethics committees may serve more as a means of institutional protection than operating in the interests of either subject or researcher. Over-protective and bureaucratic procedures can pose a danger of restricting valuable, particularly innovative, social research methods. (SRA, 2002, pp.23–4)

A balanced approach to these questions is necessary. We must be wary of accepting too readily a model of 'the researcher as exploiter' or 'the researcher as fraud'. 'In most contemporary societies there are threats to the scope of social enquiry from legislative pressure intended to protect the rights of individuals. Such legislation may lead to diluted research activity as a consequence of the fear of litigation' (SRA, 2002, p.4). Social researchers need 'to balance a concern for individual rights with the greater benefits to society of their research activity.' (p.4.). Researchers should resist the temptation to act as secular priests, making wide-ranging statements about how society should operate on the basis of relatively limited research. They should show a proper attention to the ethical issues raised in this chapter, but they should also be prepared to defend the benefits of social and political research.

Chapter 12

Conclusion: Challenging the Mainstream and the Qualitative/Quantitative Divide

The aim of this book has been to present and review the main qualitative and quantitative approaches to research in social science and discuss their application to the discipline of political science. It is important to be aware, however, that in the last two decades the adequacy of these dominant qualitative and quantitative approaches to research has been questioned by a number of critics. The most significant and vocal criticism has emerged from the feminist, anti-racist and Marxist camps and it is to these critics that our attention must now turn. We conclude by returning briefly to the issue of theoretical assumptions and the choice of methods, considering in particular the relationship between qualitative and quantitative approaches. Finally, we offer a guide for further reading with examples from each of the qualitative and quantitative areas covered in the preceding chapters.

Feminist methods?

As a discipline, political science has been slow to respond to the challenges presented by feminist theory (Randall, 1983, p.38; Meehan, 1986, p.120). In terms of research methods it could be argued that political science has yet to make a response, despite the emergence of a lively dialogue in the cognate discipline of sociology.

One of the earliest, and still most influential, feminist critiques of the social sciences was presented by Millman and Kanter (1975), who identified a number of problematic assumptions in sociological inquiry. As Sandra Harding (1986, p.85) summarizes, Millman and Kanter's criticism pointed to the 'depth and extent of the feminist charge that masculine bias in social inquiry has consistently made women's lives invisible, that it has distorted our understanding of

270

women's and men's interactions and beliefs and the social structures within which such behaviours and beliefs occur'.

Building on Millman and Kanter, Harding (1986, p.85; 1997, pp.160–70) lists five 'sources of androcentrism in social inquiry'. First, important areas of social and political inquiry have been overlooked through the use of conventional field-defining models. For instance, 'the role of emotion in social life and social structure' tends to become invisible in sociological and political analyses that focus exclusively on Weberian rationality (Harding, 1986, p.86). Second, the tendency of political science to focus on the official, public, visible and dramatic role players has obscured the 'unofficial, supportive, less dramatic, private, and invisible spheres of social organisation' (Harding, 1986, p.86), where women predominate and which may be equally important in shaping power relations and social structures. Third, research in politics and sociology has often assumed a 'single society', with respect to men and women. This tendency to generalize unproblematically about all participants fails to uncover differences in position and interests, and ignores the 'misfit between women's consciousness, desires, and needs and the roles assigned to women' (Harding, 1986, p.87). Fourth, in many political studies gender difference is simply not taken into account as a factor in behaviour. In other words, there is a persistent failure to analyse the impact of gender at the level of research design and practice. Finally, Harding notes that many quantitative research methods may systematically prevent the discovery of certain kinds of important information. The tendency to deal with 'variables rather than persons' may, according to Millman and Kanter (1975, p.xvi), 'be associated with an unpleasantly exaggerated masculine style of control and manipulation'.

In addition, the impact of the gender of the researcher is, it is argued, an important factor to consider when assessing the adequacy of results. Men do not, as a rule, have access to many women-centred aspects of social life and indirect access is often gained through other male informants. The 'reactive effect' of men researching 'women issues' (that is, their presence changing the situation they are observing) has of course been well documented in anthropological studies (Leacock, 1982; Harding, 1986, pp.90–1).

There can be no doubting the power and validity of the feminist critique. The importance of using women's experiences as resources for social analysis has implications across the disciplines of politics and international relations (see, e.g., Enloe, 1989; Tickner, 2001;

Rai, 2002). In this sense, as Harding (1997, p.164) points out, 'feminist inquiry joins other "underclass" approaches in insisting on the importance of studying ourselves and "studying up", instead of "studying down" '. Psychiatrists, Harding notes as an example, have often studied what they regard as women's peculiar mental and behavioural characteristics, but women have only recently begun to study the bizarre mental and behavioural characteristics of psychiatrists. In this way, the best feminist analysis 'insists that the inquirer her/himself be placed in the same critical plane as the overt subject matter, thereby recovering the entire research process for scrutiny in the results of research' (Harding, 1997, p.164). In other words, the class, ethnicity, culture and gender assumptions of the researcher must be available for analysis alongside the results of research. However, whilst there is general agreement that 'sexism and androcentricity' in research should be challenged (Eichler, 1988), and that the 'recovery of women's voices and experiences' is an essential task (Kemp and Squires, 1997; Hague, Mullender and Aris, 2003), there is a division within the feminist camp over the appropriateness of particular research methods. Three basic positions can be identified.

First, a large number of feminist researchers adopt a position labelled by Harding as 'feminist empiricism' (Harding, 1986, p.24). In this view, which has a counterpart in Evans' (1986, p.1) discussion of feminism and political theory, research methods are largely value-neutral. Sexism and androcentricity are caused by 'social biases' (Harding, 1997, p.166) which exist in the assumptions of researchers but not in the techniques that they employ. These prejudices can enter research at any stage from the design of research to the collection and interpretation of data. Both Roberts (1990) and Eichler (1988) appear to endorse elements of this view, with the latter concluding, 'we have not identified any method that could not be used in either a sexist or non-sexist manner. In principle, then, methods per se are neither sexist nor non-sexist; it is the way in which they are used (or misused) that makes them (non)-sexist' (Eichler, 1988, p.154). Existing methods can therefore be retained, although of course their use may be strikingly different from that of androcentric researchers. As Harding (1997, p.161) notes, feminist researchers:

> listen carefully to how women informants think about their lives and men's lives, and critically to how traditional social scientists conceptualise women's and men's lives. They observe behaviours of women and men that traditional social scientists have not

thought significant. They seek examples of newly recognised patterns in historical data.

Despite the sensitivity of this approach, it is open to the charge that sexism is not simply an individual problem but is one shaped by 'culture-wide androcentric prejudices' (Harding, 1997, p.166) and that received models of science and the scientific method are themselves inherently sexist.

The second response of the feminist movement to the 'problem of method' highlights the weaknesses of 'feminist empiricism' and seeks to confront the 'problem of gender bias on a more fundamental level' (Jones and Jonasdottir, 1988, p.4). It is a position often termed the 'feminist standpoint' approach (Harding, 1986, p.26; Nielsen, 1990, p.10). In this view, feminist empiricism is criticized for adopting a very narrow definition of 'techniques' of research that 'fails to consider the limitations of the meta-theoretical framework within which the application of research tools occurs' (Jones and Jonasdottir, 1988, p.4). Personal attitudes can of course influence the construction of research design but 'attitudes reflect more than the personal psycho-histories of given theorists' (Jones and Jonasdottir, 1988, p.5). To address the problem of sexism in research it is necessary, in this view, to 'reconstruct the methodology of political research by reformulating basic categories of political thinking in order to allow gender to infect the ways we conceptualise political reality with the insights of a feminist vision' (Jones and Jonasdottir, 1988, p.5).

This reconstruction is achieved by adopting 'feminist standpoint' epistemology which draws on Hegel's analysis of the master/slave relationship. As Harding (1986, p.26) points out, the 'feminist standpoint' proposes that men's dominating position in social life results in partial and perverse understandings, whereas women's subjugated position provides the possibility of more complete and less perverse understandings. Through analysis of feminist theory and political struggles against male domination, the 'perspective of women' can be transformed into a 'feminist standpoint': 'a morally and scientifically preferable grounding for our interpretations and explanations of nature and social life' (Harding, 1986, p.26). Standpoint theory is therefore grounded in women's experience, as understood within the feminist camp, and calls for the development of new approaches to research leading to a more complete knowledge of the position of women (Nielsen, 1990, p.25; Reinharz, 1992). Reinharz (1992, p.219) provides examples of feminist researchers creating new qualitative and quantitative methods 'because the knowledge they seek *requires* it'. Consciousness-raising, which can include small group meetings over an extended period to discuss personal experiences without professional leadership; group and individual diary writing; feminist group interviews; dramatic role-play; genealogy and network tracing; the use of literature and fiction to reveal 'direct subjectivity'; the non-authoritative research voice; multiple-person stream of consciousness narrative; and free-speaking, are all cited as examples of 'original feminist research methods' that seek to break free of existing methodological constraints (Rienharz, 1992, p.239).

Sharing the concerns of standpoint theory but with a greater emphasis on 'difference' and the 'fractured identities of modern life' is the third position on feminist methods, termed 'feminist postmodernism' or 'postempiricism' (Harding, 1986, p.27; Neilsen, 1990, p.26). From the post-modern viewpoint, standpoint theory has two central weaknesses. First, the standpoint concept implies that one group's view is more real (better or accurate) than that of other groups; but, as Nielsen (1990, p.25) recognizes, this raises the question of whether there is an accepted criterion of accuracy. The implication that the greater the oppression, the more accurate the view, seems highly implausible. Second, the post-modern view rejects the idea that there can be a single feminist standpoint, if women's (and feminists') experience is divided by class, ethnicity and culture (Harding, 1986, p.26). The 'totalizing' aspect of standpoint theory threatens to replicate the 'disastrous alliance of knowledge and power characteristic of the modern epoch', reproducing the 'problematic politics of essentialised identities' (Harding, 1986, p.27). In response, the post-modern view seeks to 'go beyond relativism and objectivism', embracing the different identities of modern life, 'the Black-feminist, socialist-feminist, women-of-color etc' (Nielsen, 1990, p.27; see also Harding, 1986, p.28).

In terms of research methods, the post-modern view seems to share standpoint theory's distrust of traditional approaches and techniques. New methods are to be sought which are capable of revealing the diversity of women's experience. In this respect Reinharz (1992, p.240) identifies a number of key themes which characterize a feminist methodology rooted in diversity:

- feminism is a perspective, not a research method
- feminists use a multiplicity of research methods
- feminist research involves an ongoing criticism of non-feminist scholarship

- feminist research is guided by feminist theory
- feminist research may be transdisciplinary
- feminist research aims to create social change
- feminist research strives to represent human diversity
- feminist research frequently includes the researcher as a person
- feminist research frequently attempts to develop special relations with the people studied
- feminist research frequently defines a special relation with the reader.

Anti-racist and Marxist challenges

Feminist critiques have also contributed to the articulation of anti-racist methodologies, and in many respects anti-racist literature follows the same categorization applied above to feminist methods. For example, whilst a number of researchers have sought to use traditional methods with sensitivity to issues of 'race' and ethnicity (Ladner, 1971; Weis, 1985; Duffield, 1988), others such as Ben-Tovim et al., (1986), have attempted to dissolve the distinction between researchers and activists and adopted an overt anti-racist standpoint (Harvey, 1990, p.180; Stanfield, 1993). In a similar vein, Collins (1991) attempts to develop an 'Afrocentric feminist epistemology'. Researching the 'black experience' from an afrocentric viewpoint involves for Collins (1991, pp.208, 212) using 'concrete experience as a criterion of meaning' and carefully developing the 'use of dialogue' as a research technique, which she claims has deep roots in an African-based oral tradition and in African-American culture. Van Dijk's (1993) attempt to analyse racism through discourse and conversational analysis provides a further example of innovative techniques adopted from an anti-racism standpoint.

A number of Marxist researchers have also questioned the validity and 'objectivity' of dominant research methods and sought to develop research from a distinctive 'working-class' standpoint. For instance, Cleaver (1979, p.11) claims that in contrast to the dominant 'passive readings of Marx', it is possible to recover a 'political reading' that 'self-consciously and unilaterally structures its approach to determine the meaning and relevance of every concept to the immediate development of working-class struggle'. This, according to Cleaver (1979, p.43), requires the use of new methods that are able to examine the 'struggles of workers themselves, not their "official" organisations (trade unions, parties, etc)'. In this respect, he cites the research produced by the Italian 'autonomia' movement focusing on the composition and political recomposition of the Italian working class (in the factory and the home) as an example of working-class standpoint research (Cleaver, 1979, p.54; T. Negri, 1988; A. Negri 1991).

Finally, in a slightly wider context, it is worth noting that the Frankfurt school of critical Marxism has also produced a sustained critique of dominant approaches to research. This critique ranges from studies questioning the validity of the notion of 'public opinion' (Pollock, 1955, excerpt in Connerton, 1976, pp.225–36), to Habermas's complex account of 'knowledge and human interests' (Habermas, 1972), in which technical, practical and emancipatory interests give rise to the possibility of three sciences: the empirical analytic, the historical hermeneutic and the critical, each dominated by particular research approaches (although only critical social science, incorporating methodical self-reflection, dissolves relations of power and ideology).

Theory, methods and the qualitative/quantitative divide

The critiques outlined above, whilst varying in emphasis, consistency and plausibility, serve to reinforce a cardinal rule: it is initial assumptions, not data, that produces interesting social science. This is not, however, to endorse a clear-cut separation between theory and methods. As we indicated in Chapter 1, research cannot be perceived as a search for 'facts' existing independently of the observer; rather, the 'inevitability of conceptualisation' means that there is a very close fit between theoretical approach and the applicability of particular research techniques. Robert Cox's (1996, p.87) oft-quoted remark, 'theory is always for someone, for always for some purpose', should, in this sense, perhaps be re-written as, 'theory and method are always for someone, for some purpose'. This issue is often one of the hardest to grasp in the design of a piece of research and is easily misrepresented as the view that theory determines research findings. However, all that is being claimed is that there is a real correspondence between social ontology, epistemology and research methodology. As Colin Hay (2002, p.63) usefully summarizes, 'ontology relates to the nature of the social and political world, epistemology to what we can know about it and methodology to how we might go about acquiring that knowledge'. In other words, before it is possible to engage in research design (and choice of methods) researchers are forced to confront the question of what is the nature and purpose of political science? (Hay, 2002, p.64)? If, for instance, the deep feminist standpoint or post-modern critique of politics is accepted, then the methods of the classic psephologist are unlikely to be of much use compared to the techniques devised to recover 'women's voices'.

It is important, however, to acknowledge that this 'purist', almost 'fundamentalist', injunction to strive for correspondence between theoretical framework and method is rarely achieved in political science. This perhaps reflects the popular view that 'a fuller expla-nation inevitably involves the use of a number of different approaches or theoretical perspectives' (Dunleavy and O'Leary, 1987, quoted in Marsh and Stoker, 1995, p.291). Methodological pluralism is, however, to be distinguished from the slide into 'perspectivism' where 'anything goes' and incompatibilities are ignored. Marsh and Stoker (1995, p.290) are right to note that diver-sity is a strength but that the positive consequences of diversity are only likely 'if the proponents of a given position are sophisticated, not only in their exposition of their own position, but also in their treatment and critique of alternative positions'.

Finally, whilst we would argue that theoretical assumptions are crucial in framing research, it is our experience that the qualita-tive/quantitative divide is rather less clear-cut than is often assumed. Marsh and Stoker (1995, p.260) are surely right to point out that rational choice theorists will emphasize quantitative methods and discourse analysts will favour qualitative approaches. Nevertheless, most 'real world research' plays down the differences and calls for both qualitative and quantitative analysis, although usually in unequal measure (Ragin, 1987; Bryman, 1988; Robson, 1993).

Bryman (1988) suggests a number of ways in which quantitative and qualitative research has been combined to useful effect. First, the 'logic of triangulation' points to the ways in which quantitative and qualitative methods may be used to examine the same research prob-lem. In this regard Burgess (1982, p.163) points out that 'triangula-tion' (or the use of 'multiple strategies') is not confined to data triangulation (multiple sets of data) or theoretical triangulation (multiple theories), but can also encompass multiple investigators working in partnership across disciplines. Triangulation can over-come the problems associated with the single-method, single-investi-gator, single-data, single-theory study but, as Burgess (1982, p.166) concludes, multiple strategies can also prove costly in terms of time and money. Second, Bryman (1988, p.134) notes that qualitative research often acts as a precursor to the formulation of problems and the development of instruments (scales and indices) for quantitative research. The most obvious sense in which this is true is the way in which qualitative research findings act as 'a source of hunches or hypotheses' to be tested by quantitative research (Bryman, 1988, p.134). Crafts (1995), for instance, has taken a number of hypotheses developed by historians and political scientists and tested their adequacy using econometric investigation techniques. Third, it is possible, though less likely, that quantitative research precedes and provides an aid to qualitative work. Bryman (1988, pp.136, 145) indicates that research by Whyte (1976) on Peruvian villages followed this pattern with an examination of survey data leading to ethnographic research on village life. In this way qualitative research enables close investigation of statistical correlations, thereby furthering our understanding of complex relationships.

There are, of course, barriers to the combined use of qualitative and quantitative research techniques in terms of expertise, resources and the compatibility of epistemological positions (Bryman, 1988, p.153). However there is sufficient overlap to question the common assumption that qualitative and quantitative methods represent opposing ideal types and that there can be little fruitful exchange between the two. In fact, there appears to be an increased tendency for most policy-based studies to adopt some form of triangulation (www.esrc.ac.uk).

This book has indicated the diverse range of research methods in political science. It is perhaps fitting that we should end not with a list of methodological injunctions but by pointing students of political science and international relations in the direction of some particularly useful examples of research in each of the areas we have covered. The list given in the next section is by no means exhaustive, merely illustrative and guided by the view that the best way to learn about research is to do it, having carefully studied some excellent first-hand accounts.

Suggestions for Further Reading

Integration of theoretical/methodological concerns and empirical analysis

Van Der Pijl, K. (1984), *The Making of an Atlantic Ruling Class* (London, Verso). A carefully researched analysis of international class formation from the turn of the nineteenth century to the end of the 1970s. It is a classic example of how Marx's discussion of capital can be used to inform detailed empirical research.

Krasner, S. (1978), *Defending the National Interest* (Princeton, NJ, Princeton University Press). On the basis of a number of case studies of American raw material policy in the twentieth century, Krasner builds a distinctive approach to US foreign policy. Notable for its treatment of state theory and its articulation of the 'statist' approach.

Gill, S. (1990), *American Hegemony and the Trilateral Commission* (Cambridge, Cambridge University Press). Interesting analysis of the changing structure of power and hegemony in the global political economy since 1945 with particular reference to the Trilateral Commission. Careful analysis of published material is supplemented with over 100 elite interviews providing a classic study of the Gramscian approach in international political economy.

Research design

de Vaus, D. (2001), *Research Design in Social Research* (London, Sage). An excellent book which emphasizes the importance of prioritizing design issues in social research. The major types of research design are described and evaluated.

Hakim, C. (2000), *Research Design: Successful Designs for Economic and Social Research* (London, Routledge). A good introduction to the problems of research design in social science research.

Milgram, S. (1974), *Obedience to Authority* (New York, Harper & Row). The classic example of experimental design aimed to discover how far people would be willing to obey instructions even though this involved inflicting pain on others.

The comparative method

Lijphart, A. (1994), *Electoral Systems and Party Systems: A Study of Twenty-Seven Democracies, 1945–1990* (Oxford, Oxford University Press). Uses aspects of electoral systems as variables, and employs both within- and between-country comparisons to draw conclusions about the nature of the relationship between electoral systems and party systems.

Hug, S. and P. Sciarini (2000), 'Referendums on European Integration: Do Institutions Matter in the Voter's Decision?', *Comparative Political Studies*, Vol. 33, No. 1, pp.3–36. Compares referenda, and attempts to link referendum results to their institutional features.

Kopecky, P. and C. Mudde (2002), 'The Two Sides of Euroscepticism', *European Union Politics* Vol. 3, pp.297–326. Refines categories of positions on European integration (from opposition to support) by comparing political parties in a number of countries.

Surveys and opinion polls

Moon, N. (1999), *Opinion Polls: History, Theory and Practice* (Manchester, Manchester University Press). A good discussion of the theory and methodology of opinion polls and why they sometimes make false election predictions.

Evans, G. and P. Norris (eds) (1999), *Critical Elections: British Parties and Voters in Long-Term Perspective* (London, Sage). This book draws on the British Election Study 1997 to analyse the impact of the 1997 General Election on party competition, social support for parties, abstentions and new electoral alignments.

Saggar, S. (2000), *Race and Representation: Electoral Politics and Ethnic Pluralism in Britain* (Manchester, Manchester University Press). A careful analysis of the electoral participation of ethnic minority voters in the UK, based on the booster sample of ethnic minorities in the British Election Survey of 1997.

Norris, P. (2002), *Democratic Phoenix: Reinventing Political Activism* (New York, Cambridge University Press). Discusses theories and trends in political activism across the world. Challenges the view that political activism is in decline. Considerable use is made of survey data.

Descriptive statistics

Dalton, R. and R. Eichenberg (1998), 'Citizen Support for Policy Integration', in W. Sandholtz and A. Stone Sweet (eds), *European Integration and Supranational Governance* (Oxford, Oxford University Press). Uses descriptive statistics to show levels of public support for the EU having policy-making capacity in different policy areas.

Holmberg, S. (1999), 'Wishful Thinking Among European Parliamentarians', in H. Schmitt and J. Thomassen (eds), *Political Representation and Legitimacy in the European Union* (Oxford, Oxford University Press). Compares MEPs' and voters' attitudes, showing that MEPs are typically out of step with public opinion. Shows interesting examples of ways to present descriptive statistics.

Curtice, J. and M. Steed (2002), 'Appendix 2: An Analysis of the Results', in D. Butler, and D. Kavanagh, *The British General Election of 2001* (Basingstoke: Palgrave). Presents descriptive statistics from the election in cross-tabular format.

Inference-making

Sartori, G. (1994) *Comparative Constitutional Engineering: An Inquiry into Structures, Incentives and Outcomes* (London, Macmillan). Compares three types of political systems (presidentialism, parliamentary systems, semi-presidentialism), and infers which type of system is preferable. Qualitative inference.

Stokes, S. (2001), *Mandates and Democracy: Neoliberalism by Surprise in Latin America* (Cambridge, Cambridge University Press). Examines the relationship between democracy and neo-liberal economic reforms through the lens of some Latin American cases, and infers under what conditions neo-liberal economic reform damages democracy, and under what conditions it does not do so. Mixes qualitative and quantitative material.

Birch, S. (2003), 'Two-Round Electoral Systems and Democracy', *Comparative Political Studies*, Vol. 36, No. 3, pp.319–44. Infers non-obvious consequences of a two-round electoral system from a study that includes a fairly large-*n* sample. Quantitative inference.

Documentary and archival analysis

Milward, A. (1984), *The Reconstruction of Western Europe 1945–51* (London, Methuen). Classic reinterpretation of European post-war reconstruction drawing on archival sources from six countries and documentary material from eleven more. Illustrates how archives can be drawn upon to build a clear argument rather than simply offer a narrative.

Gardner, R. (1980), *Sterling Dollar Diplomacy in Current Perspective*, expanded edition (New York, Columbia University Press). Carefully researched account of post-war diplomacy using official documents, newspaper reports, journals and other published material.

Goncharov, S., J. Lewis and X. Litai (1993), *Uncertain Partners: Stalin, Mao and the Korean War* (Stanford, CA, Stanford University Press).

Tripartite collaboration using a variety of archives and documentary sources from the USA, China, Korea and Russia.

The Internet and political research

White, J. (1999), *Politics on the Internet* (London: Politico's). This attempts to provide a comprehensive overview of available sites. Like all books on the Internet, the problem is one of dating.

Wright, S. (2002), 'Dogma or Dialogue?: The Politics of the Downing Street Website', *Politics*, Vol. 22, is a good discussion of some of the political issues surrounding the use of the Internet.

Elite interviewing

Rubin H. and Rubin, I. (1995), *Qualitative Interviewing* (London, Sage). This remains the most useful text on qualitative interviewing and *Political Science and Politics*, Vol. 35, No. 4, December (2002), contains a number of helpful articles on the application of the technique in the study of politics.

Deakin, N. and Parry, R. (2000), *The Treasury and Social Policy* (London, Macmillan). This book offers an excellent example of its effective application.

Jones, A. and Clark, J. (2001), *The Modalities of European Union Governance* (Oxford, Oxford University Press). This book makes effective use of interviews with over one hundred actors in the EU multi-level governance system.

Participant observation and discourse analysis

Whyte, W.F. (1993), *Street Corner Society: The Social Structure of an Italian Slum*, 4th edn (London, University of Chicago Press). This is a classic study of participant observation and is particularly valuable because of the discussion of methodological issues in the appendices. The challenges presented to the researcher by problems of access, recording observations and ethical dilemmas are sensitively analysed. The study is also enjoyable to read.

Okely, J. (1983), *The Traveller Gypsies* (Cambridge, Cambridge University Press). An excellent study which shows how groups which are difficult to access and research by 'scientific' research methods can be successfully studied by participant observation.

Budge, I. (1999), 'Party Policy and Ideology: Reversing the 1950s?', in G. Evans, and P. Norris (eds), *Critical Elections and Voters in Long-Term*

Perspective (London, Sage). An illuminating study of how content analysis can be used to measure changes in party ideology over time.

Fairclough, N. (2000), *New Labour, New Language* (London, Routledge). An important analysis of the political discourse of New Labour. It shows the importance of language in politics and how dominating the contemporary political discourse is an important ingredient of political success.

Schmidt V.A. (2002), *The Futures of European Capitalism* (Oxford, Oxford University Press). This innovative study examines how political and economic policies, practices and discourses have changed in response to globalization and Europeanization. It emphasizes the importance of political discourses in generating and legitimating changes in policy and practices.

References

Ackoff, R.L. (1953), *Design of Social Research* (Chicago, IL, University of Chicago Press).

Almond, G. (1990) *A Discipline Divided: Schools and Sects in Political Science* (London, Sage).

Almond, G. and Genco, S. (1990), 'Clouds, Clocks and the Study of Politics' in G. Almond, *A Discipline Divided: Schools and Sects in Political Science* (London, Sage).

Almond, G. and Verba, S. (eds) (1989), *The Civic Culture Revisited* (London, Sage).

Almond, G. and Verba, S. (1963), *The Civic Culture: Political Attitudes and Democracy in Five Countries* (Princeton, NJ, Princeton University Press).

Andrew, C. and Mitrokhin, V. (2000), *The Mitrokhin Archive* (Harmondsworth, Penguin).

Angstrom, J., Hedenstrom, E. and Strom, L.-I. (2003), 'Survival of the most cited? Small political science communities and international influence: the case of Sweden', *European Political Science*, Vol. 2, No. 3, 5–15.

APSA (2002), http://www.apsanet.org/pubs/ethics.cfm, 27 March.

Archer, M. (1995), *Realist Social Theory* (Cambridge, Cambridge University Press).

Armer, M. (1973), 'Methodological Problems and Possibilities in Comparative Research', in M. Armer and A. Grimshaw (eds), *Comparative Social Research: Methodological Problems and Strategies* (London, John Wiley).

Armstrong, J. and Jones, S. (1987), *Business Documents* (London, Mansell).

Asian Development Bank (2002), http://www.adb.org (August).

Atherton, L. (1994), *Never Complain, Never Explain: Records of the Foreign Office and State Paper Office 1500–c. 1960* (London, PRO).

Bachrach, P. and Baratz, M. (1970), *Power and Poverty* (Oxford, Oxford University Press).

Bales, R.F. (1951), *Interaction Process Analysis* (Reading, MA, Addison-Wesley).

Bank of England archives, various.

Barnes, J.A. (1977) *The Ethics of Inquiry in Social Science* (Delhi, Oxford University Press).

Barnes, J.A. (1979), *Who Should Know What? Social Science, Privacy and Ethics* (Harmondsworth, Penguin).

Barrow, M. (1996) *Statistics for Economics, Accounting and Business Studies* (London, Prentice Hall).

Barry, B. (2000) 'The Study of Politics as a Vocation' in J. Hayward, B. Barry and A. Brown (eds), *The British Study of Politics in the Twentieth Century* (Oxford, Oxford University Press).

Baumgartner, F.R. and Jones, B.D. (1993), *Agendas and Instability in Amercian Politics* (London, University of Chicago Press).

284

Becker, H. S. (1963), *Outsiders: Studies in the Sociology of Deviance* (New York, Free Press).

Beckham, V. (2001), *Learning to Fly* (Harmondsworth, Penguin)

Bell, C. (1977), 'Reflections on the Banbury Restudy', in C. Bell and H.J. Newby, *Doing Sociological Research* (London, George Allen & Unwin).

Bell, C. and Newby, H.J. (eds) (1977), *Doing Sociological Research* (London, George Allen & Unwin).

Benn, T. (1989), *Against the Tide: Diaries 1973–1976* (London, Hutchinson).

Benton, T. (1977), *Philosophical Foundations of the Three Sociologies* (London, Routledge & Kegan Paul).

Ben-Tovim, G., Gabriel, L., Law, I. and Stredder, K. (1986), *The Local Politics of Race* (London, Macmillan).

Berelson, B. (1952), *Content Analysis in Communication Research* (New York, Free Press).

Berelson, B. and Salter, P. (1946), 'Majority-Minority Americans: An Analysis of Magazine Fiction', *Public Opinion Quarterly*, Vol. 10 (summer), 168–90.

Berger, P. and Luckmann, T. (1967), *The Social Construction of Reality* (Harmondsworth, Penguin).

Berry, J.M. (2002) 'Validity and Reliability Issues in Elite Interviewing', *Political Science and Politics*, Vol. 24, pp. 679–82.

Beynon, H. (1973), *Working for Ford* (Harmondsworth, Penguin).

Bhaskar, R. (1979), 'On the Possibility of Social Scientific Knowledge and the Limits of Naturalism', in J. Mepham and D.-H. Ruben (eds), *Issues in Marxist Philosophy Volume Three* (Brighton, Harvester).

Bhaskar, R. (1989), *The Possibility of Naturalism : A Philosophical Critique of the Contemporary* (London, Harvester Wheatsheaf).

Billard, L. (2000), 'The Census Count: Who Counts? How Do We Count? When Do We Count?', *Political Science and Politics*, Vol. 33, 767–74.

Billig, M. (1978), *Fascists: A Social-Psychological View of the National Front* (London, Academic Press).

Birkenhead, E. (1961), *The Prof in Two Worlds* (London, Collins).

Blais, A., Gidengil, E., Nadeau, R. and Nevete, N. (2003), 'Campaign Dynamics in the 2000 Canadian Election: How the Leader Debates Salvaged the Conservative Party', *Political Science and Politics*, Vol. 36, 45–50.

Blyth, M.M. and Vargese, R. (1999) 'The State of the discipline in American Political Science: be careful what you wish for?', *British Journal of Politics and International Relations*, Vol. 1, 345–65.

Boelen, W.A.M. (1992), 'Street Corner Society: Cornerville Revisited', *Journal of Contemporary Ethnography*, Vol. 21, No. 1, 11–51.

Bowley, A.L. (1913), 'Working Class Households in Reading', *Journal of the Royal Statistical Society*, Vol. 78, 672–701.

Brittan, S. (1964), *The Treasury under the Tories* (Harmondsworth, Penguin).

Bromund, T.R. (2002) 'A Guide to Planning and Conducting Research in Contemporary British History on the Internet', *Contemporary British History*, Vol. 16, 109–22.

Bruyn, S.T. (1962), 'The Methodology of Participant Observation', *Human Organisation*, Vol. 21, 224–35.

Bryman, A. (1988), *Quantity and Quality in Social Research* (London, Routledge).

Bryman, A. (2001) *Social Research Methods* (Oxford: Oxford University Press).

BSA (1994), *Statement of Ethical Practice*, http:www.socresonline.org.uk/info/ethguide/html.

Budge, I. (1999), 'Party Policy and Ideology: Reversing the 1950s?', in G. Evans and P. Norris (eds), *Critical elections and Voters in Long-Term Perspective* (London, Sage).

Budge, I. and Laver, M. (eds), (1992), *Party Policy and Government Coalitions* (London, Macmillan).

Budge, I., Crewe, I. and Fairlie, D. (1976), *Party Identification and Beyond* (London, John Wiley).

Budge, I., Klingemann, H.-D., Volkens, A., Bara, J. and Tanenbaum, E. (2001), *Mapping Policy Preferences. Estimates for Parties, Electors, and Governments 1945–1998* (Oxford, Oxford University Press).

Budge, I., Robertson, D. and Hearl, D. (eds), (1987), *Ideology, Strategy and Party Change: Spatial Analyses of Post-war Election Programmes in 19 Democracies* (Cambridge, Cambridge University Press).

Bulmer, M. (2001) 'The Ethics of Social Research', in N. Gilbert (ed.), *Researching Social Life* (London: Sage).

Burgess, R.G. (ed.) (1982), *Field Research: A Sourcebook and Field Manual* (London, Unwin Hyman).

Burgess, R.G. (1984), *In the Field: An Introduction to Field Research* (London, Routledge).

Burgess, R.G. (1993), *Research Methods* (Walton-on-Thames, Nelson).

Burnham, P. (ed.) (1997), *Surviving the Research Process in Politics* (London, Pinter).

Burton, F. (1978), *The Politics of Legitimacy: Struggles in a Belfast Community*, (London, Routledge & Kegan Paul).

Butler, D. (1969), *The Sunday Times*, 28 September.

Butler, D. and Kavanagh, D. (1998), *The British General Election of 1997* (London, Macmillan).

Butler, D. and Kavanagh, D. (2002), *The British General Election of 2001*, (Basingstoke, Palgrave).

Butler, D. and Stokes, D. (1969, 2nd edn 1974), *Political Change in Britain: Forces Shaping Electoral Choice* (London, Macmillan).

Campbell, J. (2001), *Margaret Thatcher, Volume 1* (London, Pimlico).

Campbell, P. (1999), 'Publications: Pressure to Publish, Selective Practice by Journals, Citation Indices as Factors Producing Scientific Misbehaviour', in Max-Planck-Gesellschaft (ed.), *Ethos der Forschung: Ethics of Research* (Munich, Generalverwaltung der Max-Planck-Gesellschaft).

Cantwell, J. (1993), *The Second World War* (London, HMSO).

Carr, E. (1964), *What is History?* (Harmondsworth, Penguin).

Carson, D. (ed.) (2001), *Directory of Genealogical and Historical Libraries, Archives and Collections in the US and Canada* (Niwot, Iron Gate).

Catterall, P. (1994), 'Autobiographies and Memoirs', in P. Catterall and H. Jones (eds), *Understanding Documents and Sources* (Oxford, Heinemann).

Catterall, P. and Jones, H. (eds) (1994), *Understanding Documents and Sources* (Oxford, Heinemann).

Chalmers, A. (1980), *What is This Thing Called Science?* (Buckingham, Open University Press)

Chalmers, A. (1990), *Science and its Fabrication* (Buckingham, Open University Press).

Charlton, T., Coles, D. and Hannan, A. (1999), 'Behaviour of Nursery Class Children Before and After the Availability of Broadcast Television: A Naturalistic Study of Two Cohorts in a Remote Community', *Journal of Social Behaviour*, Vol. 14, 315–24.

Charlton, T., Gunter, B. and Coles, D. (1998), 'Broadcast Television as a Cause of Aggression? Recent Findings from a Naturalistic Study', *Emotional and Behavioural Difficulties*, Vol. 3, 5–13.

Chen, P. and Hinton, S.M. (1999), 'Sociological Research Online', 4, http://www.socresonline.org.uk/socresonline/4/3/chen.html.

Chester, N. (1975) 'Political Studies in Britain: Recollections and Comments', *Political Studies*, Vol. 24, 151–64.

Clark, A. (1994), *Diaries* (London, Phoenix).

Clarke, P. (2002), *The Cripps Version* (London, Allen Lane Penguin).

Cleaver, H. (1979), *Reading Capital Politically* (Brighton, Harvester).

Coleman, W.D. and Tangermann, S. (1999) 'The 1992 CAP Reform, the Uruguay Round and the Commission: Conceptualizing Linked Policy games', *Journal of Common Market Studies*, Vol. 37, 385–405.

Collins, P. (1991), *Black Feminist Thought* (London, Routledge).

Colville, J. (1987), *The Fringes of Power: Downing Street Diaries 1939–1955: Volume 2: October 1941–1955* (Sevenoaks, Sceptre).

Congressional Directory 107th Congress, http://www.access.gpo.gov (August 2002).

Connerton, P. (ed.) (1976) *Critical Sociology* (Harmondsworth, Penguin).

Cook, C. and Waller, D. (1994), *The Longman Guide to Sources in Contemporary British History, Volume 1: Organisations and Societies* (London, Longman).

Cook, C., Leonard, J. and Leese, P. (1994), *The Longman Guide to Sources in Contemporary British History Volume 2: Individuals* (London, Longman).

Cowell-Myers, K. (2002), 'Problems in Interviewing Northern Ireland Legislators', *British Politics Group Newsletter,* No. 107, 9–10.

Cox, R. (1996), 'Social Forces, States and World Orders', in R. Cox with T. Sinclair, *Approaches to World Order* (Cambridge, Cambridge University Press), 85–123.

Crafts, N. (1995), ' "You've Never Had it So Good?" British economic policy and performance, 1945–1960', in B. Eichengreen (ed.), *Europe's Post-war Recovery* (Cambridge, Cambridge University Press).

Crookham, A. (1998), *The Trades Union Congress Archive 1960–70* (Warwick, Modern Records Centre).

Crookham, A. *et al.* (1997), *The Confederation of British Industry and Predecessor Archives* (Warwick, Modern Records Centre).

Crossman, R. (1975), *The Diaries of a Cabinet Minister, Vol. I, Minister of Housing 1964–66* (London, Hamish Hamilton and Jonathan Cape).

Dahl, R.A. (1961), *Who Governs: Democracy and Power in an American City* (New Haven, CT, Yale University Press).

Daly, F., Hand, M.J., Jones, M.C., Lunn, A.D., McConway, K.J. (1995) *Elements of Statistics* (Milton Keynes, Open University Press).

Daniel, W. (1968), *Racial Discrimination in England* (Harmondsworth, Penguin).

de Vaus, D. (2001), *Research Design in Social Research* (London, Sage).

Daugbjerg, C. (1998) *Policy Networks under Pressure* (Aldershot: Ashgate).

Deakin, N. and Parry, R. (2000), *The Treasury and Social Policy* (London, Macmillan).

Devine, F. (1992), *Affluent Workers Revisited: Privatism and the Working Class* (Edinburgh, Edinburgh University Press).

Devine, F. (1995) 'Qualitative Analysis', in D. Marsh and G. Stoker (eds), *Theory and Methods in Political Science* (London, Macmillan), 137–53.

Dexter, L.A. (1970), *Elite and Specialised Interviewing* (Evanston, IL, Northwestern University Press).

Docherty, D.C. (2002), 'Out of Town? Alone? Need Someone To Talk To?', *British Politics Group Newsletter*, No. 107, 7–9.

Dogan, M. and Pelassy, G. (1990), *How to Compare Nations* (Chatham, NJ, Chatham House).

Downs, A. (1957) *An Economic Theory of Democracy* (London, HarperCollins).

Dreijmanis, J. (1983) 'Political Science in the United States: The Discipline and the Profession', *Government and Opposition*, Vol. 18, 194–217.

Duffield, M. (1988), *Black Radicalism and the Politics of De-industrialisation* (Aldershot, Avebury).

Dunleavy, P., Margetts, H., Barstow, S., Callaghan, R. and Yared, H. (2002), *Progress in Implementing E Government in Britain: Supporting Evidence for the National Audit Office Report Government on the Web II* (London, National Audit Office).

Duverger, M. (1954), *Les Partis Politiques*, 2nd edn (Paris, Colin).

Eichler, M. (1988), *Nonsexist Research Methods* (London, Unwin Hyman).

Easton, D. (1965) *A Systems Analysis of Political Life* (New York, John Wiley).

Enloe, C. (1989), *Bananas, Beaches and Bases: Making Feminist Sense of International Politics* (London, Pandora).

EPS Net (2003) 'The Bologna Declaration and Political Science Curriculum. Statement by the Executive Council': http://www.epsnet.org/mem_ only/kisok-plusl/open_espnet.htm

Evans, J. (1986), 'Feminism and Political Theory', in J. Evans *et al.*, *Feminism and Political Theory* (London, Sage).

Fairclough, N. (2000), *New Labour, New Language?* (London, Routledge).

Farrell, D. (2001), *Electoral Systems: A Comparative Introduction* (Basingstoke, Palgrave).

Federal Electoral Commission (2002), http://www.state.nd.us (August).

Fenno, R.F. Jr (1990), *Watching Politicians: Essays on Participant Observation* (Berkeley, CA, IGS Press).

Feyerabend, P. (1975), *Against Method: Outline of an Anarchistic Theory of Knowledge* (London, NLB).

Filmer, P., Phillipson, M., Silverman, D. and Walsh, D. (1972), *New Directions in Sociological Theory* (London, Collier-Macmillan).

Foucault, M. (1980), *A History of Sexuality. Vol. 1* (New York, Random House).

Fowler, S. (1995), *Sources for Labour History* (London, PRO).

Freeman, D. (1984), *Margaret Mead and Samoa: The Making and Unmaking of an Anthropological Myth* (Harmondsworth, Penguin).

Friedman, T. L. (1989), *From Beirut to Jerusalem* (New York, Random House).

Friedman, T. L. (2002), *Longitudes and Attitudes* (New York, Farrar, Straus & Giroux).

Gallagher, M., Laver, M. and Mair, P. (2001), *Representative Government in Modern Europe: Institutions, Parties and Governments*, 3rd edn (London, McGraw-Hill).

Gamble, A. (2002), 'Political Memoirs', *The British Journal of Politics and International Relations*, Vol. 4, No. 1 (April) 141–51.

Gans, H.J. (1967), *The Levittowners: Ways of Life and Politics in a New Suburban Community* (London, Allen Lane).

Garfinkel, H. (1967), *Studies in Ethnomethodology* (Englewood Cliffs, NJ, Prentice Hall).

Gavin, N. and Sanders, D. (1997), 'The Economy and Voting', in P. Norris, and N. Gavin (eds), *Britain Votes 1997* (Oxford, Oxford University Press).

Geddes, B. (1990), 'How the Cases You Choose Affect the Answers You Get: Selection Bias in Comparative Politics', in J. Stimson (ed.), *Political Analysis 2* (Ann Arbor, MI, University of Michigan Press).

Gibson, R., McAllister, I. and Swenson, T. (2002), 'The Politics of Race and Immigration in Australia: One Nation Voting in the 1998 Election', *Ethnic and Racial Studies*, Vol. 25, No. 5, 823–44.

Gilland, K. (2001), 'Ireland and the International Use of Force' in P. Everts and P. Isernia (eds), *Public Opinion and the International Use of Force* (London, Routledge).

Giulianotti, R. (1995), 'Participant Observation and Research into Football Hooliganism: Problems of Entrée and Everyday Risks', *Sociology of Sport Journal*, Vol. 12, 1–20.

Gold, R. (1958), 'Roles in Sociological Field Observation', *Social Forces*, Vol. 36, No. 3, 217–23.

Goldstein, K. (2002), 'Getting in the Door: Sampling and Completing Elite Interviews', *Political Science and Politics*, Vol. 24, 669–72.

Goldthorpe, J.H., Lockwood, D., Bechofar, F. and Platt, J., (1968), *The Affluent Worker: Political Attitudes and Behaviour* (Cambridge, Cambridge University Press).

Gould, P. (1998), *The Unfinished Revolution* (London, Little, Brown).

Grant, W. (1995), *Autos, Smog and Pollution Control* (Aldershot, Edward Elgar).

Grant, W. (2001), 'Environmental Policy and Social Exclusion', *Journal of European Public Policy*, Vol. 8, 82–100.

Grant, W. and MacNamara, A. (1996), 'The Relationship Between Bankers and Farmers: An Analysis of Ireland', *Journal of Rural Studies*, Vol. 12, 427–37.

Green, E. (1994), 'Business Archives', in P. Catterall and H. Jones (eds), *Understanding Documents and Sources* (Oxford, Heinemann).

Grix, J. (2001) *Demystifying Postgraduate Research* (Birmingham, University of Birmingham Press).

Grix, J. (2002), 'Introducing Students to the Generic Terminology of Social Research', *Politics*, Vol. 22, No. 3 (September), 175–86.

Gujariti, D.N. (1995) *Basic Econometrics*, 3rd edn (New York, McGraw-Hill).

Habermas, J. (1972), *Knowledge and Human Interests* (London, Heinemann Educational).

Hague, R. and Harrop, M. (2001), *Comparative Government and Politics: An Introduction*, 5th edn (Basingstoke, Palgrave Macmillan).

Hague, G., Mullender, A. and Aris, R. (2003), *Is Anyone Listening?* (London, Routledge).

Hakim, C. (2000) *Research Design: Successful Designs for Social and Economic Research*, 2nd edn (London, Routledge).

Hall, R. (1989), *The Robert Hall Diaries 1947–1953*, edited by A. Cairncross (London, Unwin Hyman).

Hall, R. (1992), *The Robert Hall Diaries, 1954–1961*, edited by A. Cairncross (London, Unwin Hyman).

Hall, P. and Soskice, D. (2001) 'An Introduction to Varieties of Capitalism', in P. Hall and D. Soskice (eds), *Varieties of Capitalism: The Institutional Foundations of Comparative Advantage* (Oxford, Oxford University Press).

Hall, P. and Taylor, R. (1996), 'Political Science and the Three New Institutionalisms', *Political Studies*, Vol. 44, 936–57.

Hall, P. and Taylor, R. (1998), 'The Potential of Historical Institutionalism: A Response to Hay and Wincott', *Political Studies*, Vol. 46, 958–62.

Hall, S. (1983), 'The Great Moving Right Show', in S. Hall and M. Jacques (eds), *The Politics of Thatcherism* (London, Lawrence & Wishart).

Harding, S. (1986), *The Science Question in Feminism* (Milton Keynes, Open University Press).

Harding, S. (1997), 'Is there a Feminist Method?', in S. Kemp and J. Squires (eds), *Feminisms* (Oxford, Oxford University Press), 160–70.

Harrison, L. (2001), *Political Research: An Introduction* (London, Routledge).

Harrop, M. and Miller, W. (1984), *Elections and Voters: A Comparative Introduction* (London, Macmillan).

Harvey, L. (1990), *Critical Social Research* (London, Unwin Hyman).

Hay, C. (2002), *Political Analysis: A Critical Introduction* (Basingstoke, Palgrave).

Hay, C. and Wincott, D. (1998) 'Structure, Agency and Historical Institutionalism', *Political Studies*, Vol. 46, 951–7.

Hayward, J. (1991), 'Political Science in Britain', *European Journal of Political Research*, Vol. 20, 301–22.

Hayward, J. (2000), 'British Approaches to Politics: The Dawn of a Self-Deprecating Discipline' in J. Hayward, B. Barry and A. Brown (eds), *The British Study of Politics in the Twentieth Century* (Oxford, Oxford University Press).

Heath, A. and McDonald, S. K. (1988), 'The Demise of Party Identification Theory?', *Electoral Studies*, Vol. 7, 95–107.

Heath, A., Jowell, R. and Curtice, J. (2001), *The Rise of New Labour* (Oxford, Oxford University Press).

Heclo, H. and Wildavsky, A. (1974) *The Private Government of Public Money* (London, Macmillan).

Heclo, H. and Wildavsky, A. (1981), *The Private Government of Public Money*, 2nd edn (London, Macmillan).

Held, D. (1980), *Introduction to Critical Theory* (London, Polity).

Hennessy, P. (2002), *The Secret State* (London, Allen Lane).

Heritage, J. (1984), *Garfinkel and Ethnomethodology* (Cambridge, Polity Press)

Hertz, R. and Imber, J.B. (1995), 'Introduction', in R. Hertz and J.B.Imber (eds), *Studying Elites using Qualitative Methods* (London, Sage).

Hetherington, M.J. and Nelson, M. (2003), 'Anatomy of a Rally Effect: George W Bush and the War on Terrorism', *Political Science and Politics*, Vol. 36, 37–42.

Hoinville, G., Jowell, R. *et al.* (1978), *Survey Research Practice* (London, Heinemann Educational Books).

Holsti, O.R. (1969), *Content Analysis for the Social Sciences and Humanities* (Reading, MA, Addison-Wesley).

Horkheimer, M. (1976), 'Traditional and Critical Theory', in P. Connerton (ed.), *Critical Sociology* (Harmondsworth, Penguin).

Howarth, D. (1995), 'Discourse Theory', in D. Marsh and G. Stoker (eds), *Theory and Methods in Political Science* (London, Macmillan).

Howarth, D. (2000), *Discourse* (Milton Keynes, Open University Press).

Humphreys, L. (1970), *Tearoom Trade* (London, Duckworth).

Ilonszki, G. (2002), 'The State of the Discipline in Eastern and Central Europe: Introduction', *European Political Science*, Vol. 1, No. 3, 24–4.

Inter-Parliamentary Union (2002), http://www.ipu.org/wmn-e/classif.htm (August).

Jenkins, R. (2001), *Churchill* (London, Macmillan).

Jones, K. and Jonasdottir, A. (1988), 'Introduction: Gender as an Analytic Category in Political Theory', in K. Jones and A. Jonasdottir (eds), *The Political Interests of Gender* (London, Sage).

Kalleberg, A. (1966), 'The Logic of Comparison: A Methodological Note on the Comparative Study of Political Systems', *World Politics*, Vol. 19, 69–82.

Kavanagh, D. (1991), 'Why Political Science Needs History', *Political Studies*, Vol. 39, 3.

Keat, R. (1981), *The Politics of Social Theory : Habermas, Freud and the Critique of Knowledge* (London, Routledge & Kegan Paul).

Keat, R. and Urry, J. (1975), *Social Theory as Science* (London, Routledge & Kegan Paul).

Kemp, S. and Squires, J. (eds) (1997) *Feminisms* (Oxford, Oxford University Press).

Kent, G. (2000), 'Informed Consent', in D. Burton (ed.), *Research Training for Social Scientists* (London, Sage).

Kerlinger, F.N. (1986), *Foundations of Behavioural Research: Educational and Psychological Enquiry* (London, Holt, Rinehart & Winston).

Kimmel, A. (1988), *Ethics and Values in Applied Social Research* (London, Sage).

Kinder, D. and Kiewiet, D. (1979), 'Economic Discontent and Political Behaviour: The Role of Personal Grievances and Collective Economic Judgements in Congressional Voting', *American Journal of Political Science*, Vol. 23, 495–527.

King, G., Keohane R. and Verba, S. (1994), *Designing Social Inquiry: Scientific Inference in Qualitative Research* (Princeton, NJ, Princeton University Press).

Kitzinger, J. (1994), 'The Methodology of Focus Groups: The Importance of Interaction between Research Participants', *Sociology of Health and Illness*, Vol. 16, 103–21.

Klingemann, H.-D., Hofferbert, R. and Budge, I. *et al.* (1994), *Parties, Policies and Democracy* (Boulder, CO, Westview Press).

Klockars, C.B. (1975), *The Professional Fence* (London, Tavistock).

Köeln Univeristy (2002), http://www/za/uni-koeln.de (August).

Koen, C. (1997), 'Beginning Research: the First Year', in P. Burnham (ed.), *Surviving the Research Process in Politics* (London, Pinter), 25–34.

Kranzler, J. (2003), *Statistics for the Terrified* (Englefield Cliffs, NJ, Prentice Hall).

Krueger, R.A. and Casey, M.A. (2000), *Focus Groups: A Practical Guide for Applied Research* (London, Sage).

Krull, W. (1999), 'Publications: Pressure to Publish, Selective Practice by Journals, Citation Indices as Factors Producing Scientific Misbehaviour?', in Max-Planck-Gesselschaft (ed.), *Ethos der Forsching: Ethics of Research* (Munich, Generalverwaltung der Max-Planck-Gesellschaft).

Kuhn, T. (1962), *The Structure of Scientific Revolutions* (London, University of Chicago Press).

Ladner, J. A. (1971), *Tomorrow's Tomorrow* (Garden City, NY, Doubleday).

Lakatos, I. (1970), *Criticism and the Growth of Knowledge* (London, Cambridge University Press).

Lamont, N. (2000) *In Office* (London, Time Warner).

Laslett, P. and Runciman, W. (eds) (1962), *Philosophy, Politics and Society; A Collection* (Oxford, Basil Blackwell).

Laver, M. (ed.) (2001), *Estimating the Policy Positions of Political Actors* (London, Routledge).

Laver, M., Benoit, K. and Garry, J. (2003), 'Extracting Policy Positions from Political Texts Using Words as Data', *American Political Science Review*, Vol. 97, No.2, 311–31.

Layton-Henry, Z. (2003), 'Transnational Communities, Citizenship and African Caribbeans in Birmingham', in J. Doomernik and J. Knippenberg (eds), *Migration and Immigrants: Between Policy and Reality* (Amsterdam, Aksant).

Lazarsfeld, P., Bereleson, B. and Gaudet, H. (1944), *The People's Choice* (New York, Columbia University Press).

Leacock, E. (1982), *Myths of Male Dominance* (New York, Monthly Review Press).

Leech, B.L. (2002a), 'Interview Methods in Political Science', *Political Science and Politics*, Vol. 35, 663–4.

Leech, B.L. (2002b), 'Asking Questions: Techniques for Structured Interviews', *Political Science and Politics*, Vol. 35, 665–8.

Lewis-Beck, M. (1988), *Economics and Elections: The Major Western Democracies* (Ann Arbor, MI, University of Michigan Press).

Lewis-Beck, M. (1995), *Data Analysis: An Introduction* (London, Sage).

Lewis-Beck, M. and Lockerbie, B. (1989), 'Economics, Votes, Protests: Western European Cases', *Comparative Political Studies*, Vol. 22, 155–77.

Lichbach, M. and A. Zuckerman, (1997), 'Research Traditions and Theory in Comparative Politics: An Introduction', in M. Lichbach and Zuckerman, A. (eds), *Comparative Politics: Rationality, Culture and Structure* (Cambridge, Cambridge University Press).

Lichtman, A. and French, V. (1978), *Historians and the Living Past* (Wheeling, Illinois, Harlan Davidson).

Lieshout, R.H. and Reinalda, B. (2001), 'The Dutch PSA 1950–2000', *European Political Science*, Vol. 1, No. 1, 60–5.

Lijphart, A. (1971), 'Comparative Politics and the Comparative Method', *American Political Science Review*, Vol. 65, 682–93.

Lijphart, A. (1994), *Electoral Systems and Party Systems: A Study of Twenty-Seven Democracies, 1945–1990* (Oxford, Oxford University Press).

Loftland, J. and Loftland, L. (1984), *Analysing Social Settings: A Guide to Qualitative Observation and Analysis* (Belmont, CA, Wadsworth).

Lowe, R. (1997), 'Plumbing New Depths: Contemporary Historians and the Public Record Office', *Twentieth Century British History*, Vol. 8, No. 2, 239–65.

Lowi, T.J. (1964), 'American Business, Public Policy, Case Studies and Political Theory', *World Politics*, Vol. 16, 655–93.

Ludlam, S. (1995), 'CD-ROMS for Political Scientists', *Political Studies*, Vol. 43, 439–68.

Lukes, S. (1974), *Power: A Radical View* (London, Macmillan).

Lunt, P.K. and Livingstone, S.M. (1992), *Mass Consumption and Personal Identity* (Buckingham, Open University Press).

MacKuen, M., Erikson, R. and Stimson, J. (1993), 'Macropartisanship', in R. Niemi and H. Weisberg (eds), *Controversies in Voting Behaviour*, 3rd edn (Washington, DC, Congressional Quarterly Press).

Macleod, I. (1969), *The Times*, 30 October.

Mair, P. (1996), 'Comparative Politics: An Overview', in R. Goodin and H.-D. Klingemann (eds), *A New Handbook of Political Science* (Oxford, Oxford University Press).

Malinowski, B. (1922), *Argonauts of the Western Pacific* (London, Routledge & Kegan Paul).

Mann, M. (1981), 'Socio-Logic', *Sociology*, Vol. 15, No. 4, 544–50.

March, J.G. and Olsen, J.P. (1984), 'The New Institutionalism: Organizational Factors in Political Life', *American Political Science Review*, Vol. 78, 734–49.

Margetts, H. and Dunleavy, P. (2002), *Cultural Barriers to E Government* (London, National Audit Office).

Markus, G. (1993), 'The Impact of Personal and National Economic Conditions on the Presidential Vote: A Pooled Cross-Sectional Analysis', in R. Niemi and H. Weisberg (eds), *Controversies in Voting Behaviour*, 3rd edn (Washington, DC, Congressional Quarterly Press).

Marsh, C. (1988), *Exploring Data: An Introduction to Data Analysis for Social Scientists* (Cambridge, Polity Press).

Marsh, D. and Stoker, G. (eds) (1995), *Theory and Methods in Political Science* (London, Macmillan).

Marsh, D. and Stoker, G. (eds) (2002), *Theory and Methods in Political Science*, 2nd edn (London, Macmillan).

Matchette, R. et al. (1995), *Guide to Federal Records in the National Archives of the United States* (Washington, DC, NARA).

May, T. (1997), *Social Research: Issues, Methods and Process*, 2nd edn (Buckingham, Open University Press).

McAdam, D., McCarthy, J.D. and Zald, M.N. (1996), *Comparative Perspectives on Social Movements: Political Opportunities, Mobilising Structures and Cultural Feelings* (Cambridge, Cambridge University Press).

McAllister, I. (2000), 'Keeping Them Honest: Public and Elite Perceptions of Ethical Conduct among Australian Legislators', *Political Studies*, Vol. 48, 22–37.

McCarville, P. (2002), 'Second Generation Irish Identity in Birmingham', unpublished PhD thesis, University of Warwick.

Mead, M. (1954), *Coming of Age in Samoa* (London, Pelican).

Meehan, E. (1986), 'Women's Studies and Political Studies', in J. Evans (ed.), *Feminism and Political Theory* (London, Sage).

Miliband, R. (1976), 'Teaching Politics in an Age of Crisis', *The Times Higher Education Supplement*, 19 March, 17.

Milgram, S. (1963), 'A Behavioural Study of Obedience', *Journal of Abnormal and Social Psychology*, Vol. 65, 371–8.

Milgram, S. (1974), *Obedience to Authority* (New York, Harper & Row).

Mill, J.S. (1910), *Utilitarianism, Liberty and Representative Government* (London, J. M. Dent).

Miller, A.J.S. (1952), 'The Participant Observer and Over-Rapport', *American Sociological Review*, Vol. 17, No. 1, pp. 97–9.

Miller, W. (1983), *The Survey Methods in the Social and Political Sciences: Achievements, Failures, Prospects* (London, Pinter).

Milliken, J. (1999), 'The Study of Discourse in International Relations: A Critique of Research and Methods', *European Journal of International Relations*, Vol. 5, No. 2, 225–54.

Millman, M. and Kanter, R. (eds) (1975), *Another Voice: Feminist Perspectives on Social Life and Social Science* (New York, Anchor Books).

Moon, N. (1999), *Opinion Polls: History, Theory and Practice* (Manchester, Manchester University Press).

Moran, Lord (1966), *Winston Churchill: The Struggle for Survival 1940–1965* (London, Constable).

Morgan, J. (1981), *The Backbench Diaries of Richard Crossman* (London, Hamish Hamilton).

Mowat, C. (1971), *Great Britain Since 1914* (London, Hodder & Stoughton).

Moyser, G. and Wagstaffe, M. (1987), *Research Methods for Elite Studies* (London, Allen & Unwin).

Negri, A. (1991), *Marx Beyond Marx* (London, Pluto).

Negri, T. (1988), *Revolution Retrieved* (London, Red Notes).

Newby, H. (1977), 'Appendix: Editorial Note by Howard Newby', in C. Bell and H.J. Newby (eds), *Doing Sociological Research* (London, Allen & Unwin).

Nielsen, J. (1990), 'Introduction', in J. Nielsen (ed.), *Feminist Research Methods* (London, Westview Press).

Niemi, R. and Jennings, K. (1993), 'Issues and Inheritance in the Formation of Party Indentification', in R. Niemi. and H. Weisberg (eds), *Controversies in Voting Behaviour*, 3rd edn (Washington, DC, Congressional Quarterly Press).

Norris, P. (1997), *Electoral Change Since 1945* (Oxford, Basil Blackwell).

Norris, P. (2002), *Democratic Phoenix: Reinventing Political Activism* (Cambridge, Cambridge University Press).

Norris, P., Curtice, J., Sanders, D., Scammel, M. and Semetko, H.A. (1999), *On Message: Communicating the Campaign* (London, Sage).

NSI (2002), http://www.nsf.gov/home/about/creation.htm.

Northern Ireland Social and Political Archive (2002) 'Northern Ireland Life and Times Survey': http://www.ark.co.uk.

Oakley, A. (1981), 'Interviewing Women: A Contradiction in Terms', in H. Roberts (ed.), *Doing Feminist Research* (London, Routledge & Kegan Paul).

Office of the French President (2002), http://www.elysee.fr/actus/elections (August).

Okely, J. (1983), *The Traveller-Gypsies* (Cambridge, Cambridge University Press).

Organisation for Economic Co-operation and Development (2002), http://www.oecd.org (August).

Oxford University Press (1999), *Margaret Thatcher: Complete Public Statements 1945–1990 on CD Rom, Users Handbook* (Oxford, Oxford University Press).

Padfield, M. and Proctor, I. (1996), 'The Effect of Interviewer's Gender on the Interviewing Process: A Comparative Enquiry', *Sociology*, Vol. 30, No. 2, 355–66.

Park, A., Curtice, J., Thomson, K., Jarvis, L. and Bromley, C. (eds) (2002), *British Social Attitudes Survey: The 19th report* (London, Sage and the National Centre for Social Research).

Parsons, T. (1949), *The Structure of Social Action*, 2nd edn (New York, Free Press).

Paterson, W. and Grix, J. (2000), 'Postscript: Interviewing in Germany', *University of Birmingham Discussion Papers in German Studies*, No. IGS2000/11.

Payne, S.L. (1951), *The Art of Asking Questions* (Princeton, NJ, Princeton University Press).

Pennings, P., Keman, H. and Kleinnijenhuis, J. (1999), *Doing Research in Political Science. An Introduction to Comparative Methods and Statistics* (London, Sage).

Peters, G. (1998), *Comparative Politics: Theory and Methods* (London, Macmillan).

Peters, B. Guy (1999), *Institutional Theory in Political Science* (London, Pinter).

Pettigrew, A. (1985), *The Awakening Giant: Continuity and Change in Imperial Chemical Industries* (Oxford, Basil Blackwell).

Phillipson, M. (1972), 'Phenomenological Philosophy and Sociology' in P. Filmer *et al.*, *New Directions in Sociological Theory* (London, Collier-Macmillan).

Phoenix, A. (1994), 'Practising Feminist Research: The Intersection of Gender and "Race" in the Research Process', in M. Maynard and J. Purvis (eds), *Researching Women's Lives from a Feminist Perspective* (London, Taylor & Francis).

Platt, J. (1981), 'Evidence and proof in documentary research', *Sociological Review*, Vol. 29, No. 1, 31–66.

Plummer, K. (1983), *Documents of Life* (London, Unwin Hyman).

Plutzer, M. (2002), 'Becoming a Habitual Voter: Inertia, Resources and Growth in Young Adulthood', *American Political Science Review*, Vol. 96, 41–56.

Pollock, F. (1955), 'Empirical Research into Public Opinion', reprinted in P. Connerton (ed.) (1976) *Critical Sociology* (Harmondsworth, Penguin).

Popper, K. (1957), *The Poverty of Historicism* (London, Routledge & Kegan Paul).

Popper, K. (1959), *The Logic of Scientific Discovery* (London, Hutchinson).

Popper, K. (1963), *Conjectures and Refutations: The Growth of Scientific Positivism* (Oxford, Basil Blackwell).

Pressman, J. and Wildavksy, A, (1973), *Implementation* (Berkeley, University of California Press).

Presthus, R.V. (1973), *Elite Accommodation in Canadian Politics* (London, Cambridge University Press).

Presthus, R.V. (1974), *Elites in the Policy Process* (London, Cambridge University Press).

Prinati, M. (1983), 'The State of the Discipline: One Interpretation of Everyone's Favorite Controversy', *Political Studies*, Spring, 189–96.

Pryce, K. (1979), *Endless Pressure* (Harmondsworth, Penguin).

Przeworski, A. and Teune, H. (1970), *Logic of Comparative Social Inquiry* (New York, Wiley).

PSA (2002), *2002 Member's Handbook* (Newcastle, PSA).

Psephos (2002), http://www.psephos.adam-carr.net (August).

Public Record Office (1996), *Current Guide* (London, PRO).

Punch, K.F. (1998), *Introduction to Social Research; Quantitative and Qualitative Approaches* (London, Sage).

Purdie, B. (1990), *Politics in the Streets* (Belfast, Blackstaff Press).

Raab, C. (1987), 'Oral history as an instrument of research into Scottish educational policy-making', in G. Moyser and M.Wagstaffe (eds), *Research Methods for Elite Studies* (London, Allen & Unwin).

Radcliffe-Brown, A.R. (1964), *The Andaman Islanders* (New York, Free Press).

Ragin, C. (1987), *The Comparative Method: Moving Beyond Qualitative and Quantitative Strategies* (Berkeley, CA, University of California Press).

Rai, S. (2002), *Gender and the Political Economy of Development* (Cambridge, Polity).

Randall, V. (1983), 'Teaching about Women and Politics', *Politics*, Vol. 3, No. 1, 38–43.

Ranney, A. (ed.) (1968) *Political Science and Public Policy* (Chicago, Markham).

Rasmussen, E. (1985) 'A Periphery Looks at Its Centres: The Case of Danish Political Science', *Scandinavian Political Studies* (yearbook), 319–28.

Reinharz, S. (1992), *Feminist Methods in Social Research* (Oxford, Oxford University Press).

Report of a Committee (2000), 'Political Science at the NSF: The Report of a Committee of the American Political Science Association', *Political Science and Politics*, Vol. 23, 895–8.

Ricci, D.M. (1984), *The Tragedy of Political Science* (New Haven: Yale University Press).

Rimington, S. (2001), *Open Secret* (London, Hutchinson).

Rivera, S.W., Kozyreva, P.M. and Sarovskii, E.G. (2002), 'Interviewing Political Elites: Lessons from Russia', *Political Science and Politics*, Vol. 24, 683–8.

Roberts, H. (1981), 'Introduction', in H. Roberts (ed.), *Doing Feminist Research* (London, Routledge).

Robson, C. (1993), *Real World Research* (Oxford, Basil Blackwell).

Rogowski, R. (1993), 'Comparative Politics', in A. Finifter (ed.), *Political Science: The State of the Discipline* (Washington, DC, APSA).

Rosamond, B. (2002), 'Plagiarism, Academic Norms and the Governance of the Profession', *Politics*, Vol. 22, 167–74.

Rose, R. (1971), *Governing Without Consensus: An Irish Perspective* (London, Faber & Faber).

Rowntree, S. (1941), *Poverty and Progress: A Second Social Survey of York* (London, Longman, Green & Co.).

Roy, D. (1970), 'The Study of Southern Labor Union Organizing Campaigns', in R. Habenstein (ed.), *Pathways to Data* (Chicago, IL, Aldine).

Royal Commission on Population (1949), Cmnd 7695 (London, HMSO).

Rubin, H.J. and Rubin, I.S. (1995), *Qualitative Interviewing: The Art of Hearing Data* (London, Sage).

Saalfeld, T. (2002), 'Methodology and Methods in German Political Science: From "Normative Pathos" to "Normality" ' in J. Grix (ed.), *Approaches to the Study of Contemporary Germany: Research Methodologies in German Studies* (Birmingham, Birmingham University Press).

Saggar, S. (2000), *Race and Representation: Electoral Politics and Ethnic Pluralism in Britain* (Manchester, Manchester University Press).

Sampson, A. (2000), *Mandela* (London, HarperCollins)

Sanders, D. (1995), 'Behavioural Analysis', in D. Marsh and G. Stoker (eds), *Theory and Methods in Political Science* (London, Macmillan).

Sapsford, R. (1996), 'Extracting and Presenting Statistics' in R. Sapsford, and V. Jupp (eds), *Data Collection and Analysis* (London, Sage).

Sartori, G. (1994), *Comparative Constitutional Engineering: An Inquiry into Structures, Incentives and Outcomes* (London, Macmillan).

Sayer, A. (1992), *Method in Social Science* (London, Routledge).

Schmidt, V. (2002), *The Futures of European Capitalism* (Oxford, Oxford University Press).

Schofield, N. (1996), 'Survey Sampling', in R. Sapsford and V. Jupp (eds), *Data Collection and Analysis* (London, Sage).

Schwartz, M. and Schwartz, C. (1955), 'Problems in Participant Observation', *American Journal of Sociology*, Vol. 60, No. 1, 343–53.

Scott, D. (1975), 'The National Front in Local Politics: Some Interpretations', in I. Crewe (ed.), *British Political Sociology Yearbook*, Vol. 2 (London, Croom Helm), 214–38.

Scott, J. (1990), *A Matter of Record* (Cambridge, Polity).

Service, R. (2000), *Lenin: A Biography* (London, Macmillan).

Seyd, P. and Whiteley, P. (1992), *Labour's Grassroots: The Politics of Party Membership* (Oxford, Clarendon Press).

Seyd, P. and Whiteley, P. (2002), *New Labour's Grassroots: The Transformation of the Labour Party Membership* (Basingstoke, Palgrave).

Seyd, P., Whiteley, P. and Parry, J. (1996), *Labour and Conservative Party Members 1990–92: Social Characteristics, Political Attitudes and Activities* (Aldershot, Dartmouth).

Shils, E. (1979), 'Privacy in Modern Industrial Society', in M. Bulmer (ed.), *Censuses, Surveys and Privacy* (London, Macmillan), 33–6.

Short, P. (1999), *Mao: A Life* (London, Hodder & Stoughton).

Shuckburgh, E. (1986), *Descent to Suez: Diaries 1951–56* (London, Weidenfeld & Nicolson).

Siim, B. (2000), *Gender and Citizenship: Politics and Agency in France, Britain and Denmark* (Cambridge, Cambridge University Press).

Smith, S. (2000), 'The Discipline of International Relations: Still an American Social Science?', *British Journal of Politics and International Relations*, Vol. 2, 374–402.

SRA (2002) *Ethical Guidelines 2002* (http://www.the-sra.org).

Somit, A. and Tanenhaus, J. (1967), *The Development of American Political Science: From Burgess to Behavioralism* (Boston, Allyn & Bacon).

Stacey, M. (1960), *Tradition and Change: A Study of Banbury* (Oxford, Oxford University Press).

Stacey, M., Batestone, E., Bell, C. and Murcott, A. (1975), *Power, Persistence and Change: A Second Study of Banbury* (London, Routledge & Kegan Paul).

Stanfield I, J. (1993), 'Epistemological Considerations', in J. Stanfield and R. Dennis (eds), *Race and Ethnicity in Research Methods* (London, Sage), 16–38.

Stanfield II, J. and Dennis, R. (eds) (1993), *Race and Ethnicity in Research Methods* (London, Sage).

Stedward, G. (1997), 'On the Record: an Introduction to Interviewing', in P. Burnham (ed.), *Surviving the Research Process in Politics* (London, Pinter), 151–65.

Stewart, D.W. and Shamdasani, P. (1990), *Focus Groups: Theory and Practice* (London, Sage).

Stoker, D. (1995), 'Introduction', in D. Marsh and G. Stoker (eds), *Theory and Methods in Political Science* (London, Macmillan).

Swann, B. and Turnbull, M. (1971), *Records of Interest to Social Scientists 1919 to 1939 Introduction* (London, HMSO).

Swann, B. and Turnbull, M. (1978), *Records of Interest to Social Scientists 1919–1939 Employment and Unemployment* (London, HMSO).

Taylor, A. (1993), *Women Drug Users: An Ethnography of a Female Injecting Community* (Oxford, Clarendon Press).

Teer, F. and Spence, J. (1973), *Political Opinion Polls* (London, Hutchinson University).

Thain, C. and Wright, M., (1995) *The Treasury and Whitehall* (Oxford, Clarendon Press).

Thatcher, M. (1993), *The Downing Street Years* (London, HarperCollins).

Thomas, R. (1996), 'Statistical Sources and Databases', in R. Sapsford and V. Jupp (eds), *Data Collection and Analysis* (London, Sage).

Thomas, R.J. (1995), 'Interviewing Important People in Big Companies', in R. Hertz and J.B. Imber (eds), *Studying Elites Using Qualitative Methods* (London, Sage), 3–17.

Tickner, J. A. (2001), *Gendering World Politics: Issues and Approaches in the Post-Cold War era* (New York, Columbia University Press).

Todal Jenssen, A. (1999), 'All that is Solid Melts into Air: Party Identification in Norway', in H. Narud and T. Aalberg (eds), *Challenges to Representative Democracy: Parties, Voters and Public Opinion* (Bergen, Fagbokforlaget).

Tourangeau, R., Rips, L. and Rasinski, K. (2000), *The Psychology of Survey Response* (Cambridge, Cambridge University Press).

Twine, R.W. and Warren, J.W. (eds) (2000), *Racing Research, Researching Race: Methodological and Dilemmas in Critical Race Studies* (London, New York University Press).

UN (2002), *Human Development Report* http://www.un.org, http://www.undp.org (August).

Upton, G. and Cook, I. (2002), *Oxford Dictionary of Statistics* (Oxford, Oxford University Press).

Van Dijk, T. A. (1993), 'Analysing Racism Through Discourse Analysis', in J. Stanfield and R. Dennis (eds), *Race and Ethnicity in Research Methods* (London, Sage), 92–134.

Vickers, R. (1995), 'Using Archives in Political Research', in P. Burnham (ed.), *Surviving the Research Process in Politics* (London, Pinter), 167–76.

Wallace, H. (2000), 'Studying Contemporary Europe', *British Journal of Politics and International Relations*, Vol. 2, 95–113.

Wallis, R. (1977), 'The Moral Career of a Research Project', in C. Bell and H.J. Newby (eds), *Doing Sociological Research* (London, Allen & Unwin) 149–67.

Ward, H. (1995), 'Rational Choice Theory', in D. Marsh and G. Stoker (eds), *Theory and Methods in Political Science* (London, Macmillan).

Ward, H. (2002), 'Rational Choice', in D. Marsh and G. Stoker (eds), *Theory and Methods in Political Science*, 2nd edn, (Basingstoke, Palgrave Macmillan).

Watson, J.D. (1968), *The Double Helix* (Harmondsworth, Penguin).

Webb, S. and Webb, B. (1932), *Methods of Social Study* (London, Longmans, Green and Co.)

Weis, L. (1985), *Between Two Worlds: Black Students in an Urban Community College* (Boston, Routledge & Kegan Paul).

Whitaker, B. (1979), *The Foundations: An Anatomy of Philanthropic Bodies* (Harmondsworth, Penguin).

Whiteley, P., Seyd, P. and Richardson, J. (1994), *True Blues: The Politics of Conservative Party Membership* (Oxford, Clarendon Press).

Whyte, W. F. (1976), *Power, Politics and Progress: Social Change in Rural Peru* (New York, Elsevier).

Whyte, W.F. (1993), *Street Corner Society: The Social Structure of an Italian Slum*, 4th edn (London, University of Chicago Press).

Wilkinson, G. (1994), 'Newspapers', in P. Catterall and H. Jones (eds), *Understanding Documents and Sources* (Oxford, Heinemann).

Winch, P. (1958), *The Idea of a Social Science and its Relation to Philosophy* (London, Routledge & Kegan Paul).

Wright, P. (1987), *Spycatcher* (Richmond, Victoria, Heinemann Australia).

Wright, S. (2002), 'Dogma or Dialogue? The Politics of the Downing Street Website', *Politics*, Vol. 22, 135–42.

Yahoo! (2002a), http://uk.docs.yahoo.com/info/howto/chapters/7/4.html, 12 June.

Yahoo! (2002b), http://uk.docs.yahoo.com/info/howto/chapters/8/1.html, 12 June.

Yahoo! (2002c), http://uk.docs.yahoo.com/info/howto/chapters/8/2.html, 12 June.

YouGov (2002a), http://www.yougov.com/corp.jsp, 12 June.

YouGov (2002b), http://www.yougov.com/method,jsp;jspessionid=qwz09as9zi, 12 June.

Index